The Arthurdale Community School

The Arthurdale Community School

Education and Reform in Depression-Era Appalachia

SAM F. STACK JR.

UNIVERSITY PRESS OF KENTUCKY

Copyright © 2016 by The University Press of Kentucky
Paperback edition 2020

Scholarly publisher for the Commonwealth,
serving Bellarmine University, Berea College, Centre College of Kentucky,
Eastern Kentucky University, The Filson Historical Society, Georgetown College,
Kentucky Historical Society, Kentucky State University, Morehead State
University, Murray State University, Northern Kentucky University, Transylvania
University, University of Kentucky, University of Louisville, and Western
Kentucky University.
All rights reserved.

Editorial and Sales Offices: The University Press of Kentucky
663 South Limestone Street, Lexington, Kentucky 40508-4008
www.kentuckypress.com

Library of Congress Cataloging-in-Publication Data
Names: Stack, Sam F., 1954– author.
Title: The Arthurdale Community School : education and reform in
  depression-era Appalachia / Sam F. Stack, Jr.
Description: Lexington : University Press of Kentucky, [2015] | Includes
  bibliographical references and index.
Identifiers: LCCN 2016006695| ISBN 9780813166889 (hardcover : alk. paper) |
  ISBN 9780813166902 (pdf) | ISBN 9780813166896 (epub)
Subjects: LCSH: Arthurdale Community School (Arthurdale, W.V.)—History. |
  Community and school—West Virginia—Arthurdale—History—20th century. |
  Place-based education—Appalachian Region—History—20th century. |
  Educational change—Appalachian Region—History—20th century. |
  Depressions—1929—Appalachian Region.
Classification: LCC LD7501.A74 S73 2016 | DDC 371.009173/40975482—dc23
LC record available at http://lccn.loc.gov/2016006695

ISBN 978-0-8131-7912-4 (pbk. : alk. paper)

This book is printed on acid-free paper meeting
the requirements of the American National Standard
for Permanence in Paper for Printed Library Materials.

Manufactured in the United States of America.

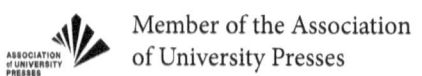

To my family,

Linda, Katie, Ashley, and Sam

Contents

Introduction   1

1. Progressive Education and the Depression   9
2. Back to the Land and the Arthurdale School   23
3. Elsie Ripley Clapp and the Community School   43
4. Beginning a Community School   61
5. The Struggle to Survive   87
6. From Community School to Traditional   107
7. The End of a Dream?   127

Acknowledgments   145
Notes   147
Bibliography   181
Index   193

Photographs follow page 86

Introduction

The concept of community and its restoration forms the basis of the story of Arthurdale and its community school. The story takes place in the heart of Depression-era Appalachia, within the federal New Deal subsistence homestead policy meant to remedy the economic plight of north-central West Virginia coal miners displaced by the decline of the coal industry. Economic concerns were certainly central to the reformist attitude of the New Dealers, but they were also concerned about the social impacts of the Depression. In the case of Arthurdale, the dissolution of community was undergirded by concerns of identity and place, the glue that in some way holds us all together. While Arthurdale was an attempt to help displaced coal miners regain a sense of dignity, it was also an economic experiment to help the unemployed start over, this time in control over their destiny. They needed to be a part of something, making a contribution, feeling like they belonged. The New Deal reformers always saw Arthurdale as an experimental community, a place to try out ideas in social and community planning, but they also saw it as a place where the school served as the center of the community. The community and its school were conceptualized in terms of cooperation rather than competition, of people working together rather than looking out only for themselves. Reformers saw the time in the coal camps as disruptive of and undermining community, in essence promoting the survival of the fittest. The American philosopher John Dewey, an adviser to the Arthurdale project, envisioned community as, in Matthew Flamm's words, the "establishment of democratically conceived group-relationships," the point being that "the democratic ideal of a multiplicity of perspectives acting in concert depends upon the maintenance of a true pluralism of group loyalties, upon the emergence of heterogeneous 'publics' instead on one homogeneous 'public.'"[1] The community school at Arthurdale attempted to follow Dewey's philosophy and his desire to use the school to restore community life, community itself forming the basis of democracy and the democratic way of life. Dewey claimed that the materialism of the 1920s had led the nation along a pattern of economic distress and that by 1929 capitalism had shown its true colors and was not workable. The Arthurdale School, under the direction of Elsie Ripley Clapp, a Dewey disciple and former student, held to a philosophy progressive in nature. Schooling had to be more than an acquisition of credentials; it also had to be a way for both adults and children to regain their sense of identity and place. The Arthurdale School expressed this in its curriculum, which covered Appalachian folklore, history, culture, music, and handicrafts. The school stressed attention to partnering with the community, being attentive to its needs, its history and culture. It was designed from the first to be the center of community life and activity. Its philosophy of education claimed a democratic purpose and one that ideally gave students a sense of identity and community.

Dewey, Clapp, and others knew that progressive education was not reaching most American children owing to the fact that it was practiced largely in university lab schools, urban schools, and private schools. Progressive education, or what was often called the *new education,* had not reached the poor and working-class children of America. While *The Arthurdale Community School* is an institutional history, it is also the story of curriculum history, of how subject matter can be developed to meet the needs of the community, attentive to the surrounding economic, social, and political forces. While the Arthurdale community experiment is well-known by New Deal historians, the school is often overlooked as just a small facet of the community. In reality, it was one of its most central facets and can give insight into many of the contemporary problems in American education, one being the alienation many students feel from schooling. Like many students today, Arthurdale children had found their previous experiences in school to be alienating, feeling no connection between what they were being taught and the real world. There was a clear attempt in the Arthurdale School to be attentive to their interests and experiences but also to guide those interests and experiences into the mastering of traditional subject matter. A historical case study of a historical institution such as the Arthurdale School allows the student of education to see how teachers, students, parents, and administrators worked together to structure a community school. David Tyack, Robert Lowe, and Elisabeth Hansot write: "The depression posed a challenge to the everyday beliefs by which people gave meaning to their lives, for the crisis of the old order was partly material, partly ideological."[2] While this book chronicles the story of a school and community instituted by federal policy, it is really the story of people and their ideas, how ideas are understood and put forth—the ideas of community, identity, and place. We often look for examples or blueprints to follow as educators, but the Arthurdale teachers understood that this was impossible since all communities and cultures are different. That is, there is no one right way to teach a given subject.

This story is told in chronological order to give the reader a sense of how this experimental community and its community school were developed over time and how the educators, students, and community members responded to creating the first federal subsistence homestead community. It is a story of overcoming the hurdles that can disrupt the educational process, a story of both success and failure. And, finally, it is a story of building community and giving people hope in desperate and discouraging times.

The Arthurdale School claimed to embody progressive education principles and was founded in the throes of the greatest economic depression America has ever known. The progressive education historian Arthur Zilversmit writes: "While we know a great deal about the theories of progressive educators and their claims that these ideas were influencing the programs of thousands of schools, we know little about how progressive principles fared in individual schools. To understand the real impact of progressive education, we need to look at specific schools and classrooms."[3] This book seeks to help remedy the historical void, chronicling the story of an experiment by progressive educators in rural north-central West Virginia who applied the philosophy and pedagogy of John Dewey in building a community school. The concept of community is central to Dewey's vision of democracy, and the building of community is what he perceived to be the ultimate goal of the school. It is not so much the study of progressive education alone that is important here but the attempt to better understand the concept of community as a central theme in progressive education. Why is this important? Because I accept Dewey's contention that community is absolutely necessary for democracy to work effectively and that it involves shared interest, hope, trust, tolerance, respect, open communication, and a willingness to sacrifice self-interest and self-indulgence for the benefit of the common good. Our society seems to be characterized by mistrust, alienation, a lack of political engagement, and a lack of respect for the other. Community implies self-sacrifice over self-indulgence and commitment over loose associations that are easily broken. Educators have a crucial role to play here in helping students and adults build community and grow the foundation for democracy. We need in education what Michael Johanek and John Puckett refer to as a "community-centered approach," one that benefits "students morally, intellectually, and motivationally."[4]

The current focus of educational reform, driven by economic interests over democratic ones, is the antithesis of a community-centered approach and has been largely detrimental to both the urban and the rural poor and certainly the poor in Appalachia. I first briefly address the state of progressive education in the late 1920s and the 1930s, the context in which the Arthurdale School was formed. Since Dewey's conception of community is the philosophical foundation of the Arthurdale School, it too will be discussed.

Dewey claimed that his own ideas were shaped by life experiences, experience being an ongoing interaction or transaction in and with the environment that became central to his views on teaching and his pragmatism.[5] What experiences shaped Dewey and his thoughts on education? Born in 1859, a year that marked a transition in American thought and history,[6] Dewey claimed that his childhood in Burlington, Vermont, gave him particular insight into the changing nature of America, which was moving from a largely rural, agrarian society to an urban one. Educated in the local Burlington public schools and matriculating from the University of Vermont in 1879, he left Vermont to teach in the boom town of Oil City, Pennsylvania, later returning to Vermont to take a position at the Lakeview Seminary in Charlotte. After much soul searching as to the direction he wanted his life to take, he decided to return to school, earning a Ph.D. in philosophy from Johns Hopkins in 1884. His experimentation in education began during his time at the University of Chicago (1894–1904), where he headed the academic areas of philosophy, psychology, and pedagogy and he and his wife, Alice Chipman Dewey, directed the university lab school from 1896 to 1904. His pedagogy was shaped by his belief that, through its focus on materialism and individualism, the Industrial Revolution had resulted in the dissolution or loss of a sense of community. He held that one of the primary goals of formal schooling should be to restore community life.

Community as Dewey understood it is a complex concept but fundamental to an understanding of his pedagogy and the goal of participatory democracy. Throughout his intellectual career Dewey showed great concern with the individualism and materialism in American society that was continually stimulated by capital and industrial growth. From 1860 to the end of the nineteenth century, the urban population of the United States had doubled, and by 1920, 50 percent of Americans lived in cities.[7] Concern with social change and its impact were not new to philosophy or social science in the late nineteenth century and can be found in the works of Karl Marx, Émile Durkheim, Jane Addams, Ferdinand Tönnies, Max Weber, Herbert Spencer, and George Herbert Mead. All worried that the changes wrought by the Industrial Revolution had adversely affected basic forms of human association, particularly the family and even the church.[8] The family and the church had been the primary means by which children were socialized, inculcating in them habits of cooperation, responsibility, occupation, and interdependence. With the growing complexity of society, including the changing nature of the division of labor, the goals of socialization and who was responsible for it became unclear, resulting in what many characterized as the dissolution of community.[9]

Dewey's lifelong friend and colleague George Herbert Mead wrote: "The child is a member of the community, but he is a particular part of the community with a particular heredity and position which distinguishes him from anybody else. He is what he is in so far as he is a member of the community, and the raw materials out of which this particular individual is born would not be a self but for his relationship to others in the community of which he is a part." He elaborated: "That which constitutes the personality lies in this sort of give and take between members in a group that engage in a cooperative process. It is this activity that had led to the humanly intelligent animal."[10] Clearly, Mead emphasized the social nature of the child as fundamental in the formation of identity, identity being necessary to understanding one's role in the community.

The disruption by scientific, technological, and economic change of social cohesion resulted in what Dewey saw as a Hegelian form of alienation. Alienation implied a sense of separateness, a feeling of being lost and not sensing one's contribution to or personal connection with society generally. With association and interaction disrupted, community ceased to exist. Reiterating Mead, Dewey informs us that we are human because we are social, there being a need for shared and common values. Shared action and common values form the basis for community, or "cooperation on the part of individuals for addressing the ills of common life and for the selection and achievement of goals which are felt to be good."[11] (One begins to see how the school came to be the vehicle for attempts to reestablish community.) And, in order to share values, one must engage in some form of communication, whether direct, that is, in oral or written form, or indirect, that is, through art (even children's art), music, or dance.[12]

While communication and community help form the basis of democracy, they are also crucial to the educational experience. That is, while democracy disperses authority to its community members, it is crucial that one balance the needs of the individual against the needs of the society as a whole. James Campbell writes: "The life of the democratic community requires effects and involvement on the part of the citizenry that would preclude the kind of isolated existence [that individualism advocates]."[13] Within the democratic environment we can fulfill the potential of the self only within the social context. Implied in this fulfillment is experience, the transaction and interaction mentioned previously. While there may at times be a sense of nostalgia in his work, at times a bit of romanticism, Dewey was really calling for feeling and emotion, guided by intelligence, to help humankind deal with rapid social and economic change. He sought in a sense of functionalism an institution to foster through experience this use of intelligence. The progressive school would come to be associated with what was termed the "new education" or progressive education.

In my attempt to grasp the understanding and practice of the Arthurdale School I will address the following questions throughout the book.

1. How did the concept of the community school develop, and how was it conceptualized and practiced at Arthurdale?
2. How did economic, social, and political forces affect the implementation of the Arthurdale School?
3. How did Elsie Ripley Clapp and her contingent of progressive educators interpret the community school in light of John Dewey's conception of democracy? Where did they succeed, and where did they fail?
4. What led to the decline of the progressive community school at Arthurdale, and how did this decline reflect national trends in education?
5. What can we learn from the historical study of the Arthurdale School that can enhance our understanding of contemporary educational practices?

This book is divided into seven chapters. Chapter 1 situates Arthurdale within the discourse of progressive education during the late 1920s and the early Depression era. It describes the reactions of educators as they coped with the educational problems that were brought on by the Depression and that set the stage for the Arthurdale School. Chapter 2 addresses the origins of the back-to-the-land movement, the reformist agenda of the New Deal planners, and how the Arthurdale School was conceived as part of this national experiment in community planning. It also addresses the progressive notion of using the school to restore community life by focusing on identity and a sense of place in an economically depressed region in Appalachia. Chapter 3 briefly discusses the life and impact of Elsie Ripley Clapp, the director of community affairs of the Arthurdale project and the principal of the Arthurdale School. It explores her background and her intellectual development, both of which guided her work at Arthurdale. Her understanding of progressive education and her philosophy of the community school are addressed, as is her attempt to apply Dewey's philosophy of education in the new homestead community. Chapter 4 chronicles the first year of the Arthurdale School. It looks at its establishment within a subsistence homestead as well as its philosophy, teachers, and curriculum during its first year. Much stress is placed on the attempt by the educators to use the school to give homesteaders in the community a sense of identity and place. Chapter 5 chronicles the second and final year of the progressive contingent of educators at Arthurdale. Emphasis is placed on the problems faced by the school, but its successes are also discussed. It also investigates reasons why the progressive philosophy was largely abandoned after two years. Chapter 6 chronicles the philosophy and practices of the school after the departure of Clapp and her contingent of progressive educators, outlining what changed and what remained the same. Chapter 7 evaluates the attempt to establish a community school in this first subsistence homestead community and what we might learn from the experiment.

The progressive education historians Susan Semel and Alan Sadovnik suggest that not only historians but also educational reformers "should study the child-centered progressive school for models of what worked, what failed, and why": "The majority of contemporary progressive curriculum and pedagogic reforms, including whole-language, authentic assessment, integrated curriculum, and multicultural education [called *intercultural education* in the early progressive schools] appear in some form in almost all the early progressive schools in the early part of the twentieth century." They also discuss some contemporary concerns of modern progressive educators: that teachers are respected as knowledgeable professionals in control of what they teach; that the curriculum is balanced and dedicated to the needs and interests of the children being taught; that attention is paid to the home and the culture of the children and that the fact that they learn best through experience is heeded; that decision making is a shared event; that critical inquiry is fostered; and that in the long run education should serve as a "model of democracy and humane relationships, confronting issues of racism, classism, and sexism," preparing children for global citizenship.[14] The Arthurdale School was attentive to the majority of these concerns, but, as Kathleen Weiler points out, like most progressive schools it "failed to address the realities of the world children were to enter as adults, the brutalities and inequities of this world, the racism, exploitation of workers, political and business corruption, effects of imperialism and colonialism." On a positive note, Weiler goes on to suggest that progressive educators sought a "respect for each student, confidence in every child's ability to know, a belief that learning should be joyous and creative—are admirable."[15]

While the successes and failures of the Arthurdale School are addressed in this book, there is also an attempt to build on our own understanding of progressive education and how this historical experiment can inform current theory and practice. What follows is the story of the Arthurdale School.

1

Progressive Education and the Depression

What actually was progressive education? How was it conceived during the 1930s when the Arthurdale School was formed? Subsumed under the larger progressive reform movement during the Theodore Roosevelt, Howard Taft, and Woodrow Wilson administrations, progressivism implied a sense of optimism that human beings could change or alter their circumstances if they chose to do so. Underlying this assumption was the emancipation of the individual from exploitative and oppressive conditions. Within education, progressivism came to mean an attempt to deal with the effects of industrialization, immigration, and urbanization, being attentive to the social sciences and how they could lead to enhanced learning and a better grasp of the human condition. A French teacher, Mme Necker de Saussure, may have been the first to use the terms *education* and *progressive* together. There is little question that the work of Necker de Saussure in 1832 was influenced by Rousseau, Locke, Pestalozzi, and Froebel, who also influenced many American common school reformers such as Horace Mann and Calvin Stowe. It emphasized the child's freedom to develop naturally in alignment with nature and paid attention to interest as a motivation for "invention and creative activity." She saw the teacher as a guide rather than an authoritarian figure, designed rather than completed, and attentive to studies of child development, health, and physical growth as well as the need to connect the home and the school. About the time of the Colonel Francis Parker School and the famed Dewey Lab School in Chicago in the mid-1890s, British periodicals were using the term *progressive education* in describing an education attentive to the growth of the child, widening interests, and self-direction of activity. In the more modern sense, the term *progressive* was associated with the work of Colonel Francis W. Parker, who from 1875 to 1902 challenged the traditional methods of elementary education. Influenced by Pestalozzi and Froebel, Parker attacked the formalism of subject matter and began to seek "recognition of the child's own desires, interests, and emotions as basic factors in learning," and he protested against mechanical drill, memorization, and routine. His methods came to be known as the "new education fad."[1]

The progressive education historian Lawrence Cremin states that "progressive education began as part of a vast humanitarian effort to apply the promise of American life—the ideal of government by, of, and for the people—to the puzzling new urban industrial civilization that came into being during the latter half of the nineteenth century."[2] But in its literal meaning *progress* implies a move forward, in essence a move to improve the quality of life, but it also implies that men created the problems that inquiry and intelligence could resolve if there was enough will. Grounded in a more scientific approach, fully utilizing inquiry and intelligence, was Dewey's theory of democracy and what he believed could be fostered by the school as the natural extension of the community.[3] The school could meet not just the needs of the child but also those of society. This tension between the needs of the child and those of the social order defines the divisive nature of progressive education, so diverse that in reality it was never a united movement. Regardless of that diversity, the progressive education historian William Reese claims that progressive educators held some beliefs in common: "They proclaimed that children were active, not passive, learners; that children were innocent and good, not fallen; that women, not men, best reared and educated the young; that early education, without question, made all the difference; that nature, and not books alone, was perhaps the best teacher; that kindness and benevolence, not stern discipline or harsh rebukes, should reign in the home and classroom; and, finally, that the curriculum needed serious reform, to remove the vestiges of medievalism. All agreed that what usually passed for education was mind-numbing, unnatural, and pernicious, a sin against childhood."[4]

In 1929, with the onset of the Depression, Harold Alberty attempted to articulate several points he believed were characteristic of progressive schools. The first of the characteristics was the concept that "the child is creative by nature" and that the school should create the climate to nurture that impulse. Second was the interest in "the flowering of personality and a sense of social responsibility," nurtured by freedom, physical activity, and intelligence. Third was that the "self-initiated activity of the child rather than learning imposed by the teacher must dominate the school's program." Progressives tended to see the traditional school as a passive, docile institution that focused on "listening" over critique and reflection, although this perception could vary.[5]

Owing to the diversity of progressive education, Cremin refuses to specifically define it, but, in attempting to make sense of the Arthurdale School, it is necessary to try and understand how the educators at Arthurdale conceived the concept and how they practiced their profession. It is important to try and sort through the general conceptions and themes of progressive education in the late 1920s and the 1930s to understand education at Arthurdale. Regardless of the intellectual diversity, most progressive educators at the time could agree that schools needed to be attentive to the health, vocation, and family life of their students. They believed that the social sciences, mostly psychology and sociology, could provide research to nurture growth through attention to how children actually learned. Because of perceived differences in how children learned, more attention was directed to individualized instruction. The ultimate goal was preparation for participatory democracy, although the means of getting there varied greatly.[6]

Just prior to the Depression, one of the best-known progressive educators and perhaps one of the most influential, William H. Kilpatrick, argued that the school was crucial in the process of learning about democracy, a place for practicing it. Kilpatrick described the typical school of his day as "largely autocratic": "Our pupils have on the whole practiced not democracy but obedience, not to say subservience to autocracy." Such docility meant to accept without question what was doled out by the teacher, who had gathered the "fruits from the tree of knowledge," chewed them, and, according to Kilpatrick, helped the students "swallow easily and readily." Kilpatrick believed that the school should be a place of experience, where learning was characterized by activity, with a teacher who understood and "sympathize[d] with childhood," creating conditions conducive to growth. He attempted to nurture experience through what he termed the *project method*.[7]

From 1924 to 1929 the Progressive Education Association (PEA), initially formed in 1919 as the professional organization of progressive education, listed seven guiding principles. The first principle was the freedom to develop naturally, emphasizing the needs of the community. Freedom did meant not license but opportunity for initiative and self-expression based on interesting subject matter. Second was the principle of interest guiding all work. Interest, a type of emotional attachment, was to be developed through experience and knowledge, seeking correlation of subject matter and a conscious sense of achievement. The third principle emphasized the teacher as a guide and not a taskmaster. Teachers needed to encourage use of the senses, the training of observation, judgment, and reflection, to make sense of acquired information and the drawing of adequate conclusions via logic. Progressives tended to believe that classes functioned best for both teachers and students when they were small. The fourth principle, the scientific study of pupil development, emphasized the use of objective and subjective forms of assessment. This assessment included "those physical, mental, moral, and social characteristics which affect both school and adult life and which can be induced by the school and the home." Principle 5 stressed the importance of and attention to the child's physical development, including "much more room in which to move about, better light and air, clean and well-ventilated buildings, easier access to the out-of-doors and greater use of it." Principle 6 addressed cooperation between the home and the school, guided by the "natural interest and activities of the child . . . especially during the elementary years." Principle 7 classified the role of the progressive school in education movements as "a laboratory where the ideas, if worthy, need encouragement; where tradition alone does not rule, but the best of the past is leavened with the discoveries of today, and the result is freely added to the sum of educational knowledge."[8] As we proceed through the story of the Arthurdale School, it will become clearer how these seven principles affected its theory and practice.

    The historian Patricia Graham points out that throughout its history progressive education appealed mostly to the middle and upper middle classes and was conducted in private or university lab schools.[9] Within this context I address four primary groups of progressive educators active during the Depression era: the social reconstructionists, the administrative progressives, the child-centered progressives, and the community school progressives. It was the latter group that led the school at Arthurdale. Arthur Zilversmit believes that progressive education centered itself on the child: "A progressive school was one that followed a child-centered rather than a subject-centered curriculum, a school which mobilized children's natural desire to learn."[10] There was an attempt to meet the emotional and physical needs of the students and to make sure that children had some say in the direction and content of their education. However, Zilversmit appears to be describing the more child-centered camp of progressives, a camp that often seemed to follow Rousseau more than Dewey. Child-centered progressives tended to challenge traditional grading or assessment and stressed physical activity, working in small groups, emphasizing freedom, and placing an emphasis on the interest of the child in guiding the curriculum. They often emphasized the role of the individual over the role of the individual in society. Margaret Naumburg provides an example of the child-centered approach: "Individual children, in all their human variety, must be the learning center of our changing schools, and the crux of the problem of our new education moves from controlling the machinery of organization and the collection of facts to creating a living organism, a new society, within the school itself." Naumburg lauded Kilpatrick's project method but was critical of an article by Dewey in the *New Republic* in which he tied individualism to capitalism.[11] Yet in many ways the child-centered progressives were reacting—at times in an extreme fashion—to the drill and recitation of traditional educational practice. They failed in Dewey's view because they ignored the centrality of experience, misunderstood freedom as an absolute, and could and should have paid more attention to the mastering of subject matter.[12]

Centered at Teachers College, Columbia University, and Ohio State University, the social reconstructionists envisioned the school as a tool for social, political, and economic reform. Led by George Counts, Harold Rugg, Boyd Bode, John Childs, Laura Zirbes, and others, they challenged teachers to lead the charge for social, economic, and political reform. Counts heavily criticized the child-centered progressives in his *Dare the School Build a New Social Order?* (1932) and voiced his concerns about inequity in school. Supporting Dewey, he believed that schools should foster cooperation and community rather than individualism and competition.[13] This meant involving students in locating and finding solutions for problems in the community and society at large and furthermore challenging "any institutions that distracted the growth of the individual member of society."[14] While vocal, the social reconstructionists were small in number and had little influence on America's teachers.

The administrative progressives, in turn, tended to be male and well educated and to have ties to business and capital. They had their greatest impact on school organization and management and often based their principles on the ideology of business. In describing them, David Tyack writes: "Their social perspective tended to be cosmopolitan, but paternalistic, self-consciously modern in its deference to the expert and its quest for rational efficiency, yet at times evangelical in its rhetorical tone." The administrative progressives favored a top-down model, placing decisions in the hands of the experts, those with the knowledge needed to make decisions. Standardization was their watchword, they prized organization and efficiency, and they taught proper work habits such as punctuality, respect for authority and experts, and time management, including the proper use of recreation.[15]

The community school progressives counted among their number Elsie Clapp, who held the title of principal and director of community affairs at Arthurdale. Clapp knew many child-centered educators and had worked with them, spending time with Caroline Pratt at the City and Country School.[16] She was familiar with George Counts, William Kilpatrick, and the social reconstructionists at Teachers College and would argue with Counts over his understanding of education as imposition and the idea that the community school could serve as a force for social reconstruction. While attentive to the needs of the child in terms of cognitive and physical development, Clapp was also concerned about social development and role in the community. Like Dewey, her former mentor, she held strongly to the belief that American industrialization had disrupted community life and that the school could serve as a tool giving students a clearer sense of identity, of their role in democratic society. She felt that the school should serve the community by constituting an "embryonic" society, making use of interest, but coupling it with knowledge of subject matter. Teachers played a crucial role by being attentive to the life and culture of the community, helping create a common or public spirit. They were to be a visible and integral part of the community.[17] The school was for the community-centered progressives an extension of the community where the child became self-fulfilled, but within the context of a shared existence, nurturing a spirit of service, part of the democratic ethic. Through the school the community-centered progressives attempted to create solidarity and cohesiveness characterized more by *Gemeinschaft* than by *Gesellschaft*.[18] Of these four groups identified above, the community school educators seem to be the least studied.

These various progressive groups sought to "make children competent members of society," as Alan Ryan puts it, but they differed greatly on what constituted competence and the role of the individual in society. For the child-centered progressives competence was the activation of interest, for the administrative progressives it was institutional efficiency and preparation for work, for the social reconstructionists it was the integration of knowledge with social and political action, and for the community-centered progressives it was a greater understanding of identity and place within a common culture.[19] Dewey viewed competence—and essentially education—

as the process by which individuals gain "sound" and "discriminating" judgment. Education was meant to cultivate the "habit of suspended judgment, of skepticism, of desire for evidence, of appeal to observation rather than sentiment, discussion rather than bias, inquiry rather than conventional idealization."[20] These are clearly characteristics of participatory democracy. From these brief descriptions, it is clear progressive education was characterized by diversity. Regardless of its diversity, progressive education shared, according to Patricia Graham, five central principles: "commitment to child centeredness in education; belief in the responsibility of the school in society; conviction of the need to evolve a philosophy of progressive education; orientation toward research as the basis for practice; a trend to homogeneity in the character of supporters and consequent increasing isolation from the American mainstream."[21]

Earlier, in the 1920s, the thrust in progressive education was a concern for the physical and emotional development of children; the 1930s, by contrast, placed much more emphasis on the school as a tool of social reform.[22] Graham argues that in the 1930s the PEA was characterized by two main, but related, educational problems: "the role of the school in the social order and the need for total reform of the school curriculum." She notes that the seven guiding principles outlined above were put aside by 1929, the PEA refusing to take action on the more political issues, probably owing to the dominance of the child-centered camp. Adding to the confusion, PEA president Burton Fowler wrote in 1930: "Although our association has never promulgated or approved anything like a program, either of principles or procedure, we do endorse, by common consent, the obvious hypothesis that the child rather than what he studies, should be the centre of all education effort and that a scientific attitude toward new educational ideas is the best guarantee of progress. In such a crusade of sane educational adventure we urge all forward-looking educators, both teacher and parents, to enlist."[23] Clearly, Fowler was among the child-centered progressives, but his call was far from uniting and failed to address the dire social and economic conditions of the Depression and their growing impact on American schools. He placed the emphasis on the child and not the role of the child in the social order. It is this dichotomy that adds to the confusion of purpose in progressive education.

In 1930, the primary organ for progressive education, the journal *Progressive Education,* listed the following educational goals: the child's physical well-being, the opportunity for initiative and self-expression, the development of group consciousness through the school as a community, the use of interest to motivate work, basing the curriculum on the needs of the child, using the teacher as a guide, and developing alternative forms of assessment. It further emphasized cooperation between the home and the school and the concept of the school as experimental, in essence a type of educational laboratory.[24] More specifically, the tension between the camps in progressive education made any attempt to compromise difficult. The divisive nature of the various schools of thought also made it more difficult to affect the nation's public schools, which most American children attended. Cognizant of the changing Depression-era political and economic affairs, Kilpatrick emphasized an education that would help the rising generation become better able to take care of the more rapid changes in affairs. He criticized his colleagues in progressive education for being "too satisfied with the existing state of affairs," which he believed failed to "encourage thinking on the part of children." Criticizing the child-centered camp, he noted that freedom and interest did not constitute "an automatic panacea or device to be applied without thought." True education should help the child "grow as a whole, while and because he learns more and more adequately to face the realities and possibilities of life."[25] C. A. Bowers refers to the child-centered camp as "the cult of the child." "They were for the most part men and women of action," he notes, "not careful thinkers concerned with the exposition of educational and philosophical issues or with the exploration of the limitations and dangers of the ideas they were applying in their classroom with such great energy."[26] However, by 1932 the leadership of the PEA changed, with a former school superintendent from Illinois, Frederick C. Redefer, at the helm, assisted by a group of "more socially and politically aware educators."[27]

One of those educators was the Ohio State professor Laura Zirbes. In May 1931, she addressed the American Association of University Women in a reformist tone. Zirbes believed that the progressive elementary school should be "more concerned with the development of world citizenship and adjustability to a changing social order than it is with the transmission of a fixed social heritage and maintenance of the status quo." She referred to the progressive school as the "soil of democracy" and challenged those who saw it as mere innovation or fad. Like Dewey and Kilpatrick, she criticized those who equated democracy with absolute freedom or license, a clear critique of the child-centered camp. While freedom allowed for self-direction, it needed to be guided by the teacher and coupled with social responsibility. In conclusion, Zirbes found the movement in progressive education lacking a solid foundation and momentum, "which serious investigation and critical evaluation provide." Most prophetic, she described traditional education as remote, disconnected from life, and characterized by piecemeal learning, competition over cooperation, repetition, unfamiliarity, regimentation, and drill. She advocated for a more experimental approach to teacher training and argued for greater teacher voice in educational matters.[28]

In November 1931, Boyd Bode contended that progressive education should envision the school "as an agency for securing wider participation, by the pupil, in the life of the community," but he was not yet sure that progressive education had succeeded. He believed that an aspect of this failure was the misplaced confidence progressives had placed in the "significance of interests for the selection of subject matter." For Bode, this focus on interest had undermined "genuine participation on the part of pupils to achieve a personal philosophy of life or social outlook, as a basis for effective participation in the life of the community." An outcome of this should be an enhanced application of inquiry and problem solving to the pressing questions of human life, specifically, the problems being brought on by materialism and an acquisitive society and resulting in great "privation and suffering."[29]

In April 1932, Stanwood Cobb, the editor of *Progressive Education,* noted that, in "this rapidly changing world, what is most needed are clear power[s] of analysis and of evaluation." In an era when intelligent problem solving seemed to be lacking in dealing with social and economic problems, Cobb sought an education "gifted with creativeness," with students "capable of thinking out new ways and modes of living." And he included in his editorial an excerpt from Dewey's *Philosophy and Civilization.* "We are living in a period of depression," Dewey wrote: "The intellectual function of trouble is to lead men to think. The depression is a small price to pay if it induces us to think about the cause of the disorder, confusion, and insecurity which are the outstanding traits of our social life."[30]

Yet perhaps the greatest challenge to progressive education in the 1930s came from the Teachers College professor George Counts, who in a controversial 1932 address to the PEA claimed that "the great weakness of Progressive Education, lies in the fact that it has elaborated no theory of social welfare unless it be that of anarchy or extreme individualism." Once again the target was the child-centered camp of progressive education. Counts noted that progressive education held sway only in private and university lab schools and that it was a fad of the middle class. In the most quoted statement from the address, he called for progressive education to "emancipate itself from the influence of [the middle] class, face squarely and courageously every social issue, come to grips with life in all its stark reality, establish an organic relation with the community, develop a realistic and comprehensive theory of welfare, fashion a compelling and challenging vision of human destiny, and become less frightened than it is today of the bogeys of imposition and indoctrination."[31]

Interestingly, one respondent to Counts's published address was Elsie Ripley Clapp, at the time the principal of the Rogers Clark Ballard School, just outside Louisville, Kentucky. Agreeing with Counts that the progressives had neglected social problems or were "not fully informed about them," Clapp felt that this neglect could be remedied by "a willingness to participate fully in our own communities, the best education for all of us."[32] She seemed disturbed by Counts's use of the term *indoctrination,* although from her previous social welfare experience she was quite aware of the social class he was preoccupied with and the economic concerns he was attempting to address. Like most progressives, Clapp did not invest her energy in attempts to change the economic system; rather, she envisioned her growing concept of the community school as a means to challenge the status quo. She envisioned the community school as the means of reconstructing society. Her idea of the community school was a happy medium between the child-centered progressives and the social reconstructionists. Social theory could, she felt, best be put to work at the local level.[33] This belief was clearly evident at Arthurdale.

Stimulated by Counts's challenge, and feeling the necessity to act owing to the economic conditions, the PEA formed the Committee on Social and Economic Problems to "promote within schools and their affiliated bodies, thoughtful and systematic study of the economic and industrial problems confronting the world body." Members of the committee included Merle Curti, Jesse Newlon, Sidney Hook, Goodwin Watson, George Counts, and Rexford Tugwell, soon to become the head of the New Deal's Resettlement Administration, which would oversee Arthurdale and the other homestead projects. Tugwell, among other reformers, "advocated reshaping America into a planning society with an organic economy, and such a society was akin to that envisioned by the social reconstructionists."[34] Although dominating the discourse for a short time, the committee had no effect on the policies of the PEA. Alex Baskin writes: "The fact that the Committee on Social and Economic Problems was unable to issue its report as the official policy of the PEA was an excellent indication of how shallow went the roots of social reconstructionist thought in the organization." Caution still dominated radical social and economic change among progressive educators, yet the reconstructionist rhetoric continued.[35]

In a 1932 address in Nice, France, the social reconstructionist Harold Rugg called for more than an "understanding of our rapidly changing civilization" but "nothing less than thoroughgoing social reconstruction." "We must become students of economics, social, and political life," Rugg argued, "as well as students of artistic self-expression, and of growing childhood." He went on to critique what he termed the laissez-faire "marriage of politics and economics that had produced enormous inequalities in wealth and social income, resulting in the exploitation of people throughout the world and class conflict." He called for attention to the "two fold concept of socially useful and creative labor," the true instrument for social reconstruction, rather than the labor of the individual or the creation of capital. "I cannot accept the conclusion," he wrote, "that bodily education and especially creative handcraft, must come to have a place in the new education coordinate with that of literary education. . . . If the labor is creative, that is if it is an original, honest, expression of the worker, of his moods, of his comprehensions of and feeling for life."[36] Dewey and Clapp would have agreed, and many of Rugg's concerns were eventually addressed by the community planners and educators at Arthurdale.

By early 1934, and roughly five years following the stock market crash, it became clearer that progressive educators were cognizant not only of the economic problems of the Depression but also the moral. "We now know that unless we can direct our best intelligence," wrote the American Committee on Economic Policy, "to economic problems a lot of us are going to stop eating, shiver in somebody's cast off coat, sleep on the sidewalks of bankrupt cities, and get none of the extras that are an important part of civilized living. We live in a country that could in reality provide its citizens with a hundred billion dollars worth of goods a year—and more. Only a race of fools would be content to starve in the shadow of so magnificent a plenty."[37] Continuing this theme, PEA president Willard Beatty reported that 2.3 million public school students "who desire an education have been forced out of American schools," that two thousand schools had closed or been forced to implement shortened terms, that two hundred thousand teachers were without jobs, and that many of those with jobs were being paid less than the "common laborers under the National Recovery Act." He called for federal aid to be made available to local school districts for "schoolhouse alteration and construction, especially in rural areas where grants may be used to speed up consolidation, and thus aid in the elimination of the wasteful and unsanitary one-room school."[38] These were desperate times for American education.

In an article in the same issue of *Progressive Education* in which Beatty's report appeared, Harold Rugg once again attempted to clarify the role of the educator during the Depression. Rugg believed that the teacher must step up to deal with present conditions since politicians and financiers had "revealed their inability ... to create and operate sound economic and political government." "Apparently," Rugg continued with a desperate challenge, "there is no one but the professional educator to lead the country in carrying on the democratic tradition of fostering a scientific study of society."[39]

Norman Woelfel, an associate editor of the *Social Frontier*, the journal of the social reconstructionists, suggested in *Progressive Education* that educators share their work with workers and implied a cooperative effort to work toward a "better vision" for America. He noted his concern that organizations such as the National Education Association had voiced little concern for helping in the "reconstruction of American society." He went so far as to challenge teachers to "not blindly shrink from the fact that it may require some use of force against those of present privilege."[40] In the same issue of *Progressive Education*, the historian Merle Curti broadly asked, "Why are American educators socially conservative?" Curti suggested that Christian ethics, humanitarian ideals, capitalism, the frontier process, and scientific thought and method might be part of the answer. In a postmodern sense of critique, he claimed that "devotion to science" made educators think they could be objective and neutral, allowing them to turn their backs on pressing social problems and leaving them squarely in "the socially conservative camp." Educators, Curti felt, needed to take a serious look at the claims that education was the great social cure-all, "the road to utopia."[41]

The majority of teachers, many fearful of retribution and job loss and struggling daily to survive, did not heed the reformist call of the social reconstructionists. Helen Hefferan, a member of the Chicago Board of Education, challenged what she felt were deliberate attacks by the city's business elite on Chicago schools. These attacks resulted in the closing of kindergarten programs, the elimination of physical education and manual training programs, the loss of the successful junior high system, and the firing of three hundred elementary school principals. The so-called citizen's committee led by Chicago's business elite "under the guise of unselfish civic service

... took advantage of the financial plight of the public bodies to impose a ruthless program of economy on the school in the city," Hefferan noted.[42] The *Chicago Tribune* strongly supported the business committee's decisions. Like many teachers throughout the nation, Chicago teachers were hurting. Chicago teacher Edith Smith described her personal situation: "I was much better off than some. I never went hungry as did those who depended for lunch upon big green apples from their pupils. There were many that lost their homes and some that lost their health. I lost only my insurance, my automobile, and my self-respect. I did lose one thing more, but that is not be regretted—my faith in the status quo. Few of us are the sweet, complacent, non-thinking 100 per centers we used to be."[43]

Rural schools in the hinterland were also experiencing great difficulty. According to a report published by the National Education Association in 1933, a total of 1,884 schools housing over 100,000 pupils would not open in the fall of 1933. By the spring of 1934, it was estimated that 20,000 more schools would close. Some schools relied, as we have seen, on shorter terms, and some were open for fewer than three months of the year. The schools were a reflection of the disillusionment growing in America. For the first time in the history of the United States, those leaving the country outnumbered those arriving, a statistic that changed only in 1936 with the growth of fascism.[44]

Given the dire economic situation in America in 1933, the goals of the common schools were being overwhelmed by the necessity of economic survival. Yet Americans as a whole never seemed to lose hope that education was a part of the solution and that the system and the common school ideals of opportunity, as limiting as they could be in terms of race and class, could still offer hope. It is this hope in this era of disillusionment that forms the foundation of understanding the Arthurdale homestead community and the creation of its community school.

2

Back to the Land and the Arthurdale School

Without the Great Depression, the Arthurdale community and its progressive school would never have existed. While some Americans had prospered during the Roaring Twenties, most were just getting by. The turn of the twentieth century and the defeat of the Central Powers in World War I provided Americans with a sense of optimism that the values they held—such as hard work, frugality, and charity—were superior to European custom and tradition. There was a belief in the power of the self to triumph over the odds if one only worked hard enough, a faith in the pioneer spirit. This belief seem strengthened by the growing individualism and materialism of the 1920s, undergirded by a naive concept of equality of opportunity.

The crash of the stock market on 28 October 1929, known as Black Friday, shook American optimism to the core. Within a span of four years, from 1929 to 1933, the gross national product dropped from $103 billion to $55.6 billion, personal income fell from $85.9 billion to $47.0 billion, and estimated unemployment (no one really knew how many were out of work) soared from 3.2 percent of the civilian labor force to 24.9 percent. Profits of corporations after taxes fell from $8.6 million to -$2.7 billion. "Income produced in agriculture declined by over one-half, manufacturing by almost two-thirds, and construction by four-fifths."[1] It was clear to some that the laissez-faire economic system was gone forever, that rugged individualism was a thing of the past.[2] Discontent coupled with a revolutionary spirit seemed everywhere. Alex Baskin notes:

> The revolutionary mood of the nation was everywhere present. The unemployed factory worker and the foreclosed farmer, the discon-

tented veteran and the evicted mother, young and old, Americans questioned the worth of an economic system which permitted hunger in the midst of surplus farm products and unemployment in the shadow of great factories where furnaces had been stilled. The contradiction was present everywhere and visible. The wealthy recognized the troubled nature of the country and heard the discordant voices in the land. They could see the breadlines, the apple sellers, the hunger marchers, and the street corner agitators.

Lloyd's of London was selling insurance against riot and commotion to wealthy Americans.[3]

The confidence of the 1920s was beginning to be replaced by suspicion, fear, and mistrust. Life savings had seemed to vanish overnight; what one had earned and deposited for another day appeared stolen. Studs Terkel described this fear as coupled by an underlying shame, certainly among those who had held to the middle-class values of hard work leading to success and prosperity. "I didn't want to go on relief," a salesman told Terkel. "Believe me, when I was forced to go to the office of the relief, the tears were running out of my eyes. I couldn't bear myself to take money from anybody for nothing."[4] In their study of the model community Middletown, the sociologists Robert and Helen Lynd found families putting up a fake front, what they termed a *brave social front,* to hide their shame for holding onto a fake sense of values, a foreboding feeling that somehow they had failed. David Tyack writes of such people: "They had saved money only to find their banks collapsed—they had worked hard only to find themselves in the bread lines. They had trusted business leaders only to find them at first mindlessly optimistic and then as bewildered as ordinary people."[5]

There was plenty of blame to go around. Unfortunately, as Arthur Schlesinger put it, by fostering policies that led to oversaving by Americans, the federal government "had ignored the dangerous balance between farm and business income, between the increase in wages and the increase in productivity . . . ignored irresponsible practices in the securities market . . . ignored the private debt in the banking and the financial system . . . and had mistaken class interest for national interest." Militancy was on the horizon, and on 6 May 1930 the Communist Party declared International Unemployment Day. While the protestors achieved their goal in inciting the police to attack them, most Americans seemed more interested in their day-to-day survival than in challenging capitalism and advocating its overthrow. Rather than changing the system, the majority preferred to attack those who they believed had corrupted the system. One perceived way to resolve the problem was to seek effective leadership, and President Herbert Hoover was not fitting the bill. In reality, Hoover cannot be blamed for all the ills of the Depression, but his slow and confused response, owing to his conviction that state and local organizations could meet relief efforts and that the economy would soon turn around, certainly did not help matters. His name became associated with hate: tent cities were called *Hoovervilles*, newspapers *Hoover blankets*, broken-down cars *Hoover wagons*, jackrabbits *Hoover hogs*, and empty pockets *Hoover flags*.[6]

The state Board of Children's Guardians found horrifying instances in West Virginia: "One farmer cremating his dead infant because he could not afford a funeral. A mother, insane from hunger and worry, drowned her two children. A ten-year-old girl, whose father had been arrested, had been alone for five days, except for the companionship of a small brown dog and black hen. She had a cataract in one eye and was almost blind in the other. She had gone barefoot in the winter; one of her toes had frozen but had healed."[7] The early years of the Depression were hitting the coal industry in West Virginia, Pennsylvania, and Kentucky hard. According to Jerry Bruce Thomas, the expansion of the coal industry in West Virginia led to the economic ills of "market gluts, chronic losses, frequent bankruptcies, and low wages," with "miners, their families, the coal mining communities," and West Virginia suffering in the process.[8] Miners often responded to wage cuts with strikes, although their militancy had little effect. The Depression came as a shock to an industry that had greatly prospered since World War I. By the 1930s the coal industry was no longer the "object of wonder and amazement."[9] In 1930, membership in the United Mine Workers was half what it had been in 1920, and, by 1932, the union's strike fund was exhausted.[10] While some of the strikes in the coal camps were supported by the Communist-backed National Miners Union, they had little influence on changing the deplorable conditions in the coal camps. However, they did garner media publicity. By 1932 coal production was the lowest since 1904, with 300,000 coal miners out of work nationwide and general wages less than $2.50 per day. These conditions were only exacerbated when industrial decline was coupled to rural poverty, many living in isolation "remote from modern communication and commercial markets."[11] John L. Lewis, the head of the United Mine Workers, called for federal intervention to save the coal industry, casting aside the capitalist notions of laissez-faire, competition, and rugged individualism. Even the Chamber of Commerce and the president of General Electric were calling for some sort of intervention in or management of the economy.

While the Hoover administration had attempted to meet some relief needs in the depressed coalfields, such as the feeding of children, the effort was far from enough. In the north-central region of West Virginia, relief was under the direction of Clarence Pickett of the American Friends Service Committee (AFSC). Handicraft shops—including the Mountaineer Craftsmen's Cooperative, a weaving and furniture-making enterprise that employed roughly fifty men and women—were created, but serious federal intervention did not come until the election of Franklin Roosevelt in 1932.[12]

Appealing to the masses, FDR had campaigned on the platform that selfishness and greed had resulted in the Depression and that he favored greater opportunity and a more equitable distribution of wealth. Underlying his concern over individualism were still a degree of optimism and his desire to rebuild American identity through community. A new vision of the American dream could be realized.[13] Inauguration day, 4 March 1933, was not the traditional one of celebration but clouded by gloomy skies and despair. Herbert Hoover, frustrated, hurt, shamed, and virtually impossible to reelect, found himself paralyzed in the midst of the economic crisis. He refused to offer the traditional welcome to the president-elect, who seemed angry at and insulted by the snub. As millions listened to FDR on radio, they heard him boldly state: "Let me assert my firm belief that the only thing we have to fear is fear itself—nameless, unreasoning, unjustified terror which paralyzes needed efforts to convert retreat into advance." He swore on the Roosevelt family Bible, opened to the thirteenth chapter of First Corinthians: "For now we see through a glass darkly; but then face to face: now I know in part; but then shall I know even as also I am known. And now abideth faith, hope, charity, these three; but the greatest of these is charity." In his inaugural address Roosevelt also floated the idea of population redistribution, which directly tied to his thoughts on subsistence homesteads and the building of community.[14]

In June 1933, roughly two months after his inauguration, FDR signed into law the National Industrial Recovery Act (NIRA). The act declared the Depression "a national emergency productive of widespread unemployment and disorganization of industry," one that "burdens interstate and foreign commerce, affects the public welfare, and undermines the standards of living of the American people."[15] It was strongly supported by American capitalists, including Gerard Swope of General Electric and Harry Harriman, the president of the Chamber of Commerce, who helped draft the legislation. It suspended the antitrust laws, expected companies to adhere to fairness in competition, pushed fixed wages and prices, protected consumers, and allowed for the right of workers to join unions and participate in collective bargaining. In essence, in attempting to please everyone, the NIRA pleased only a few and did little to help the economic slump. It was declared unconstitutional by the Supreme Court in 1935.[16] Regardless of its unconstitutionality, the NIRA set the tone for the New Deal.

In 1933, the Federal Emergency Relief Administration (FERA) estimated that over 4.5 million Americans were stranded in areas and communities where they could no longer make a living wage. Many reformers believed that these people could become self-supporting if moved to rural settings where they could grow their own food and support each other though cooperatives. While the very notion of going back to the land had a Jeffersonian ring to it, the modern back-to-the-land movement was attractive to many in Britain during the late nineteenth century. The English Industrial Revolution had triggered a massive rural-to-urban migration that resulted in cities characterized by overpopulation, pollution, unemployment, widespread disease, and what some perceived as a loss of community. Charles Dickens captures this new type of city in his description in *Hard Times* (1854) of the fictional Coketown.[17] The British back-to-the-landers sought a substitute for the social Darwinism they saw all around them, attracting those who felt that "conventions and proprieties seem suffocatingly restrictive, preventing the expression of natural feelings and simple pleasure." Even fashion and social conduct seemed repressive and confining to them. They sought simplicity and believed that simplicity could be coupled with a return to nature as the only "viable alternative," "the earth as the source of all goodness." Characteristic of this return to nature was a revived interest in local gardening, weaving, folklore, music, and art.[18] A similar movement developed in the United States after the Civil War when, "confronted with postwar unemployment and depression," the nation was attempting to provide for its disabled war veterans. Through the Homestead Act of 1862 Congress sought a rural solution to urban growth and unemployment. The Panic of 1873 brought further attention to rural migration.[19]

Liberty Hyde Bailey, a progressive educator at Cornell's Agricultural School, furthered championed and was an ardent spokesman for what he termed *country life*. He believed that agriculture was "not only the rock foundation of democracy" but also "the very basis of humanity, morality, and justice." For Bailey it was the farm that had made America great, not the city or the industrial capitalists. The farm was the moral compass of the nation. Bailey showed concern about the perceived antagonism between city life and country life, seeking cooperation rather than conflict. Rather than a true back-to-the-land movement, Bailey preferred a back-to-the-village movement where people could farm their own land but also work in or near the city as wage laborers. He did not favor the romantic impulse in the English movement, sensing that industry was here to stay, but he did hope to satisfy what he characterized as the "desire for a nature connection."[20]

There was a bit of mysticism and even spiritualism to American concerns about rural life. Just prior to the Depression, L. L. Bernard, a sociologist at the University of Chicago, noted that the "fundamental values of farm life are mainly spiritual." These "fundamental values" included the discipline of farm life and the solidarity of family life. According to Bernard: "Country life offers . . . a greater spiritual completeness, although on the whole a simpler and more primary spiritual context. Justice, right, obligation, evil, duty, all principles and elements of character, appear relatively simple."[21] The materialism and industrialism of the Roaring Twenties seemed to forge quite a diverse group of back-to-the-landers in America. This eclectic group included capitalists such as Henry Ford, decentralists like Ralph Borsodi, church groups, both Protestant and Catholic, and southern agrarians.[22] While Ford believed that the family farm was antiquated and generally could not provide for complete economic sustenance, he also believed that industrial problems could be remedied by decentralizing industry, providing not only salvation to the farmers but also salvation from industrial blight.[23] On the other hand, Ralph Borsodi, an author and social thinker, reacted strongly against what he characterized as "this ugly civilization" brought on by urban sprawl and industrialization. Borsodi held much in common with the British back-to-the-landers and, according to Paul Conkin, "attracted the sympathy of many of those that had strong inclination toward familialistic and nativist doctrines, or who reacted violently against the more novel aspects of modern city and industrial life." He was actually the first to receive federal subsistence homestead funds for his experimental community in Dayton, Ohio. Catholic and Protestant reformers tended to favor farms of the subsistence type, showing concern about the moral decadence of city life, while, as Conkin notes, the southern agrarians "took a stand in behalf of their ideal agrarian society, the Old South." Faced with the gradual industrialization of the South, they sought to maintain a society that valued "art, agriculture, manners, authority, simplicity, tradition, breeding, leisure, religion, romanticism," all of which were "under attack."[24] By the time of the Depression, the notions of going back to the land and of subsistence farming were part of American social reformist discourse but not yet formal policy.

One year prior to the crash of the stock market, sensing the problems of urban America, Elwood Mead, a professor and engineer as well as head of the Federal Bureau of Reclamation, further articulated the importance of rural society. He argued for planned rural settlements that offered agricultural sustenance but also recreational, social, and economic cooperatives. "[The ideal rural settlement] required the grouping of farmers around a village or community center," he noted, "which would contain stores, the church, and school, cooperative markets, and a community building." Mead believed in community planning by agricultural experts and community homes that could be efficiently and economically constructed.[25]

Following the crash, the publisher Benarr McFadden, another supporter of a rural solution, challenged Congress. "Gentlemen," he began, "I think that unless something is done to relieve the serious unemployment we have everywhere we do not know what may happen to us." Warning his audience of political unrest, he noted: "Firebrands of some kind may start most anything. Idleness is always dangerous, but when idleness is associated with hunger, and children are crying for bread, we cannot blame the people for being desperate. If we take those people to the land and provide them with implements that will interest them, that will occupy their time profitably, and have their children grow up in the country, we will do a great service. It does not make any difference whether those people have much to wear; they will be satisfied with enough to eat."[26]

The back-to-the-landers held several notions in common, though the movement was far from united. They generally believed that a full economic recovery was not possible and that rural America needed to absorb the unemployed. While no one had a clear perspective on what a back-to-the-land program might look like, it was typically seen by most as only a temporary and even an experimental relief measure.[27] Prospective transplants to the rural communities came to be known as *homesteaders,* borrowing from the nineteenth-century American pioneer spirit to start over and build anew. Part of the plan was to nurture and build community, not just relocate those stranded. It was also important that "the physical equipment, the houses, the school, the community center, the recreation facilities—community house, parks, playground—the workshops and industries be so constructed and so located in relation to each other to develop naturally a beautiful community and a happily coordinated community life."[28] Building this type of community required attention to the culture and history of the homesteaders.

FDR believed that the subsistence homestead experiment was worth a try, and he found "a sympathetic and powerful supporter" in Senator John H. Bankhead of Alabama, a southern agrarian. While in early 1933 Bankhead's initial homestead bill failed to gain enough support, an amendment (Section 208, Title II) to the NIRA that he introduced passed in May of that year, ensuring that, when the NIRA itself passed the next month, a federal relief effort would be mounted.[29] Section 208 reads: "To provide for aiding the redistribution of the overbalance of population in industrial centers $25,000,000 is hereby made available to the President, to be used by him through such agencies as he may establish and under such regulations as he may make, for making loans for and otherwise aiding in the purchase of subsistence homesteads. The moneys collected as repayment of said loans shall constitute a revolving fund to be administered as directed by the President for the purposes of this section."[30] As the historian Paul Conkin notes, it authorized the president to move those stranded "away from industrial centers by providing loans or other aid to enable families to purchase subsistence homesteads," creating in essence a type of back-to-the-land movement.[31] Roosevelt in turn authorized Secretary of the Interior Harold Ickes "to set up homesteads for the redistribution of the population in industrial centers by making loans for and aiding the purchase of the subsistence homesteads."[32] The Division of Subsistence Homesteads, established within the Department of the Interior, was also charged "to engage in any kind of charitable, educational, advisory or relief activity and in any other instructional or social activity whatsoever in connection with subsistence homestead projects, purposes and activities stated in this certificate of incorporation."[33] The act referred to the subsistence homesteads as "demonstration projects" that were to be located in "principal" problem areas. These projects were to be carried out "with a maximum of local initiative and responsibility associated with adequate Federal supervision and guidance and protection for the federal funds advanced."[34]

The basic idea behind homestead subsistence farming was that the homesteaders would grow their own food—thus placing less pressure on the declining agricultural production in the United States—and find part-time work to supply enough money to buy whatever else they needed. History had shown, the reformers believed, that, during times of economic depression, farm families tended to survive better than others owing to their ability to grow their own food. While subsistence farming was family based, the concept also connected the individual to the community through cooperatives and "local networks of exchange."[35] That is, a type of bartering system was to be established in which labor could be exchanged for labor. The first director of the Division of Subsistence Homesteads was Milburn Lincoln Wilson, a strong advocate of the subsistence homesteads even though he disliked the term *subsistence*. For Wilson, *subsistence* meant "a rather low, self-sufficing standard of living" rather than "the opportunity to have dignified, wholesome and well-rounded, abundant lives."[36] Raised on a farm, Wilson had graduated from Iowa State, the state land grant institution, and he had practical experience as a farmer that he combined with the improved agricultural efficiency and production techniques to which his professional experience had exposed him. And, as head of the Department of Agriculture and Economics at Montana State, he had established relationships with farmers, agricultural educators, and government officials nationwide. He was among the New Deal back-to-the-land advocates influenced by Richard Ely, a group that also included Elwood Mead and Rexford Tugwell, both crucial influences in the subsistence homestead movement.[37]

Wilson believed that American industry needed to be decentralized. That is: "Industrial cities [should be] built in which the workers, instead of living on town lots or in crowded apartment or tenement houses, will live in suburban communities."[38] Considered an expert on cooperative agricultural communities, Wilson had discussed his ideas about community planning with FDR when the latter was governor of New York. One major concern was the increasing migration from rural areas to urban, placing enormous pressure on cities to meet the needs of those displaced by the Depression.[39] Roosevelt had shown an interest in community planning as early as 1913 when he suggested that suburban farms be provided for city dwellers. In an address before the American Country Life Conference on 19 August 1931, he spoke about the better distribution of populations away from cities. "From many of the larger centers of population," he noted, "I receive appeals from families who, springing from an agriculture background, have tried the ups and downs of city life and who are now ready to exchange its uncertainties for the comparative assurance of a livelihood given by the smaller community." He always attempted to make clear that the subsistence homestead program was designed not to fully eliminate the relief problem but "to make available homes and small farms to persons who were in a position to pay the government for them in small monthly installments, although they might be temporarily unemployed or seasonally out of a job." Essentially, he saw the program as offering hope in desperate times, and for many these were desperate times.[40]

Rexford Tugwell, the future head of the Resettlement Administration, which eventually took over the subsistence homestead program, concluded that FDR believed that people were better off in the country than the city. "In fact," Roosevelt reported in 1932, "I might almost say that the political salvation of the country lies with the country men and boys, not because they are more honest or more patriotic than their brothers in the cities, but because they have more time to think and study for themselves."[41] He was suggesting an intermediary type of community, communities established by "the state alone or by the state with the cooperation and assistance of private capital," "wholly new rural communities of homes for workers on good agricultural land within reasonable distance of which facilities shall be offered for the establishment of new industries aimed primarily to give cash wages on a cooperative basis during the non-agricultural season."[42]

Wilson was also familiar with the work of Ralph Borsodi, who began subsistence farming in 1920. Borsodi was known for economic independence, self-sufficiency, and his hostility to urban life.[43] As a progressive reformer, Wilson, like Ely and John Dewey, was deeply concerned over the crass materialism of the 1920s and the period's growing individualism. His democratic temper convinced him that materialism and individualism could result in the fragmentation and possible dissolution of the American democratic experiment. As Paul Conkin writes: "[Wilson] desired the economic activity, social stability, neighborliness, lack of social pressure and the social participation of America's agricultural past, while he believed that much of city life was unnatural, leading to frustration, toward nervous systems and decreased physical vitality." Wilson's democratic views further emphasized local control of the subsistence homestead projects rather than centralized control by bureaucrats in Washington, no matter how honest and idealistic the reformers might be.[44]

This democratic vision went beyond mere economic solutions, such as the construction of houses and farm plots, to include the building of community. Conkin writes: "Democracy was the nearest thing to an absolute to Wilson." And, in most Deweyan fashion, Wilson feared that the values of republicanism were under attack in the modern capitalist era. His notion of community embodied economic security, social security, and stability undergirded by a sense of contribution beyond the individual but for the larger common good. The slum and urban congestion were symptoms of an illness that could be treated by decentralization and subsistence farming.[45] Wilson and the federal homestead subsistence supporters "had consciously aimed at something more than a group of carefully engineered and designed rural houses located in a rather odd, city-rural pattern." They put their "emphasis on creative endeavors, such as handicrafts, with less social competition and more stability and security, and capping it all, with as many as possible of the community activities organized on a cooperative rather than a competitive basis."[46] Wilson envisioned the production of handicrafts in an aesthetic and practical way, as a form of individual creativity and expression, but he also thought handcrafts might provide extra income for the subsistence homesteaders. He described his idea of the subsistence homestead as follows: "This new pattern of life therefore is a sort of village life, but more than this it may develop the handicrafts and skills of which we have, but little in this country."[47] For progressive reformers like Wilson, capitalism had reached its zenith; something else needed to be tried, and in the Depression era subsistence homesteads were considered possible and practical. Wilson was far from alone in his critique of capital. Rexford Tugwell noted: "We have depended too long on the hope that private ownership and control would operate somehow for the benefit of society as a whole. That hope has not been realized."[48]

"The federal government is justified, we believe," wrote John Pratt Whitman, on behalf of the Committee on Administration of Subsistence Homesteads, to Secretary of the Interior Ickes, "in a large degree of experimentation which may well lead a whole people into a better and wiser way of life. We humbly recommend, therefore, that time, through available funds be generously contributed toward a successful outcome of the Subsistence Homestead projects." Whitman's report emphasized a harmonious relationship, cooperative buying, cooperative agriculture, and cooperative consumption.[49] Such views struck a strong Jeffersonian tone on the virtues of rural/agrarian life. As Jefferson had articulated: "Cultivators of the earth are the most valuable citizens, they are the most virtuous, and they are tied to their country and wedded to its liberties and interest by the most lasting bonds."[50] For these reformers, there was something special about the soil, which represented a connection to nature, nostalgia for another time, one simpler, more personal, communal, and cooperative.

The practical goal of the subsistence homestead movement was to construct modest homes, financed through long-term contracts and low interest rates, and, where educational facilities were not available, establish them along with a community center.[51] The projects were to be located in areas where the homesteaders could obtain sufficient cash income to make their monthly house payments as well as meet other family needs. Wilson stated: "Subsistence Homesteads are of such a character as to provide principally food for a family and not to engage in commercial agricultural production of those commodities of which there is a surplus."[52] All homesteads were to be organized into cooperatives guided by the laws of the individual state, and all homesteaders were to be members of a cooperative. "The existence of such cooperatives of homesteaders," wrote the federal planner Nathan Margold, "will enable the carrying out of several experimental forms of community organization which are being considered."[53]

One of the strongest supporters of the federal subsistence homestead projects was First Lady Eleanor Roosevelt. She visited the coal camps of Scotts Run, in north-central West Virginia just outside Morgantown, in August 1933 following an invitation from her close friend Lorena Hickok, an Associated Press reporter. Working for FERA at the time, Hickok had come to see the coalfields of Scotts Run at the invitation of Clarence Pickett, who headed up relief efforts for the AFSC in the Scotts Run area and would play a key role in the Arthurdale experiment. Educated at Penn College in Iowa, Hartford Theological Seminary, and Harvard, Pickett was serving at the time as the executive secretary of the AFSC, a post he had held since 1929. In 1932, Mrs. Roosevelt had invited him to the White House to discuss the plight of mining families. She was familiar with his work in vocational rehabilitation and subsistence gardening in the north-central West Virginia area.[54] Scotts Run mining camps were typical of those in Appalachia generally. The historian Ron Eller writes: "The typical mining camp was located on the lower slopes and valley floor between two high ridges. Not much more than a crevice in the earth, this natural location provided little space for the necessary structure of a mining town and often contributed to the confined and congested appearance of the camp itself."[55] Hickok had described Scotts Run as "not fit for pigs."[56] Another observer called the area "the damndest cesspool of human misery I have ever seen in America."[57] Families were living close to starvation, with inadequate diets, respiratory disease, and dysentery. Scotts Run had changed drastically from 1900 to 1920, the portion of the population working as coal miners growing from 1 to 63 percent. In his study of industrial development in the town, Phil Ross writes: "Stripped of its industrial glory, Scotts Run became a bleak reminder to the public, the industry, and New Deal policy makers of the fallacy of unchecked development."[58] Ron Lewis further notes: "The Great Depression, of course, was a national calamity, and Scotts Run residents suffered more than most Americans from the maladies of unemployment, ignorance, ethnic and racial prejudice, and the other corollaries of abject poverty."[59] Scotts Run provided a clear example of the transition from a rural/agrarian world to an industrial one, a change not lost on the subsistence homestead reformers.[60] But the reformers were also attentive to what they saw as the human waste, including "worthless men, injured men, trouble makers, and men without morals."[61] Mrs. Roosevelt visited Scotts Run with Hickok and Pickett as they observed the problems of the community. Unrecognized by the coal miners and their families, she quizzed them about their lives, and she took notes. Most likely they saw her as a social worker engaged in relief work, and they knew how important that was to their survival. She commented: "The conditions I saw convinced me that with a little leadership there could develop in the mining areas, if not a people's revolution, at least a people's party patterned after the forms of the previous parties born of bad economic conditions."[62] She sensed the urgency of the situation and conveyed that sense to the president on returning to Washington.[63] As Secretary of the Interior Ickes explained things: "Our subsistence problem ... is divided toward making families, now on relief, self-supporting citizens. The situation among the bituminous coal miners is desperate indeed. According to reliable sources at least 200,000 coal miners have been permanently displaced from the industry. Relief for them is costing both federal and local agencies large sums. Continued relief is, as you know, demoralizing. Those people must be given a new start in life and afforded an opportunity to become self-supporting once more."[64]

Bituminous coal production in the United States had reached its height in 1923. In that year there were, as Eller notes, over 700,000 men working in nearly 12,000 mines, with a possible production of nearly a billion tons. However, by late 1923 production slowed owing to a decrease in demand, and the slow market continued through the 1920s. Not surprisingly, many smaller mines began to close, leaving the towns that had built up around them with neither jobs nor electricity. According to Eller: "By 1930, unemployment, destitution and despair stalked the coal fields. Although coal production recovered again with the outbreak of World War II, employment in the Appalachian coal fields never again reached the halcyon days of the twenties."[65]

By the time Mrs. Roosevelt visited the area, Scotts Run had become a hotbed of violence, with tension growing between the United Mine Workers and the Communist-backed National Miners Union. The Roosevelt administration, including the First Lady, was clearly attuned to the potential for violent class conflict and viewed the miners of Scotts Run as a viable population to be considered for the first homestead subsistence project. Mrs. Roosevelt's compassion for the people of the area and her detailed descriptions directly influenced FDR and Ickes in choosing a north-central West Virginia location for the first subsistence homestead project—Arthurdale. She envisioned the project as "an agricultural experimental station . . . to be run by local corporations but with the advice of the federal planners." With a budget of only $25 million, the project was, she knew, just a start, but the community—two hundred long-term unemployed coal miners and their families—could serve as a model for others. Rexford Tugwell agreed with her, writing optimistically: "Our subsistence homesteads program will provide some exceedingly useful experiments."[66]

The selection of Arthurdale as the first federal "demonstration project" was announced on 12 October 1933 by the secretary of the interior. In a press release issued that day, Ickes described the purchase of the eleven-hundred-acre Arthur farm in Preston County, West Virginia, roughly twenty-five miles southeast of Morgantown. "The settlement will be self-governing," Ickes declared, "with administration to be patterned after the New England town meeting plan. A school will be established which will also serve as a community center." He emphasized the importance of handicraft industries and factory labor coupled with homestead subsistence farming, claiming: "The project is in many ways one of the most significant in this period. It will serve as a means of measuring the possibilities of decentralizing industry in this country where the evils of over-urbanization have become all too evident in this depression. It will undertake to return to usefulness, security and to a high degree of self-sufficiency a group of men and their families who are victims of the period of planlessness and helter-skelter development and misuse of natural resources which I hope we are leaving behind."[67]

Initially known as the Reedsville Experimental Project, the settlement soon became known as Arthurdale, after the farm family from whom the federal government purchased the land.[68] The miners were given farm lots, they were expected to build the homes they were to live in, and they were also expected to participate in "cooperative enterprises including farming, processing, and commercial activities."⁶⁹ The project's experimental nature was made clear in a position paper that Mrs. Roosevelt prepared:

> It was from the start a laboratory in every way. . . . This plan was thought of as the place where new types of rural schools might be tried; the place could serve as an object lesson to communities of a similar kind throughout the country. . . . There were certain things if improvements in community living in rural centers which might be tried there [sic]. . . . The fact [is] that rural life has actually not held sufficient attraction for youth because of the lack of opportunity for both recreational and educational activities, and community life which would be of real social value was practically impossible under our present rural conditions. Under this head I put the nursery school, recreational facilities, the connection between school and community centers, handicraft work, and certain adult educational plans which might lead to more satisfactory living.⁷⁰

Part of this experimental community, a laboratory in many ways, was a school that could, Mrs. Roosevelt felt, be a potential model for schools throughout rural America.

Clearly viewed as a champion of the people, Mrs. Roosevelt was receiving inquiries about the homestead project and its school shortly after its announcement. Typically coal camp schools "were poor, understaffed, and scarcely adequate for the education needs of rural mountaineers." The character of these schools did not, however, imply that the destitute mining families they served did not place great faith in public education and seek quality "schooling" for their children.⁷¹ A group of women in the Scotts Run area wrote to Mrs. Roosevelt offering advice on and assistance in planning for the project: "We have heard that there is no school near the new colony. We consider it very important to have a schoolhouse—also a community house which could be used for a kindergarten on week day mornings, for a recreation and reading room in the evenings and as a place for worship on Sundays." They closed the letter thanking Eleanor for her help in building this "happy and hard working community."⁷²

Becoming a homesteader at Arthurdale was far from easy. The selection process was complex and under the direction of an advisory committee of faculty members from West Virginia University. Owing to the political nature of the subsistence projects, the Roosevelt administration sought to select families who could make the project a success. Because of the experimental nature of the community, the advisory committee sought homesteaders of "intelligence, perseverance, and foresight." By November 1933, between six and seven hundred applicants were seeking homesteads. Clarence Pickett suggested the application process be suspended owing to the large number of applicants.[73] The overwhelming response from people seeking to gain admission to Arthurdale surprised the federal planners, revealing a need greater than could possibly be met. Those selected as homesteaders were subjected to interviews, some of them very personal, along with an eight-page application. They were expected to be in good mental and physical health, have some knowledge of farming and animal husbandry, and have some formal education. As families were interviewed, notes were taken on the furniture and the neatness of their homes. Potential homesteaders were asked numerous questions. Could the men leave the home to go and work on the Arthurdale project? Would the children be satisfied to attend the local Reedsville grade school and Masontown High School (as plans originally called for)? Did they have the courage and nerve to face up to the harsh winters in Preston County? What did they want their children to become? How far in school did they wish them to go? Did they get along with their neighbors? Did their children get along with the neighbors? What were their attitudes toward farming? What was their nationality? Homesteaders were also asked to trace their hands for possible defects and show evidence of manual labor. They were tested on their knowledge of seeds and planting cycles, asked agricultural questions such as the difference between "a layer and a loafer" and how often the poultry house should be cleaned. They were questioned about their knowledge of cows, pigs, and horses. They were asked about their preferred forms of recreation, what games they liked to play, their ambitions, church affiliation, and even whether they returned tools after borrowing them.[74]

The goal of the selection committee was to provide homesteads only to those deemed to be "safe risks."[75] The politically charged nature of Arthurdale pushed planners to select only those homesteaders who could make the project successful but also not cause problems. At this point in the process, the potential homesteaders were asked to sign the following pledge: "If you were given an opportunity to own a farm in the new rural community, we will consider your signature below and a pledge of your loyalty to and cooperation with the management of the project in all requests and direction which may be necessary to develop this rural community along solid lines, economically, industrially, and socially." Clarence Pickett emphasized the importance of moral character in the selection of the homesteaders.[76]

Following interviews with over five hundred applicants, the West Virginia University College of Education faculty member and professor of agriculture Howard B. Allen expressed the difficulty of directing former coal miners into farming: "Relief must be brought to the distressed miners without embarrassing sorely perplexed farmers . . . and any successful program must be ultimately self-sustaining [with the] prospect of seeking an adjustment of higher standards of living without burdening disproportionately the rest of society."[77] A native of Buffalo, New York, Allen held his academic credentials from Cornell, earning a Ph.D. in 1932. His academic specialties were agricultural education and industrial arts, both strongly emphasized in the Arthurdale community and school. Allen concluded that many of the Arthurdale applicants lacked the material resources to begin farming and recommended continuous supervision and education and federal financing to ease the transition. Still, he strongly believed that the application process accomplished the "effective sorting" the federal planners were seeking. He was so confident that he wrote to Clarence Pickett on 18 December 1933 suggesting that any "trained person could prepare a similar plan for selectively recruiting 'safe risks' for any of [his] numerous projects." He also offered his assistance in the planning of further projects by the government.[78]

The highly selective application process and limited number of homesteads available led to a flood of letters to various federal officials, including Eleanor Roosevelt, whom many saw as a champion of the poor and willing to help them.[79] Nevertheless, only fifty families were initially selected owing to the number of houses being planned.[80] It made sense, therefore, to chose only those most likely to succeed. And it is likely that the project manager, Bushrod Grimes, had a strong influence on the selection process owing to his prior work in the mining camps.[81] The homesteader contract stated that the property to be turned over to the homesteaders could not be used for an "unlawful purpose." This included the use of, the keeping of, or the selling of liquor. The property was to be properly maintained and kept free of fences, outbuildings, weeds, and shrubs. If homesteaders broke their contract by not paying rent, the government could terminate the agreement.[82]

The homesteaders selected for Arthurdale were all Caucasian, about half of them miners, and some others who had knowledge of woodworking, sawmill operation, and farming.[83] Roughly 25 percent of the applicants were African American, yet none were selected. This can partly be explained by the fact that, owing to an 1872 change to the West Virginia constitution, schools in the state were required by law to be segregated. Another contributing factor was the belief, perpetuated by the Arthurdale Homesteader's Club, that those "clamoring for admission are not Negroes, but are of mixed blood and far inferior to the real Negroes who refuse to mix with the white race."[84] Also, some miners who preferred an all-white community saw African Americans as strike breakers.[85] Coal companies in West Virginia had used racism to stem union growth, fostering tensions between whites, blacks, and immigrants "in order to forestall immigration by segregating the men and playing one group off against another." However, before the Civil War, black miners often worked side by side with white miners and had been part of coal production in Appalachia. Indeed: "In 1920, 43% of the black miners employed in the US worked in West Virginia, but the vast majority worked in the southern region of the state."[86] The NAACP challenged the racial bias of the selection process, and W. E. B. DuBois challenged the use of federal funds to establish segregated subsistence homesteads. DuBois sought a share of the funds to underwrite African American homestead projects, and a few were started, yet Arthurdale remained segregated.[87]

Prior to the occupation of the first home, Mrs. Roosevelt visited a mining camp and in response to the experience offered her conception of the advantages of a subsistence homestead. She, and the federal planners, felt that the mining camps disrupted individual initiative and community. She told the story of the mother of a coal family working hard to survive who had planted a garden and was canning what she grew: "It was easy to see that here was a young woman who was trying hard to bring up a healthy family and who had the standards of good and well-planned farm living in her mind."[88] For Mrs. Roosevelt, this young woman embodied the spirit of subsistence homesteading—families not competing with local agricultural interests but providing food for themselves. Indeed, the homesteaders were prevented from selling their crops for cash. As one journalist noted: "The central nature of the subsistence homestead problem therefore is to demonstrate the economic values of a livelihood that combines part time wage work and part time gardening or farming."[89] Mrs. Roosevelt echoed this notion when she wrote that the ideal was for "one member of the family to be employed in a factory a sufficient number of days in the year to bring in the amount of money needed to pay for the things families must have and cannot produce for themselves." Accordingly, all lots awarded to the homesteaders consisted of five acres, including pasture and a comfortable house. At the time, Mrs. Roosevelt believed that the local county schools could take care of educating the children of the homesteaders, although that was to change. Concluding her remarks, she suggested: "If the West Virginia experiment succeeds it may be the model for many other similar plans throughout the United States."[90]

The first home was ready for occupation on 10 March 1934 and was described as a "cheery dwelling with all conveniences."[91] The first families began to move in on 28 April 1934, as noted publicly by FDR: "This project provided an experimental ground for community planning, home construction, community farming and education, and for other activities which presented some particular problems, the solution of which would be beneficial to the entire subsistence homestead program."[92] The federal subsistence homestead program was now coming to life.

The Roosevelt administration as well as Mrs. Roosevelt placed great faith in education as part of the subsistence homestead experience, in large measure because the project was designed to help the underprivileged. In broadly describing the New Deal planners' educational philosophy, the historian David Tyack writes: "They had a strong commitment to schooling as a means of social change and an avenue of equality of opportunity. But classroom instruction was only part of the New Deal style in education. The New Deal education innovators had a deep faith in the democratization of culture and of learning . . . and stressed how people can learn from working cooperatively."[93] What was learned from experimental schools like Arthurdale could serve as a model for the public education system at large.

For the federal planners, it was crucial that the children of the Arthurdale homesteaders have adequate access to education. Early plans called, as we have seen, for them to be transported to a local county school in the Reedsville area, but that school could not accommodate the growing number of children in the new homestead community.[94] This inadequacy resulted in the development of a school specific to the needs of the homestead community. Mrs. Roosevelt was a primary influence on this new school's planning process and most likely was not disappointed that the Arthurdale community would have its own school. She believed that the distinct nature of this community required a special kind of school, one best based on a progressive education philosophy. While the progressive education movement was never monolithic, as previously noted the Arthurdale School accepted some aspects of its philosophy and challenged others. A component of this philosophy integrated early childhood education, adult education, and handicraft training.[95] Health, recreation, and household economy were also deemed worthy of attention. The Arthurdale planners believed that the school should be the center of community life, "the pivot and center of the community," "reach[ing] out as spokes from a hub into village activities everywhere." There was an attempt to remove traditional barriers between the homesteaders and the school, and teachers were expected "to be residents of the community from the beginning and to assume economic responsibilities similar to the homesteaders": "Teachers were to be scattered among their neighbors where they could be familiar with the known problems, and with individual families on an equal basis of neighborliness."[96] While this ideal of integration was never fully achieved, that it was discussed shows a serious concern about education being key to community life. For Milburn Wilson, a form of social experimentation such as a homestead had to nurture a "democratic atmosphere throughout, with numerous committees and unending discussion": "Only this type of education could lead to the consideration and the questioning of fundamental values."[97] Yet this atmosphere could be cultivated only if it was based on an element of trust, that is, only if the homesteaders had a voice in the planning and governing structure of the project. Unfortunately, the political nature of the Arthurdale project, coupled with the nature of government bureaucracy, put this goal beyond reach.

Socialization undergirded the philosophy of the Arthurdale School, the idea being to give the students and the adults the requisite skills to participate in the local community and the larger democratic society. To build such a society, children needed to be nurtured in the habits of cooperation, interdependence, and responsibility. Knowledge was not just something one sought after or acquired but something used and shared in cooperation with others. It was communal and not something to be guarded or held for its own sake. For Mrs. Roosevelt and the reformers, the school needed to and should serve the community at large and not just schoolchildren. It could help overcome the alienation and isolation that both the children and the adults had experienced in the coal camps of Scotts Run. To create such an idealistic institution, which would become known as the Arthurdale School, in a new, experimental type of community was not an easy task, and it fell on a disciple and former student of American philosopher John Dewey, Elsie Ripley Clapp.[98]

3

Elsie Ripley Clapp and the Community School

While working at the Ballard Memorial School just outside Louisville, Kentucky, in 1933, Elsie Clapp wrote: "A community school foregoes its separateness. It is influential because it belongs to its people. They share its ideals and its work. It takes from them and gives to them. There are no bounds as far as I can see to what it could accomplish in social reconstruction if it had enough wisdom and insight and devotion and energy. It demands all these for changes in living and learning of people are not produced by imparting information about different conditions or by gathering statistical data about what exists, but by creating with people, for people."[1] Her words express a clear link between the school and the community, a type of mutual exchange and one destined to make changes in the lives of the entire community, not just the students'. Deeply influenced by her association with and reading of John Dewey, Clapp, like many of the federal homestead planners, believed that the Depression only worsened the loss of community in American society and that the school could serve as a means to restore it. Learning was, she felt, both an individual and a social process, grounded in human experience, the foundation of community and democracy as ethical association. Yet her work also calls attention to the progressive paradox, the contradiction between democratic theory and actual school practice.[2]

By 1933, Clapp was well-known in progressive education circles. From 1933 to 1934, she chaired the National Committee on Rural Education for the Progressive Education Association (PEA) and served as PEA vice president, and she served as a member of the PEA Advisory and Executive Board from 1924 to 1936.[3] Although her experience in rural education was limited to Kentucky, she would soon be extensively involved in rural education in

West Virginia through the homestead project at Arthurdale. Her experiences in rural education are documented in her two books, *Community Schools in Action* (1939) and *The Use of Resources in Education* (1952), as well as several articles.[4] To fully grasp an understanding of the Arthurdale School, one must first understand Elsie Ripley Clapp, the principal and director of community affairs, and her ideas about community schools. It was her view of progressive education that undergirded the philosophy of the Arthurdale School from 1934 to 1936 and, essentially, up to World War II.

Clapp's intellectual philosophy and her attempt to integrate theory and practice developed over a number of years from personal and extensive experience in public and private education.[5] Born in 1879 in Brooklyn, New York, Clapp spent her early years in affluent Brooklyn Heights. She described the first fourteen years of her life "as incredibly comfortable, protected, in our own world": "We lived unostentatiously perhaps, but luxuriously."[6] (Later in life, she recalled her affluent lifestyle as highly restricted, never impromptu.) Born a child of wealth, she received her early education in the home. "The real education I received in childhood," she recalled, "came through familiarity with the libraries of my father and grandfather and association with the older members of my family and exposure to their interests."[7] This education also included concertgoing, theatergoing, and dancing. Clapp began her formal education in local Brooklyn private schools and attended high school from 1894 through 1899 at the Packer Collegiate Institute in Brooklyn. Packer challenged her intellectually and socially, giving her some interaction with girls from other social classes and ethnic groups. Much of her energy was spent improving her Latin skills, reading, and translating. Following high school graduation she enrolled at Vassar.[8]

During her sophomore year of college, Clapp was diagnosed with chronic appendicitis and later phlebitis, conditions that resulted in her leaving Vassar and eventually transferring to Barnard College, where she matriculated in 1908 with a degree in English. Prior to completing her degree at Barnard, she accepted a position at the Brooklyn Heights Seminary teaching seventh- and eighth-grade English, a position she held from 1903 to 1907.[9] For five months during the 1908–1909 school year she taught at the Horace Mann School at Teachers College in New York, where she tutored fifth-, sixth-, and seventh-grade children who needed remedial work. However, because the work interfered with her classes, she took a job as a secretary for the *Journal of Philosophy, Psychology and Scientific Methods*, edited by the Columbia University professor F. J. E. Woodbridge. While finishing her undergraduate degree, she also took graduate classes in English and philosophy at Columbia. It was philosophy that captured her interest. She studied the history of philosophy with William Montague, fundamental problems of philosophy and Aristotle with Woodbridge, Plato with Wendell Bush, Kant with Arthur Lovejoy, and ethics and curriculum with John Dewey. As a graduate student, she continued to serve as the secretary for the *Journal of Philosophy, Psychology, and Scientific Methods*. Her work with the journal and her interactions with members of the Philosophy Department stimulated her intellectual growth, but her main influence came from Dewey.[10] Her association with Teachers College brought her into contact with William H. Kilpatrick, whom she described as a lifelong friend. She met Kilpatrick about the time he was moving from teaching the history of education to teaching the philosophy of education.[11] Clapp received a master's degree in philosophy from Columbia in 1909.

During 1909–1910, Clapp spent most of her academic efforts in the English Department pursuing a Ph.D., although her heart seemed always drawn to philosophy. She continued her studies with Dewey, taking from him a course on Kant that she recalled as "notable for its clarity and conciseness" and a course on the philosophy of education. During the summer of 1910, she assisted Dewey in his course Aims and Principles of Education at Teachers College, an assistantship she believed Dewey paid for out of his own pocket. Clapp continued her studies in English and in philosophy, attending, for example, Dewey's lectures on types of logical thought, but she also expressed indignation that Dewey's work was not considered as significant as that of others in the Philosophy Department: "Dewey received no support in this endeavor," she recalled. "Montague was a realist, Woodbridge called himself a metaphysical realist, and Dr. Bush was a Platonist. . . . To them, the distinctions against which Dewey inveighed were necessary and inevitable. Although his ideas apparently fascinated them, for members of the Department attended most of his lectures. They found it difficult to grasp his conception of the individual-in-the-world, acting upon it and reacting to it, living and learning."[12] She was essentially attempting to address Dewey's concept of experience, central to his pragmatism and pedagogy and influential in her future practice.

Clapp was fascinated by Dewey and continued her study with him in his courses The Logic of Experience and Philosophy and Education in Their Historic Relations. She noted: "I discovered what it is really to know a writer, and realized that the insight that discerns significant relation between education's development and the history of thought is the result of both reflection and wide knowledge and experience."[13] In the summer of 1911, she assisted Dewey in preparing for two courses, An Analysis of Experience and Theory of Experience. She appreciated and admired his patience and "willingness to receive ideas offered by his young assistant and . . . his generosity in finding in them matter relevant to his own thinking."[14]

While Clapp is best known for her work at Ballard and Arthurdale, her intellectual growth at Columbia and early articles provide insight into her ideas about progressive education and the goal of understanding the interaction of the school and the community in a rural public school setting. She recalled her first experience of reading Dewey's "My Pedagogic Creed" (1897) while a sophomore at Vassar: "I still remember the night I first read it as a sophomore at Vassar. We were all excited by it and barely believed that such an education was in existence."[15] Her understanding of Dewey's philosophy and pedagogy was enhanced by her close work with him as a student and as his teaching assistant. Dewey expressed confidence in her philosophical insight and before teaching one course asked for her assistance: "I should appreciate it if you would make any further suggestions that have occurred to you—reflections before I actually start teaching one course. I regret to say the educational course is in about the same dim and inchoate form [word illegible] that it was."[16] Soliciting Clapp's input from another course, Dewey responded to her comments:

> While things have not all come together in my mind yet, I got more help that day in what I had been trying to do and got stuck in . . . connecting the chief issues of philosophy . . . with natural perplexities of life than I can tell you. And I have found much enlightenment in what you have sent me. . . . I want to hold you to your word about future conversation.[17]

Clapp must have been elated. She and Dewey held a mutual respect for each other, a lifelong professional respect in which they never referred to each other as Elsie or John.[18] Some of their most interesting correspondence focused on the meaning of *experience,* a concept central to Dewey's pragmatism and Clapp's pedagogy. In her notes as a teaching assistant, Clapp attempted to clarify: "Do not call it experience unless the modification of conscious action. Education is a social process whereby the individual is assisted by others having foresight of consequences. All known experience is social in character and can be explained as an interaction of biological and social factors." Building on her discussion with Dewey about the nature of desire, she noted: "Education is any modification of the one who has the experience with a view to receiving more desirable; avoiding less desirable forms of further experience."[19] She eventually attempted to capture this desire—what Dewey would later refer to as *interest*—as a basis for developing the curriculum at Arthurdale, in the interest of the child and the community.[20]

In this early association between teacher and teaching assistant, Dewey began to articulate concepts such as experience, certainty, contingency, and the role of philosophy that would later be expressed in such books as *Experience and Nature, A Quest for Certainty, Experience and Education, Reconstruction in Philosophy*, and *Democracy and Education*. Through Clapp's notes on Dewey's lectures, it is easy to understand her belief that philosophy was more than the traditional search for truth and wisdom; it was a means to transform the environment to meet the needs of the individual and the community. Clapp, much like Dewey, began to see community life as composed of art, thinking, inference, cooperation, shared experience, inquiry, and free and undistorted communication. Dewey acknowledged the contributions of both William H. Kilpatrick and Elsie Clapp in the preface to his seminal work *Democracy and Education*, first published in 1916.[21] Both viewed these as characteristics of democratic society. While chaos, disorder, confusion, and conflict were a part of human social interaction, within the context of democratic society there was the freedom to interact and create conditions for accelerated social change.[22]

Clapp completed all the coursework for a doctorate in English but not the dissertation. She was examining the theory of English grammar in the sixteenth, seventeenth, and eighteenth centuries, a formidable task. However, during the preliminaries, what today might be considered a qualifying exam for candidacy, several of the English faculty members began to argue among themselves, and after an hour Clapp left the room in confusion and disgust. She refused to undergo a second examination and thus never received her degree.[23]

Frustrated by her experience, Clapp left Columbia University but soon began work as a member of the Committee on Children in the Paterson Silk Workers' strike organization. The historian Steve Golin writes: "The Paterson strike began as an attempt by workers to control the rate of production; significantly, the reduction in hours." The strikers also attacked low wages, long hours, and poor working and living conditions.[24] This job opened Clapp's eyes to a different world from affluent Brooklyn Heights and was her first true exposure to poverty and the plight of the working classes. She became well acquainted with the Lower East Side and the uptown tenement districts. "I was amazed," she wrote, "to discover how poor and crowded were the homes of those who had offered refuge to the children of their fellow workers."[25] During the strike, Clapp met Bill and Margaret Sanger, Bill Haywood of the Industrial Workers of the World, Elizabeth Gurley Flynn, William Zorach, Carla Tresca, Arturo Giovanniti, and John Reed. She learned a great deal from her observations and participation—if nothing else, gaining a growing sympathy with the plight of the working class, a sympathy that would serve her well in rural Kentucky and West Virginia.

Later in 1913, Clapp traveled south to Charleston, South Carolina, to teach in an exclusive girls' school, Ashley Hall, where she headed the English Department from 1913 to 1914.[26] While teaching at Ashley Hall and showing a growing political militancy, Clapp joined five thousand other women in the suffrage parade in Washington during President Woodrow Wilson's inauguration on 3 March 1913. Although police were everywhere, she recalled that they ignored the "hoodlums who surged out from the sidewalk and forced us to reduce the marching lines to eight abreast." With pride she noted: "But not a single woman faltered and finally we reached the Auditorium at the top of Capital Avenue."[27] Desiring to return north, Clapp left Ashley Hall in 1914 and taught English for one year at Jersey City High School. In 1915, she took a job at the Brooklyn Heights Seminary, where she remained from 1915 to 1921, serving as head of the English Department and as executive secretary to the principal.[28]

During the summer of 1921, Clapp once again entered Dewey's life, asking him if she could help him in his summer courses at Teachers College. She believed that her educational and social experiences now gave her greater insight into the philosophy of education, claiming: "The practical work I had been doing for the past six years seemed to have deepened my understanding of philosophy of education." Leaving Brooklyn Heights in 1921, she moved to Milton, Massachusetts, to teach English and history at the private Milton Academy for Girls, where she also headed the English Department from 1922 to 1923. Milton was a pleasant experience for Clapp: "Even if I was the only progressive at the school, other staff members cooperated readily with me."[29] What did the concept of progressive education mean to Clapp at the time? While still defining her philosophy of education, she was attempting to use traditional subject matter to nurture in her students the skills, problem-solving ability, creativity, and reflection that she felt necessary for life in democratic society. She incorporated her talent and interest in art in the curriculum at Milton and began to associate with other women interested in progressive education.

From 1923 to 1924, Clapp taught seventh grade at the City and Country School in New York. Begun by Caroline Pratt in 1914, the school served as an experimental institution in the middle of Greenwich Village. It attracted intellectuals, artists, and writers, many of whom were willing to place their children in an innovative educational program.[30] Close colleagues of Clapp's at City and Country included Jessie Stanton, Harriett Johnson, Marietta Johnson, and Lucy Sprague Mitchell.[31] Mitchell and Stanton remained close to Clapp throughout her educational career and were involved in the planning of the Arthurdale School. While teaching at City and Country, Clapp assisted Dewey during the 1923-1924 winter session at Teachers College. However, she was never comfortable and felt like an outsider at City and Country and found the teachers' attitude of discipleship toward Caroline Pratt distasteful. She also believed that Pratt was jealous of her extensive education and her association with Dewey.[32]

Leaving City and Country, Clapp served from 1924 to 1929 as principal of the Rosemary Junior School in Greenwich, Connecticut, which she described as "one of the oldest and largest of the conservative college preparatory schools in the east."[33] By this time, she was well entrenched in progressive circles. She described the early years at Rosemary as akin to rolling a ball uphill. Progressive education had become a fad in some circles, drawing attention from the upper middle classes as a more unique or innovative way to educate their children, a problem that often plagued it. Clapp described the situation at Rosemary: "The children, accustomed to maids and chauffeurs and to a weak and inefficient school, were both bad mannered and indolent and lacking any work habits or interests.... Some parents were hopeful, more doubtful and a few hostile." Yet, gradually, the children became more alive and interested in their work. Clapp commented that the teachers in the secondary school (called the *upper school* at Rosemary) were "astonished to find that in progressive schools, such as ours, teachers occupied a far more responsible and independent position."[34]

Clapp wrote one of her first articles in 1926 while serving as principal of the Rosemary Junior School. The article, "Subject Matters in Experimental Education," published in *Progressive Education*, was based on her experience at Rosemary. Noting the influence of Dewey, Clapp explained: "Professor Dewey suggests that the activity of a person in remaking for his own purpose, his environment is comparable to the practice of the artist in reshaping, recreating his world. For he refashions it to the end that it and he can function reciprocally, and with the result that they are in a developing and harmonious interrelation. And so he is organically, himself integrated in the process."[35] She strongly suggested that subject matter should be chosen on the basis of inquiry, experience, and the interests of the child. It was important to listen to the voices of the children, but those voices were to be guided by learning subject matter through experience and not whim. Clapp also believed that teachers should be masters of their subject matter to give children more than just a superficial understanding.[36] Teachers were to be active participants in the community, identifying with its life and interests. "The teachers were residents, neighbors," Clapp wrote. "Their life is part of the community. Their comings and goings are part of the happenings. The work of the school with the children—health matters, social matters—takes them everywhere, into homes in contact with people of every kind."[37] She also warned anyone aspiring to teach in a progressive education setting: "There is no ease, little leisure, much work, great happiness, no aloofness, take and give, learning and living—expanding work and answering growing needs."[38] Teachers were to be active in their community and experts in their subject matter, traits strongly advocated at Arthurdale.[39] No doubt, Clapp had some sense of what Dewey felt about teaching, integrating it into her own varied experiences as a teacher. Dewey tended to hold the teaching profession in high regard; however, he was also concerned about the lack of professional identity and camaraderie among teachers. Some of this was due to an institution that disempowered them and was not attentive to their experiences or voice. Dewey saw the teacher as an inquirer, politically astute and social engaged, a type of civic servant rather than a mere civil servant.[40]

Clapp continued her concerns about traditional subject matter and the approach to it in another article, "Children's Mathematics," written in 1928. She believed that math, taught in the traditional manner of facts to be learned, prevented children from understanding its value. She suggested teachers needed to be integrating material such as "looking into how men long ago counted and measured, when they figured and measured, how they recorded it, how this helped them in their living, how it helped them to get food, to build, to exchange goods, to travel, to provide, to export and import, to think out problems without having to go through physically what they wanted to do, to foresee to try other ways to get the facts they needed, to check results, to invent, to improve conditions, to plan new things, to discover lands, to analyze, to draw conclusions."[41]

Clapp saw no reason why language, art, music, and history could not be integrated into children's personal experiences, helping them better understand math, emphasizing the important role of process in learning, the freedom to make sense of information (math in this case) and its relationship to other knowledge or subject matter. Children may experience difficulty when knowledge becomes bracketed into subject matter categories, separate from human experience. Clapp's interest in literature and art helped broaden her experimentation with subject matter. Literature, art, music, and dance were integral parts of the Ballard and Arthurdale curriculum and community life.

From her experiences at the Rosemary Junior School, Clapp internalized the necessity of having a carefully selected and highly trained staff if a progressive school was to work, a belief she carried to and applied at the Ballard School in Kentucky and eventually at the Arthurdale School in West Virginia. Student teachers from Vassar were "baptized" at Rosemary in progressive pedagogy under Clapp's direction, and one student, Elisabeth Sheffield, followed Clapp to Ballard and Arthurdale. Although successful at the Rosemary Junior School, Clapp wished to apply her progressive pedagogy in a larger community setting, gaining a better understanding of the role of the school in the community. This meant taking progressive education out of the domain of private schools and university lab schools. In retrospect, and expressing the sympathy of colleagues, Clapp wrote: "The Progressive Education Association continually sought ways and means of introducing progressive methods into the public schools in which the majority of the children in our country are educated—a task rendered difficult by the size of their class groups, and especially the fact that most public school teachers then were untrained in progressive ways of thinking."[42]

Such an opportunity came in 1929 when Clapp was offered the position of principal of the George Rogers Clark Ballard Memorial School in Jefferson, Kentucky. She remained at Ballard until 1934, when she accepted a position at Arthurdale. The work at Ballard and Arthurdale represents a clear attempt to implement progressive pedagogy and build the community school in more rural settings and in a more public sphere and with Dewey's support. Both schools gave Clapp the opportunity to test her ideas about pedagogy, integrating theory and practice in a largely rural setting.

The Ballard School was a rural public school in Jefferson, Kentucky, and under the control of the Jefferson County Board of Education. Land for the school was donated by Mrs. Thurston Ballard in memory of her son, George Rogers Clark Ballard. The Ballard School comprised several consolidated one- and two-room schools in the county and in 1932 enrolled 212 students. During Clapp's tenure, the school consisted of ten grades, eight elementary and two secondary. Seventy-five percent of the children who attended came from poor rural areas and the rest from more well-to-do farm families.[43] An understanding of the Ballard School is necessary because it serves as the backdrop for the Arthurdale experiment in community education. The progressive educators, who lacked rural experience, and especially rural Appalachian experience, were strengthened by their time in Kentucky. Many of the teachers who worked with Clapp there followed her to Arthurdale. All learned from their work in Kentucky, and this is clearly evident in how curriculum was developed in the Arthurdale School.

Clapp described the rural Kentucky children as "backward in reading": "They did not seem to comprehend what they were studying, and exhibited no particular interest or curiosity. The plan however, got its start when in order to find what their interests were, we began to share in their outside-school activities." At Ballard, and later at Arthurdale, Clapp began her work in the community schools by first addressing health and recreational needs. She believed that dealing with these concerns was the first step in bringing people together, building a sense of trust between the school and the community. Once these needs were met, the teachers could focus on pedagogy largely through enhancing cultural understanding and self-realization, keys in community building. Clapp believed that the traditional focus on teacher and text had kept the children from understanding real-life experiences, which were separate from subject matter. She and her progressive colleagues felt that education needed to focus on the interests, abilities, and experiences of the children, giving them a feeling of ownership in the process, with the school as the center of the community.[44]

Clapp saw herself as implementing Dewey's "My Pedagogic Creed" through her work at Ballard and Arthurdale. In that piece, Dewey discussed education as a social process: "The school is simply that form of community life in which those agencies are concentrated that will be the most effective in bringing the child to share in the inherited resources of the race, and to use his own powers for social ends."[45] One could not harbor preconceived notions of how a community school should be structured. Because all communities were unique, all community schools were unique, and their natures had to be discovered by the study of their communities' culture, history, beliefs, and values.

Clapp received quite an awakening at Ballard owing to what she described as "her protected childhood on Brooklyn Heights."[46] Although considered by many in progressive education circles to be an expert in rural education (there were few of them), Clapp faced an enormous challenge in the situation with which she was presented in Kentucky. She expressed her concern in *Community Schools in Action*, truthfully stating: "Unfortunately, or fortunately, we knew nothing of rural education. All this we had to learn."[47]

Clapp viewed Kentucky as the "mingling of the old and new, that today makes her rich educationally, for her children still can see the things around them, the whole history of her growth and can, through it, understand the history and development of this country."[48] She believed that an understanding of the past was necessary if children were to comprehend their role in the present. In essence, cultural understanding provided the foundation for self-realization, the first step in understanding the role of the individual in a democratic community. It was necessary if students were to gain a sense of identity and place. The school as a social institution could and should enhance and nurture this understanding. Clapp explained her conception of the role of the school in the community in an article published during the Ballard years: "The fact that schools are schools of communities implies reciprocal and cooperative responsibility on the part of the community schools—cooperative endeavor for community affairs. It involves shared responsibility, the community for the school and the school for the community and this involves action of the school in community life because of its interests and investment of interest and activity as well as of money by the community in the school."[49] She later wrote: "It was in Kentucky that we came to an understanding of the nature and functioning of a community school. In Arthurdale, West Virginia, we built a community school and used it as agency for community education. It was the work in a public rural school of Jefferson County, Kentucky, and our experiences there in answering the needs of the children and families of the school district, that brought us the realization that a public school in a rural area is necessarily a socially functioning school."[50]

The location of the Ballard School, near the Ohio River and the city of Louisville, afforded a unique opportunity for learning. The school used as its subject matter what it found in the surrounding environment. For example, owing to its limited resources for the teaching of science, teachers embarked on a geological study along with the study of trees, birds, flora, natural resources, and local sources of power and energy. Clapp's belief in the social role of the school in the community was clearly evident. She sought to demonstrate to other educators a "socially functioning school using the agencies at hand and where necessary creating these, also demonstrating the organization of subject matters for use in social education."[51] For the Ballard School, this involved close association with agricultural agents and medical and dental specialists at the University of Louisville and in the community at large. Ballard also made use of a sliding-scale lunch program based on need, taught girls cooking and sewing, made home visits, taught proper planting, and emphasized public health education issues. As an example of the social role of the school, 140 of the school's 218 children received medical examinations during the summer of 1930. "The results of these examinations," Clapp recalled, "which confirmed our worst fears, came as a surprise to everyone. Of the 140 children examined, 109 had posture defects, 73 suffered from acute malnutrition, and in this undernourished group, 30 were threatened with infantile tuberculosis. . . . Unless ways and means could be found to meet these conditions half the children of Ballard would neither learn nor develop."[52]

While taking care of the health needs of the children was crucial, so was continuing to build on their cultural past. Clapp, an accomplished artist, made use of art and music throughout the curriculum. She viewed art as instrumental in helping children integrate present experience with the cultural past, and it was emphasized as a significant aspect of a child's education, not a frill. She wrote: "Art has been used with all ages in the school . . . as a means of realizing what they have been experiencing. It is freely and continuously used and is greatly enjoyed and appreciated. It has been a means of discovery, to the child's beauty in their surrounding and has constituted a personally satisfying way of uniting the child and his learning."[53]

Clapp, like Dewey, saw art as a way to express the human experience beyond the limitations of language. Art was connected to emotion and desire, but it was also the basis for intelligence through reflection and inquiry. It helped connect the past with the present, giving us the ability through thought to create, imagine, take action, or solve problems. It was for Clapp what Dewey characterized as "consumatory experience."[54] As an example of how art could be fully utilized, Clapp described a Christmas play at Ballard directed by George Beecher, a future Arthurdale teacher, as an example that combined school and community participation, a social effort that stimulated the growth of knowledge, interest, and appreciation. Clapp characterized it as a rural gathering, a sharing of talent and interest to benefit the school and the community.[55] Clapp, much like Dewey in *Art as Experience*, seemed to comprehend that art can embody democratic traits such as freedom of expression, open communication, creativity, and imagination. At Ballard, as at Arthurdale, art served as a means to involve the whole community with the school.[56]

In linking experience with interest and cultural understanding, Clapp supported studies that connected the past and the present, however, rarely from a critical perspective. In her Ballard narrative, she described an eighth-grade play that emphasized the history of Kentucky during the Andrew Jackson era. The children decided that a play might be the best means to investigate this aspect of Kentucky history. Owing to the economic importance and geographic location of the Ohio River, this led to a study of transportation, including river boats, railroads, and wagons. The children made costumes and furniture with community assistance. "The success of the plays, the intense interest," Clapp recalled, "the engagement, the growth, were due to the fact that they filled a need for all the children, satisfied desires, gave meaning to familiar things around them, as in their own past."[57] For Clapp, the play provided a means for the children to better understand their place as well as a means to involve the community in the life of the school.

The focus on cultural history served as the foundation for other grades at the Ballard School. The first grade studied farm life, while the second grade studied village communities. The third grade concentrated on Native American peoples who had inhabited the Kentucky area prior to the arrival of white settlers. The fourth grade studied pioneer life and the fifth grade transportation. The sixth grade focused on the coming of the French, English, and Spanish.[58] Unfortunately, there is no indication in Clapp's description that teachers discussed the conflict between whites and Native Americans over land and culture. The traditional depiction of native peoples as inferior or savage is present even among these progressive educators. At Ballard, this was evident in Clapp's description of a fourth-grade play written and performed by the students. They had decided to write a story about the American folk hero Daniel Boone and his family. In the play, Boone's daughter strays from camp and is captured by the "Indians." Only through the bravery, cunning, and honor of a white man is she saved. The eighth-grade study of the Jackson era also failed to discuss the "Trail of Tears"—the forced relocation of native peoples from the Southeast to Oklahoma Territory in a treacherous, deadly, and costly journey. For Clapp, her colleagues, and others associated with progressive education, there is far too often a serious failure to understand that democratic community encompasses diverse dimensions and that it cannot exist in an environment of classism, racism, and inequality. These activities failed to stimulate reflection and inquiry, essential traits of the democratic citizen. Including the Native American experience could have strengthened the understanding of democratic community and its diverse nature as well as understanding of the students' own exploitation and oppression within the Appalachian experience. While the democratic rhetoric at Ballard was strong, as it was in most progressive schools, actual practice often reveals some troubling concerns, still an issue for contemporary educators. Unfortunately, this lack of reflection followed Clapp and her band of progressive educators to Arthurdale.

Although lacking critical reflection at times, the Ballard School did at times influence the lives of the people in the community. The discovery during a study of wells by the first-grade class that several were contaminated by sewage resulted in moving those wells to higher ground, improving the drinking-water supply and, in the process, public health. This was a good example of people working together to improve the conditions of their community and gaining a new respect for the value of education. "Because of its position and the value of its work," Clapp wrote, "[the school] penetrates and affects the lives of the people. It may improve conditions in the village and in the homes, means of health, ways of living. It teaches whatever is taught about leisure . . . and improved ways of living."[59]

Concern about the loss of community intensified among progressives following the stock market crash, and this concern trickled into the philosophy of education. An important component of this philosophy was to use the school to restore community life, a life disrupted by the failure of capitalism and its values of individualism and materialism. This concern closely tied progressive education to Milburn Wilson's view of the subsistence homestead, both of which were designed to rebuild lives and communities. The Arthurdale community and its school were pet projects of Eleanor Roosevelt, who was instrumental in the planning of the school as early as January 1934. She was assisted in her planning by the College of Education at West Virginia University, which "was responsible for the plans covering the school buildings."[60] On the advice of Clarence Pickett of the American Friends Service Committee, Mrs. Roosevelt offered Clapp the job of principal of the Arthurdale School and director of community affairs. The title alone shows the perceived need for educators to be aware of and connected to the community, with the school at the center of community life.

The estimated budget for the Arthurdale School included expenses for the school plant of $163,808. This figure included construction of a nursery school, a primary and elementary school, a high school, a gymnasium, administrative buildings meant to house the health clinic and the lunchroom, three to four cottages for the teachers, and Clapp's cottage, along with grading work and sewage, water, and heating facilities. Estimated expenses for the teaching staff included salaries for Clapp, seventeen other teachers, a nurse-physician, an executive secretary, and two stenographers, with half the funds for the teachers' salaries coming from the state of West Virginia. These latter funds totaled $34,000 beyond the cost of the physical plant but did not cover Clapp's salary, which amounted to $6,000. Another $26,000 was to be supplied by outside, private sources. Other operating expenses for the school—salaries for two janitors and the cost of coal, water, and electricity—were projected at $7,000. The cost of equipment for the library, the shop, the health clinic, athletic programs, the home economics program, and the kitchen was estimated at $35,000. It was hoped that the property taxes of the homesteaders in Arthurdale could also offset some of the school expenses.[61]

Secretary of the Interior Harold Ickes was aware that Mrs. Roosevelt and Clapp wished to expand the school budget beyond what the government had planned; he estimated that their additions to the proposed budget were at least $63,000 over the approved budget. The Arthurdale project director, O. B. Smart, was, therefore, advised not to begin construction on the physical plant, although this delay meant that facilities would not be available for the children arriving in the fall of 1934 to begin school.[62] The only remedy for the cost overrun was to elicit private funds, largely under the direction of Mrs. Roosevelt and those she convinced to contribute, significantly Bernard Baruch. When actual construction on the Arthurdale School began in April 1935, the allotted budget for the physical plant alone was $125,000, far below the amount Mrs. Roosevelt and Clapp had hoped for.[63]

Clapp officially became an employee of the Arthurdale project on 7 July 1934.[64] The *Louisville Courier-Journal* reported her departure from Ballard on 13 July 1934, stating that six Ballard teachers would follow her to Arthurdale.[65] Clapp claimed that she accepted the position because "John Dewey wished to have worked out for education use a plan of community education—a cooperative enterprise of a community in and through a school."[66] She viewed the Arthurdale project as the ideal opportunity to utilize the school as a tool to restore community life. The school could grow just as the community was being built around it and with it. Clapp did show some unease with the project: "No one including myself really knew the function of a school in a homestead community project." So, as in Kentucky, she and her staff started addressing the provision of health and recreational services to build community trust. There is no doubt that the Ballard experience helped them begin their work at Arthurdale, another opportunity where the school could serve as the center of community life. Clapp had learned from Ballard that education needed to be a cooperative endeavor, a skill so necessary for problem solving during the Depression. Work needed to be shared by all, parents, students, teachers, and other members of the community.[67] This type of sharing fit well with the characteristics of the subsistence homestead and the concept of the community school.

To get a sense of the people and their culture, Clapp visited the Scotts Run area prior to the 1934/1935 school year. She described her visit in *The Use of Resources in Education*. On their departure from the area, the coal mine operators had cut off the electricity but allowed the miners to remain in their homes for fear the empty houses would become sources of firewood.[68] If anything, the plight of the people in the coal camps had worsened by the summer of 1934. Clapp saw in the people frustration, alienation, and hopelessness, but, like Mrs. Roosevelt and the federal planners, she believed that progressive education could help free the homesteaders from their misery and alienation and give them a sense of hope, encouragement, identity, and place and build community through the school. Discouraged and displaced miners complained to Clapp on her visit: "You ain't never going to make nothing of us. We're like them old apple trees out there, all gnarled and twisted." Much like the federal planners, Clapp believed the coal camp existence had "bred habits of complaint, suspicion, obedience to the boss and resource to the relief of excess and also casual and irresponsible living."[69] Although there is a degree of progressive paternalism here, Clapp did understand that the community school needed to be built on trust, a concept she believed was not fostered in the coal camp environment of competition and self-survival. She sensed the difficulty in overcoming this alienation and thought that the homestead subsistence community, coupled with the progressive schools, could give the people a greater sense of place, self-realization, and ownership. One future homesteader, Claude Hitchcock, expressed in an interview with a Pittsburgh reporter: "A mine camp is no place to bring up children. Mine camps are tough. There are all kinds of people in them. Most of them are people you wouldn't want your children to know. My kids are tickled to death about coming out here in the country. Something like this, glancing around Arthurdale, is the only chance we'd ever have to get out. Miners don't save money. In good times they spend it, and in poor times they manage to get along on what they can make."[70]

With the advice and support of the Arthurdale School National Advisory Committee (sometimes known as the Arthurdale Sponsoring Committee), Clapp earnestly began the educational experiment. Members of this committee included Mrs. Roosevelt, John Dewey, E. E. Agger of the Resettlement Administration, Fred Kelly of the Office of Education, Lucy Sprague Mitchell of the Bank Street College, Clarence Pickett, and W. Carson Ryan, a well-known figure in progressive education.[71]

The idea of subsistence farming was in 1929 not so far-fetched as it might appear today. In 1929, there were more farmers than coal miners, and many miners continued to farm even as they worked in the mines. As Jerry Thomas puts it: "More than half of all West Virginia farms were of the self-sufficing or low-income category, struggling to make it on annual incomes of $500 or less. Of the roughly 105,000 farms in the state, only about 25,000 enjoyed reasonable commercial success, earning gross annual incomes of $1,900 or more."[72] The collapse of the coal industry in north-central West Virginia filled the relief rolls and drew the attention of federal planners wishing to experiment with the concept of subsistence homesteads.

The first federal subsistence project, with its experimental progressive school, was about to begin.

4
Beginning a Community School

Similar to rural communities across America, what would become Arthurdale was surrounded by nine one-teacher schools within a four-mile radius. These schools might be described as the "cracker box type, with bi-lateral lighting, inferior equipment, and generally unattractive appearance: heated by stoves in fair conditions and partially jacketed; and provided with outdoor privies in generally fair condition and with about an acre of grounds which, however, in several instances is not highly satisfactory for playground purposes."[1] The oldest of these schools dated back to 1893.

Two committees were charged with the planning and implementation of the new Arthurdale School, the National Advisory Committee and a local advisory board called the West Virginia Advisory School Committee. The National Advisory Committee consisted of Eleanor Roosevelt, John Dewey, E. E. Agger (representing Rexford Tugwell of the Resettlement Administration), Fred Kelly of the Office of Education in Washington, Lucy Sprague Mitchell of the Bank Street College, Clarence Pickett of the American Friends Service Committee (AFSC), and W. Carson Ryan.[2] Formed first, the local West Virginia advisory committee began work in February 1934. Members included a mix of individuals from the public schools and higher education. Floyd Cox, superintendent of Monongalia County Schools, chaired the committee. Other members included Justus Deahl, superintendent of Preston County Schools; W. W. Trent, state superintendent of West Virginia schools; Leonard Hill and Howard Allen of West Virginia University; Assistant Superintendents Robert Clark and R. B. Marston; Alice Davis, the city welfare administrator; Mary Jo Barrett, a local teacher; and George Colebank, principal of the University Demonstration High School in Morgantown.[3]

It was the responsibility of the West Virginia advisory committee to plan the school program and the physical plant. Clarence Pickett claimed that the Arthurdale School was to be "integrated with the community, serving residents of all ages; its curriculum built around the community's vocational and recreational needs and possibilities; agricultural and animal husbandry projects, industrial arts and crafts, home care, social and civic enterprises, music, drama, dancing." Early childhood, elementary, secondary, and adult education "were recognized as the four major divisions of the program as it developed, but interlocking activities made even this classification somewhat arbitrary."[4] This local advisory committee, much like the federal homestead planners, perceived the Arthurdale community as a laboratory, with the learning experience of the school coming "chiefly through the vocational life of the community."[5] The program and physical plant were clearly outgrowths of a progressive philosophy and embodied many of the seven principles of the Progressive Education Association (PEA) in the 1930s. One of these principles was to enhance cooperation between the school and the home, the former being attentive to the "natural interest and activities of the child," but with the realization this could come about only through the "intelligent cooperation between parents and teachers." The PEA principles further emphasized the school as a laboratory that was meant to test educational ideas and that needed to move beyond a "child centered school," or one too focused on the whims of the individual child rather than a larger social perspective. Influenced by the Depression and the social reconstructionists, some educational progressives in this era saw students as too self-centered, "critical, but indecisive," meaning that they were not being prepared to help sort through conflicting points of view and that schools had failed to arouse "keen thinking about social problems."[6]

Two fundamental issues for progressive education in the 1930s were the role of the school in the social order and the need for reform within the curriculum. However, many progressives, including Clapp, believed that the school could not only serve as the center of community life but also reach out beyond that community as a laboratory for social and political reform. "In the twenties," notes the progressive education historian Patricia Graham, "the method, not the rationale or philosophy, had been supreme."[7] For Clapp and her progressive contingent at Arthurdale, it was rationale and philosophy that undergirded the entire educational project. Clapp's life experiences and her studies in philosophy, particularly those with John Dewey, provided her with the background to begin developing the community school in the new homestead community. Even though she was from an elite background, her experiences working with the poor through various social welfare activities and at the Ballard School had given her a sense that education could serve as a tool for individual and social reform. She believed, as did many progressives, that the Industrial Revolution had had a disruptive impact on the lives of many in America, one destructive of community life. She had seen this disruption firsthand when her father lost the family's wealth in the Depression of 1893, changing her close, loving relationship with him to one of alienation. So, much in the Deweyan fashion, Clapp saw the school as the key to the restoration of community life—community life being defined as self-identity, a sense of place, and a sense of contribution, but also as individual and social responsibility—by serving as the center of the community.[8]

Clapp knew that the people in the mining camps of Scotts Run had little hope for the future and that the subsistence homestead offered hope for only a few. Yet she believed that the community school in this homestead community could serve as the centerpiece, drawing people together, as distinct as they were, to form unity through a common purpose.[9] The journalist John Pratt Whitman described the Arthurdale School as reaching "out as spokes from a hub into village activities everywhere."[10]

In February 1934, in the parlor of the Arthur mansion with many homesteaders present, the West Virginia advisory committee presented its "Plan for the New School at Arthurdale." As the plan was presented, the homesteaders voted on each paragraph. The plan laid out the school's philosophy, its curriculum, and the role of the school administration. In the introduction it was noted that the community was experimental and that the character and success of the school depended "on the philosophy of life which is to dominate all the activities constituting the curriculum and other phases of the school program, including pre-school and adult education."[11] The school philosophy stressed a "faith in democracy and confidence in the ability of an enlightened people to govern themselves in economic and political affairs" and a confidence that democratic principles would guide both instructional and administrative activities. Children were perceived as being of unlimited potential, and learning was to be associated with the "acquisition of moral and spiritual values" rather than with "bookish and academic implications."[12] There was a strong emphasis on tempering the individualism of the homesteaders that derived from the reformers' perception of the individualism and material necessary to survive in the coal-town camps and, in fact, in American society generally. "Consequently," the advisory committee stressed, "the school should cultivate a toleration of and an appreciation for individual differences in intellect, emotions, and personal habits," leading to a more harmonious community. The committee believed that this goal could be achieved by making the school the center of community life and activity, an institution for both adults and children fostering creative expression and cooperation. This philosophy was to guide the development of the curriculum, which was "to be adapted to the special needs of the community . . . and not be hampered by traditional and formal courses of study, nor by standardized grading and the grouping of pupils."[13] The community itself was to provide the educational experiences and serve as a laboratory for experimental activities, including home and civic projects, school projects, and agricultural activities. "This means," the committee noted, "that the real learning experiences of the school will come chiefly through the vocational life of the community. . . . Lifelike problems will constitute the curriculum material, rather than the conventional schools subjects."[14] This was an understanding of vocational life that was not confined to mere job training but embraced such subject matter as art, music, home economics, citizenship, folklore, libraries, and the study of animal life.

Furthermore, the administration and organization of the Arthurdale School were to be not based on traditional practice but "progressive" and "efficient." It was clear that the West Virginia advisory committee was sensitive to the political nature of Arthurdale and that federal budget concerns were influential. The committee therefore charged: "The school was not to be established at excessive costs and should demonstrate that it is possible in West Virginia or another state that a more desirable rural school is possible without unreasonable investment of money in the program." Because of philosophical as well as budgetary concerns, the physical plant was to consist of simple buildings, generally separated and "homelike in character" and "allow[ing] the maximum amount of sun and air."[15] To build community, literally and spiritually, parents should participate in the construction of the school, as should the children, who could build much of the needed equipment in the school shop. With all working together, the homesteaders could unite in an act of shared interest and common purpose. Besides the problem of providing employment for the male homesteaders, planning continued to emphasize the importance of early childhood education (through the nursery school), adult education, handicraft education, and clearly the use of the school as the center and cementing force of community.[16]

However, not long after the approval of the school plan, Arthurdale found itself immersed in one of its many political controversies. In March 1934, the well-known progressive educator William A. Wirt claimed that certain members of the Roosevelt brain trust were planning a revolution, and he directed much of his venom toward Arthurdale. The incident that stimulated this attack on Arthurdale actually began on 1 September 1933 at a dinner party held at the home of the former Wirt associate Alice Barrows. Wirt was one of the best-known educators in the country at the time, famous for his work at the Gary School, a US Steel town in Gary, Indiana. John and Evelyn Dewey had lauded his work in their *Schools of Tomorrow* (1915). The progressive education historian Lawrence Cremin writes: "Dewey had argued in the *School and Society* that progressive education was essentially an effort to adapt the school to the circumstances, needs, and opportunities of industrial civilization."[17] Wirt's work seemed to accomplish that task, although Dewey's rhetoric is far from clear. The journalist Randolph Bourne described the Gary School as one of the best examples of progressive education.[18] It is no surprise that Wirt's criticism of Arthurdale quickly drew the attention of both progressive educators and reformers. Wirt used the forum of Barrows's dinner party to attack the policies of the New Deal and accused Barrows and others at the party of trying to foment a revolution. He specifically attacked the Arthurdale project as socialistic.

These charges led to discussion in Washington about an alleged New Deal Communist conspiracy. Subpoenaed to appear before a House subcommittee, Wirt was asked to provide the names of those he was accusing.[19] He refused to name names—with the exception of mentioning his belief that Rexford Tugwell of the Resettlement Administration, and at that time in charge of the subsistence homestead programs, was among the members of the brain trust seeking revolution.[20] While it was not mentioned at the hearing, it was clear that the Arthurdale project was becoming a politically charged issue for the Democrats and an experiment that Republicans like Wirt saw as blatant socialism. The Wirt inquiry came to an end on 18 April 1934 despite the protests of Republicans who wished to keep it open.[21] The House committee, dominated by Democrats, saw no reason to pursue Wirt's charges, while the Republicans on the committee vehemently disagreed. What Wirt had accomplished was drawing attention to what would become a growing controversy surrounding the Arthurdale project.

In spite of the controversy, school planning continued. Establishing a public school on a government-supported subsistence homestead was a unique and difficult endeavor. Clapp met with members of the West Virginia Legislative Education Committee and West Virginia state superintendent of education W. W. Trent. From this meeting it was decided that "the Arthurdale school [would] be a free, independent state school, with freedom in designing curriculum to meet the special needs of its community, that it [would] be sustained by state funds for basic salaries for the [West Virginia] teachers who were assigned to the school, and with supplementary salary assignments by the county."[22] The Arthurdale Nursery School was to be financed through the Federal Emergency Relief Administration (FERA) and other teacher salaries to be supplied through private funds. State funding for the teachers presented a problem the first year because teacher assignments in the state were based on the average daily attendance of pupils in a county the last three months of the prior school year. Only eighty-seven children of the homesteaders had attended school in Preston County, resulting in only three Arthurdale teachers being paid for by the state the first year.[23] The original plan called for half the teachers to come from the state. Obviously, this placed a burden on funding the rest of the teacher salaries, a burden largely remedied by personal funding from Barnard Baruch and Mrs. Roosevelt. The school plan was also projected to cover 200 families with 450 children—100 attending the nursery school, 200 the grade school, and 150 the high school.[24]

Shortly after meeting with state legislators and members of the West Virginia advisory committee, Clapp visited several schools in the vicinity of Arthurdale. She saw children crowded into one-room schools between Arthurdale and Morgantown and visited a two-room school and several Preston County elementary schools in Kingwood and Terra Alta. She observed in these classrooms several teachers whom she invited to join her and her progressive staff at Arthurdale. On returning to Kentucky to finish her final term at the Ballard School, Clapp attempted to describe the conditions of the mining camps and the prospect of the homestead community at Arthurdale to the teachers soon to follow her. She believed that these teachers held a philosophy similar to her own and could work in the progressive school environment. In her description, she emphasized the loss of community that had been experienced by the displaced miners, creating what she characterized as a cultural milieu of suspicion and strife: "When the mines stopped working, social contacts fell away. The men no longer had the companionship of their miner crews and the women, struggling to keep their families going had no time for visiting with each other."[25] According to Clapp, this environment was marked by fear rather than hope, parents afraid to send their children to school, and children who lacked adequate food, clothing, and shelter.

The alienation that Clapp perceived could also have been deeply rooted in rural mountain life. The historian Ronald Eller has pointed out the preindustrial, rural agrarian nature of mountain life, people generally living on small, self-sufficient family farms. While the miners generally had the power to leave the mines if they were dissatisfied, the controlling atmosphere of the company town made that decision difficult. According to Eller, the miners could be "individualistic, fatalistic, and present oriented," and their "powerless situation in the company town augmented these traits."[26] Clapp discovered these traits soon enough, and it frustrated her greatly. Nevertheless, she found that the parents still placed faith in the future and believed that a proper education could help their children rise above the darkness of the coal camps. "Somehow we must find ways to give them the schooling," she mused, "that they had missed and an education that would open to them opportunity for a life they had never known."[27]

Plans for the construction of the Arthurdale School began in February 1934, following a visit by the New York architect Eric Gugler. Gugler was a member of the architectural firm Gugler and Toombs and showed an interest in designing the project in a way that took account of the needs of a community school. His early plans for six classroom buildings, two nursery buildings, and an administrative building were estimated to cost $130,000. Eventually those plans were expanded to include a gym, a shop, and a laboratory.[28] In consultation with the West Virginia Advisory School Committee, it was decided that the school buildings "should be plain and simple and, above all, functional." In June 1934, Clapp traveled to Washington to meet with M. L. Wilson, then serving as the associate director of the Department of Agriculture and head of the Division of Subsistence Homesteads. The initial planning process made it clear to the reformers that "the school must serve adults as well as the children and make provision for enterprises such as the women's canning activities, and for community recreation and health needs."[29]

One of the central components of the Arthurdale School was meeting the needs of early childhood education. Clapp sought the expertise of Miss Jessie Stanton, who she believed "knew the needs of children better than anyone in the country" and understood what was "required for their welfare and growth."[30] Stanton agreed to serve as director of the nursery school at

Arthurdale. Born in Brooklyn, like Clapp, Stanton had experience in settlement work and had taught at Caroline Pratt's City and Country School. Prior to her Arthurdale appointment, she served as assistant director of the Harriett Johnson Nursery School in New York City.[31] During the summer of 1934, she and Clapp traveled to Scotts Run so that she could see for herself the children and their environment. Stanton was greatly affected and troubled by the poverty, suffering, and health conditions there, so much so that a trip to Arthurdale would, Clapp believed, invigorate her spirits.

On arriving at Arthurdale, Clapp and Stanton saw a community beginning to come alive. The town hall, a disused church that had been moved to the homestead, was in place and surrounded by the workshop of the Mountaineer Craftsmen's Cooperative Association, the project administration offices, and the craftsmen's forge.[32] However, even though the plans for the school buildings had been completed, construction had not yet begun because the plans had not yet received federal approval. According to Subsistence Homestead Project Manager C. E. Pynchon, the proposal submitted by Clapp, Mrs. Roosevelt, M. L. Wilson, and Eric Gugler was $63,808 over the amount originally allotted. Part of the problem was the unforeseen expense of housing the teachers and other school personnel in the community, as the proposal called for. Pynchon instructed O. B. Smart, the local project manager, not to proceed with construction until federal authorization had been secured. He did, however, realize the consequences of the delay: "We are faced with the problem of having available in the fall necessary school facilities for the children," he wrote to Harold Ickes, "whether we will have to increase the amount of appropriated funds to cover this work or find legal ways to accept private funds, if they are secured by Mrs. Roosevelt." Ickes responded three days later suggesting that Pynchon contact Mrs. Roosevelt and Louis Howe about potential changes.[33]

Shortly following this exchange it was announced that some of the homesteaders could move in to their new homes immediately.[34] In early July, Clapp was back in Washington continuing to review the plans for the school. When interviewed about the project, she emphasized her commitment to the concept of the community school, a type of partnership between the village and the school that was attentive to the health, recreational, and vocational needs of both parents and children. "In the country we work simply," she explained. "We have no program to impose, but out of a long school experience we are growing to understand the needs of communities such as this, to anticipate some of them and to meet others as they arise."[35] Part of the philosophy of the community was to provide both men and women handicrafts training. As Mrs. Roosevelt noted, some of the Arthurdale men would be "instructed in furniture making for the furnishing for the homes," that instruction to come through the community forge and Mountaineer Craftsmen's Cooperative. As for the women, they would learn to "make rugs for their homes and knit stockings."[36] But there was more to the handicraft instruction than the simple act of making. In a most progressive sense, the educators and reformers viewed that act in an aesthetic sense, seeing creativity and a connection to one's work as helping with one's own sense of being as well as helping form the foundation of community. This kind of work gave the homesteaders something they had control over, unlike that to which their time in the coal camps was devoted. While these activities could and did result in small economic gain, the primary purpose was a sense of accomplishment and human expression through art.

Having completed the necessary paperwork,[37] Clapp was officially notified on 26 July 1934 that she was to be the principal of the school and director of community affairs for the Arthurdale project. Although she was actually paid through Mrs. Roosevelt's private funds, her contract stipulated she was to be paid by the government the sum of one dollar per year. As midsummer neared, Clapp and her staff realized the school construction would not be completed in time for the start of the fall term.[38] Facilities already in existence would have to be utilized. Thus, with the help of the homesteaders, the Arthur mansion was "washed or scrubbed and painted until it was fit for children's use." A shed near the town center was turned into the school shop, and a stockroom was readied to house the high school students. A room near the assembly hall at the Town Hall became the staff headquarters. None of the school furniture ordered had arrived, so, with last-minute federal approval, "benches of the oldest American school patterns were knocked together by the men on the project."[39]

Although frustrated by the slowness of the federal bureaucracy, the teachers and the homesteaders appeared far from disheartened. "For two weeks we had all together—fathers, teachers, mothers, children—worked at everything," Clapp proudly recalled. "The school was a reality at last and it was ours—the community's school."[40] "To us it seemed a miracle," she claimed, "a school on the homestead at last, and the children in it happily learning. Nothing else really mattered, even the fact that we had virtually no equipment, few if any books, a scant number of pads and pencils, and for blackboards sheets of brown wrapping paper tacked up on the walls."[41]

The Arthurdale School was to "meet all standards laid down by the state department of West Virginia," but, because of its experimental nature, it was allowed some flexibility to deviate and "not expected to adhere rigidly to prescribed procedure."[42] Finally, the fall term was set to commence, and Clapp announced that, for grades 1–8 and the high school, school would begin on 10 September 1934 at 8:30 A.M., with students first reporting to the Arthur mansion. The nursery school was to open one week later, on 17 September.[43]

The teaching staff that began school that fall were experienced in progressive education, and several had served under Clapp at the Ballard School. They were an eclectic and highly educated group of carefully selected individuals generally well versed in the methods of progressive education. Ethel Carlisle and Eunice Jones taught grades 1–3, Elisabeth Sheffield grade 4, and Carlton Saunders and Harry Carlson grades 5 and 6. Fletcher Collins was hired to teach English, drama, and music, and Adolph Ipcar, initially hired to serve as the school registrar and accountant, would assist by teaching math as needed in the high school.[44] The teachers did not initially know much about the homesteaders. When the children were enrolled, information was sought on the educational background of the parents, the size of the families, and general health and immunization records. Staff members saw themselves as members of the community and were elected to and served on school and homesteader committees even though most had to live in nearby towns and villages owing to the housing shortage. According to a labor inventory of the homesteaders, most had held unskilled positions in the coal mines before coming to Arthurdale.[45]

One early problem faced by the Arthurdale School once it was up and running was the transportation of students. Because of the housing shortage, not all the children attending the school lived in the Arthurdale community; many remained with their families in the coal camps. The federal authorities were concerned that it might be illegal for Arthurdale as a homestead corporation to pay for the transportation of the children from and then back to the camps.[46] As Clapp later recalled, because the Preston County School Board "did not feel that it could furnish transportation for the school, the only alternative was to engage the service of one of their bus drivers after he had completed his regular school round and apportion the cost of this arrangement among the families whose children went to school by bus."[47]

Another early problem was malnutrition. While school lunches had not been budgeted for, the problem was remedied by using food grown and canned over the summer by the homesteaders. With the assistance of one of the teachers, Ethel Carlisle, who had expertise in domestic science, and the school secretary, Alice Bowie, schedules were developed that brought the mothers of the children together to prepare their lunches. Lunches tended to consist of potatoes, another vegetable, bread, and milk. Ethel Carlisle noted of the mothers: "They seem to enjoy getting together, and very often when it isn't their day to cook women drop in and help, or just visit." Alice Bowie concurred: "The mothers do a splendid job. Six or seven cook lunch and do the washing up for about a hundred and fifty children each school day, and the children help by coming to the serving door of the kitchen for their plates and returning them there."[48] The food used by the school had been planted by the men working on the construction of the homes the previous spring. They had laid out a community garden under the direction of the agricultural agent Bushrod Grimes. Only the nursery school received its food allotment from the federal government through FERA.

While the Arthurdale School was struggling with these problems, bureaucrats in Washington continued to debate the growing expense of the school and the Arthurdale project overall. By September 1934, the entire Arthurdale project had cost the federal government $601,095. C. E. Pynchon believed that, ultimately, it would require $1 million over the amount already spent, including $175,000 for the physical plant, bringing the total budget to roughly $700,000.[49] He sought to bring the cost of the physical plant within its budget of $125,000, recommending construction of "five of the six buildings, namely nursery, primary, administration, high school and recreation, at an estimated cost of $105,000.00; to allot for immediate expenditures for equipment of $4,500.00; the balance of the $125,000.00 on budget for school building and equipment to be carried as a contingency fund." To save money on the construction of roads and athletic fields and on paving the roads in front of the school, he suggested contacting the FERA, under the direction of Harry Hopkins, for funding.[50] Another point of contention was the teachers' salaries, which were essentially privately funded. On 13 December 1934, Mrs. Roosevelt wrote to Clapp expressing her concerns. Bernard Baruch had made available approximately $25,000 to the AFSC to be used for Arthurdale teacher salaries, supplementing what the federal government had budgeted for the first year of operation. For the second year Clapp had asked for $7,000 more, which disturbed Mrs. Roosevelt, who asked Clapp to clarify her request.[51]

Clapp was clearly frustrated by government red tape and what she perceived as Pynchon's incompetence. As she wrote Mrs. Roosevelt: "I think the difficulty is partly Pynchon, who has a kind of paralysis upon him due to many reasons which I can discern, which is nevertheless impeding. He just needs to be made to do the simplest things. . . . Once the written authorization is sent down to Mr. Flynn [the local project manager at Arthurdale], Mr. [Steward] Wagner [who had replaced Eric Gugler], and myself, we can put it through with speed. Both of these men are doers, I am grateful to find."[52]

While the federal officials argued about the costs, Clapp faced other troubling local problems. One of the most significant issues the educators found themselves dealing with was the children's health care, which they believed influenced the learning environment. Clapp wrote about the urgency of adequate medical, dental, prenatal, and preemptive care for the children and their families: "At Arthurdale, it was from the beginning clear that the medical demand created by malnutrition, neglect, disease, accidents, and childbirth could not be ignored. Those needs drove us to rapid action. Other agencies to meet them were not present locally. There could be no debate as to whether or not the school should undertake them."[53] She could not, however, find a physician to serve on the staff during the fall term. She did locate a nurse already employed to look after the government construction workers, but soon the nurse became overwhelmed by the community's health-care needs. Finally, the community school was able to enlist the service of another nurse, Kay Plummer, who had worked for the Henry Street nursing group in New York City and also had experience in social welfare. "Regardless of Plummer's experience and diligence," Clapp recalled, "she and I were both troubled by the responsibility developing on her in cases of sudden illness or difficult deliveries." During one difficult delivery resulting in hemorrhage, a local doctor refused to come to the project for a relief case. In desperation, Clapp appealed to Clarence Pickett, who was eventually able to hire Dr. Harry Timbres, "a gifted and able physician just returned from work in the Far East." According to Clapp, Dr. Timbres saw the homesteaders not as relief cases but as human beings, "injured by what they had been through, who needed medical care."[54] Clapp believed that the health problems of the nursery school children—many of whom suffered from scabies and impetigo—could be attributed to the poverty of the coal camps. "Their condition yielded slowly to treatment," she reported, "but to better food, to baths and physical routines, but that was spring before it was finally eradicated."[55]

Money was constantly an issue at Arthurdale. Clapp wrote to Mrs.

Roosevelt about a donation of $250 that she wanted to use "for shoes and underclothes for the older children and for musical instruments" for use in the adult orchestra. Feeling frustrated by her growing responsibility, Clapp appealed to have Clarence Pickett placed in charge of the project: "He is the logical person and we could then develop a self-help program of cooperatives." Clapp believed, as did Mrs. Roosevelt, that what she was doing at Arthurdale could serve as a model for other homestead projects throughout the country. With regard to Pickett, Mrs. Roosevelt responded: "I do not know whether that would be possible right now. There are other thoughts in the iffing [sic] which I will tell you about when I get back."[56]

During the fall of 1934, Clapp worked closely with Clarence Pickett and Eric Gugler on the architectural plans for the school. Gugler, called to the White House to oversee renovations there, was soon replaced by Steward Wagner. Clapp saw Wagner as "an able and experienced architect, who quickly grasped the School's function in the homestead community." However, owing to Washington's financial concerns, the budget initially agreed on had to be reduced, forcing a choice between what Clapp termed "the essential and the desirable."[57] Clapp constantly lobbied for the homesteaders, both traveling to Washington and writing the secretary of the interior. She knew there might have to be compromise but still clearly that wished Clarence Pickett could be placed in charge of Arthurdale, a request that seemed to irk Mrs. Roosevelt, who believed it unrealistic and did not grant it.[58]

The site chosen for the new school was, according to Wagner, "in a ravine, near a small stream with some seclusion, but yet accessible to the homesteaders." Wagner sought such seclusion so as to avoid the potential disruption of the children's education by the large number of people expected to visit the homestead. He designed the structures to match the style of the homes being constructed. The original plans had called for the use of fireproof materials, but they turned out to be too expensive. Individual heating units and septic tanks were included for each building. The recreational building, which included the gymnasium, was closest to the Town Hall to facilitate what was sure to be frequent access. The gym was to include a full-size basketball court, showers, dressing rooms, and a stage for plays and concerts with room in the wings in which to build sets and make costumes.[59] Next to the recreation building was the high school, to be utilized by both the older students and the adults. Next to the high school was the school administration building, which was to include a lunchroom, offices for the doctor and the nurse, the school bank and bookstore, typing rooms, and offices for the principal and the school secretary as well as rooms for cooking, sewing, and canning. The elementary and primary school buildings were followed, capped by the nursery school at the far end of the road.

According to Wagner, the location and attributes of the school were decided by the West Virginia advisory council. A natural setting was sought, one affording easy access to the surrounding natural world, including playgrounds, gardens, and wooded areas. The school buildings were detached owing to health concerns, and, because it was believed that sunshine and fresh air made for healthier children, they were constructed with large windows that could be opened. "The school was in effect," Clapp recalled, "a little village in itself."[60] It was viewed as a central facet of the community and key to the success of the homestead project. The life of the families was becoming more stable and secure as long as the fathers could bring home a paycheck, always an issue. Arthurdale was becoming a growing and "bustling community, a school to which we all went—a school in which everyone was, so to speak, both learner and teacher": "What the children studied at school their mothers and fathers also were learning, and what their parents learned and did taught the children. And we, the teachers, learned both from them and with them, for homesteading and building a village community were new to us, too."[61]

When school opened without the promised facilities and essentially without texts and materials, the Arthurdale teachers were forced to develop their own curriculum and learning experiences. While a problem, it did not seem to trouble the progressive education contingent, who had worked together in Kentucky and held the same educational philosophy. The Ballard experience provided an opportunity to work with rural children, and the curriculum developed at that school helped immensely at Arthurdale. Many of the first-year activities at Arthurdale paralleled the Ballard experience. The first graders under Ethel Carlisle began a study of farming, an activity that was all around them and in which all homestead families were expected to engage. The children studied threshing buckwheat, digging and husking corn, growing potatoes, and planting for spring harvest. They also engaged in block play, which originated from the work of Friedrich Froebel and was picked up by progressive educators like Caroline Pratt and adapted to their sensory-based learning theory.[62] Block play was employed at Arthurdale to nurture creativity and problem solving. Copying what they saw around them, the children constructed block trucks, barns, schools, even coal mines. Still, traditional subject matter was not neglected. Carlisle spent time every day working on reading, math, and writing skills. She reported: "The children are eager to learn and seem to get especial satisfaction from their achievements. They play well together, as they are unselfish and always ready to help each other."[63]

The second-grade teacher, Eunice Jones, discovered that her students wished to build their own miniature village, similar in character to what they saw being built around them. Jones saw no reason that this activity could not be educational, so the children began their study. Jones had noticed initially her students had problems with reading and writing, but by the end of September they were beginning to enjoy books. In building their village, they learned to communicate, plan, and work together. They collected their building materials from the construction sites on the homestead. They learned math through measuring, cutting, and sawing, and they learned to level a foundation by watching the workmen in the community. By the end of the term, the village was constructed, and the students had elected governing officials, including the mayor and councilmen. To learn how to operate their village bank, they traveled to Reedsville to observe a local bank in action. According to Jones in her half-year report, the second graders "were becoming competent and self-reliant."[64]

Fourth graders began their year by studying pioneer life, utilizing an abandoned log cabin in a meadow near the Arthur mansion that was believed to have been occupied by a slave named Watt owned by one Colonel John Fairfax, a previous owner of the land. Educators saw the opportunity to link the study of pioneer life to life in a modern homestead community. In learning how the early settlers "cleared the land, built homes, and raised crops, [the children] were learning about the very things their fathers and mothers were doing." The fourth-grade teacher, Elisabeth Sheffield, used student interest in pioneer life to enhance reading and writing even though there were still "no books, no tools, and no paints, no anything." The students began to clean out the cabin, which was dirty and neglected and had previously been used for grain storage. They developed research skills in the process of trying to locate information about the cabin. They learned how to use berries and nuts to dye wool and how to grind corn for meal, but, as Sheffield noted, in doing so "they were bringing up their work in writing, spelling, arithmetic, and reading" and showing keen interest in books. They learned to dip candles and later learned to weave and knit. They studied geography, soil and plant life, and animal husbandry. Local Reedsville women loaned the class a spinning wheel for its study of flax. Sheffield believed the study of pioneer life linked the community and the school, helping the children better understand their heritage and identity that had, she believed, been disrupted by the experiences in the coal camps.[65] The educators at Arthurdale were always sensitive to what they perceived as the dissolution of community life and the role of the school in restoring it.[66]

The fifth and sixth grades were under the direction of Carlton Saunders, the math and athletics director, and Harry Carlson, the shop teacher. The two grades were combined initially owing to the late arrival—in December—of the West Virginia teachers. Unlike the younger children, the fifth and six graders, as Clapp noted, "found regular work in school and the demands of school-community living somewhat difficult."[67] The Arthurdale educators believed that this difficulty was largely the result of previous bad experiences with schooling and some health problems that compromised their learning potential. To stimulate interest in their studies, Carlson and Saunders took a chance that the students might find a study of West Virginia interesting. The gamble worked, and, by the time the West Virginia teachers Inez Funk, Sara Liston, and Katherine Kimble arrived, the students were "engrossed in their experiences of the colonists who settled western Virginia and other regions farther west." Funk recalled the stress of learning the progressive methods that Clapp espoused. "We had to go to classes at night and work extra," she explained. Sara Liston corroborated Funk's recollection: "We had meetings every Sunday evening in Miss Clapp's home, besides the few she called through the week after school. At some of the conferences, for instance, she wanted us to take a problem child and study that child, and study far enough along that with readings, we would learn to cope with that child in ways best for his advantage and ours. We had to keep a report on that child and then she [Clapp] would ask for a written report on results.... We had to study John Dewey's methods. She wanted to know if we were understanding and applying them." Clapp was impressed by Liston—who had come to her asking how to be a more effective, creative, and imaginative teacher—and described her as "an outstanding teacher in traditional methods before she came to Arthurdale." Funk and Liston sensed the importance of community participation in the school, which both believed was enhanced by the study of pioneer life. Liston proudly noted the "night activities and after-school activities" that made the parents "[feel] close to the school." Years later, Funk recalled: "I would not take the experience for anything. It taught me a lot about working with children, how to deal with them and the things they can do." Their efforts led to the production of a loom, a churn, a flatboat, a stool, and a hornbook and some growing interest in the construction of musical instruments.[68]

The seventh and eighth grades were taught by Fletcher Collins, who held expertise in art, music, and dance. Collins attempted to unify the group since most of the children did not know each other. He had them make a scale, mural map of the Arthurdale area, including the topographical features of the community. When completed, the map was placed in the hallway of the Arthur mansion for display, but the project had served to unite the children in what Collins termed "an esprit de corps."[69] He further attempted to improve the oral language skills of his students as well as their work in math and reading. Part of the math instruction consisted of designing and building play equipment for the nursery school, including wooden blocks, sand shovels, wheelbarrows, and sawhorses for use as the fulcrums of seesaws. As part of their local studies, the seventh and eighth grades began geological studies of the area that involved understanding the local topography and plant and animal life, the growth of coal during the Carboniferous Period, and the age of dinosaurs. They also wrote a play about the Arthurdale and Scotts Run experience and performed it for an audience.

Harboring a professional interest in folklore, Collins attempted to tie Scottish and English ballads to those from Appalachia. Encouraged by Collins and Carlson as well as the community interest in square dancing, some boys wanted to learn how to make musical instruments. Collins had developed his interest in music and poetry at Yale, where he had earned a Ph.D. An acquaintance of George Beecher, whom he had met at Yale and who had previously worked with Clapp in Kentucky, Collins was officially hired at Arthurdale as the head of music and drama. He continued to explore music and poetry at Arthurdale, collecting Appalachian ballads and learning to play the fiddle.[70] He found a local craftsman, Bert Nicholson, to help the boys learn to craft their fiddles. Nicholson, who used only a chisel, a penknife, and a hacksaw to construct his instruments, taught the boys about the proper woods to use for tone, spruce and maple being preferred over the scarce wood the boys had collected. Carlson and Collins were, with the assistance of Bert Nicholson, able to create a learning environment integrating subject matter using music, drama, literature, poetry, history, science, and math through regional studies of the area. Collins, Beecher, and Carlson believed that music was a means by which to engage the community and bring people together. Owing to the lack of housing for teachers the first year, the Beecher and Carlson families lived together, and on Sunday mornings the home was filled with music. Collins and Sheffield "would also come over," as would "other people that had a talent for musical instruments," recalled Harry Carlson. "Sunday was a tremendously wonderful experience."[71]

Arthurdale also welcomed nineteen students between the ages of fifteen and twenty-one to its high school. They were divided into four grades and offered three main courses of study meant to address their interests and experiences. The first course included science and math as they related to life experiences and home economics. The second included shop, math, spelling, history, economics, and practical calculations and also covered typing and shorthand. The third focused on art, literature, music, and library work. The high school met the first year in a homestead project shed located near the community center. George Beecher, the high school principal, claimed that the students and parents were actually grateful for this working environment. "We had no books, no lab equipment," he noted, "in fact no accessories of any kind." Still he was not deterred. With a sense of optimism he wrote: "Perhaps I should mention as an asset the brand new environment of a West Virginia mountain glade, being reclaimed for the life of a community, itself in the formative period."[72]

After early discussions with the older students, it was clear that most of them saw education as preparation for entering the job market. "All they wanted . . . out of school, really, was training for jobs which they felt confident despite the scarcity of work, were waiting for them," wrote a disheartened Clapp.[73] These students were grouped not by age or grade but by "line of endeavors" and the "experiment [of educating them] undertaken because it seemed more likely than any other plan to organize—reorganize—high school work along fruitful lines."[74] Botany students began to collect local flora and mount them, working with Bushrod Grimes, who supplied them with the reference materials they needed (he also advised the homesteaders on their subsistence farming). Students studying electricity with Harry Carlson installed a telephone connection between the shop and the science room. Other students in library work built bookcases and began to collect books and catalog them. (Although small, the library served the entire community.) Collins immersed his students in Wordsworth, Shelley, Whitman, and Emerson, having them read the poems aloud to improve their diction. "These boys and girls have an ingenious talent in all their writing," he declared, "quite unspoiled by contact with conventional literary styles and techniques."[75] This type of talent found itself exhibited through a play written by the high school students called *The Gold Rush*. The students had been studying western history with Adolph Ipcar and reading western novels by Bret Harte in Collins's classes. (Essentially trained as an accountant, Ipcar had graduated from the City College of New York in 1926 with degrees in accounting and philosophy. He served at Arthurdale as the high school math and history teacher.)[76] In searching for a performance venue, the students "found an ideal place for an outdoor theater in the wooded glade near the old sawmill—level ground which could be easily cleared for a stage, surrounded by sloping hillsides that would accommodate the audience."[77] Collins and the other high school teachers found that the students who had come to school listless and apathetic in the fall were now full of excitement and enjoyment over their capacity to learn and create. The end of the first semester seemed promising, and Clapp described the first community Christmas in a letter to Mrs. Roosevelt: "Such joy, I wish you could have seen it. The toys you gave reached every boy and girl, baby. And, best of all, out of their abundance, the homesteaders on their own initiative made up several Christmas boxes for some people near us who are very poor and miserable. . . . I am so glad that the homesteaders' impulse was to think of others."[78]

However, this success was tempered by the outcome of efforts to help a group of male students aged fifteen to twenty-six who had left school prior to the creation of the homestead community. Many of them had lost their jobs when the mines closed and, on moving with their families to Arthurdale, were unable to find work. Clapp and her staff realized that they had a problem on their hands and met to resolve the lack of education for this group of young people. Classes were started in carpentry, electricity, math, typing, science, reading, and writing. However, as Clapp noted, "the group's response was lukewarm, and attendance slight and irregular." Over the Christmas break, a school-to-work plan was created that had Bushrod Grimes hiring the boys on his work crews if they attended night school, and the plan offered some promise. "There were of course, grumblings when nonattendance at night school lost them work hours," Clapp recalled, "but we hardened our hearts and held them to the arrangement, and slowly they grew accustomed to coming regularly to classes and to working each day."[79] Adolph Ipcar offered night classes in practical math and keeping farm accounts, and Elizabeth Sheffield taught the students a class in English that sought to improve their reading and writing skills. Harry Carlson taught a few of the night school boys basic electricity, showing them how to construct a compass, a telephone, a telegraph, and a sound amplifier. Carlton Saunders, in charge of athletics, taught the boys how to play basketball, and they competed against each other and against local high school teams. While the night school was designed to attract predominately boys, some girls attended Sheffield's English class, some studied typing with Alice Bowie, some took pottery classes with Ethel Carlisle, and some studied home economics with Mary Sedman, who directed the nursery school.

Overall, the educators seemed pleased with their effect on the young adults in the night school. "Night School," according to Clapp, "bridged the gap in their lives between the mine camp and the homestead and tided them over till spring." "Harmed as they unquestionably were by idleness and by life in the cesspool conditions of the abandoned mine camp," she asserted, "they had an innate sweetness of nature, an unquestionable and infectious gaiety."[80] "School is swinging along," she wrote to Malvina Schneider, Eleanor Roosevelt's secretary, "night school also for boys and girls of 16 to 25. Also a full program of music, plays, and programs for the adults—our orchestra is slowly forming. Our singing groups run from 30 to 100. February 7 is a play. February 14 our educational program its music planned by the homesteaders."[81]

Unfortunately, many of the gains made with the older boys were lost when government planners decided that only one male in a family could be employed in the construction work going on in the homestead community. The problem of keeping the homesteaders employed continued to plague Arthurdale, and, as director of community affairs, Clapp often found herself in disagreement with and frustrated by federal officials. On 5 April 1935, Assistant Secretary of the Interior Oscar Chapman wrote to Clapp: "If therefore we are to have the school ready for the fall, it seems to me to be evident that it will be wise to allow the school to be built on contract." That is, only those few homesteaders with "highly developed skills" were to be employed. In closing his letter, Chapman wrote: "I hope that it may meet with your approval." Clapp scribbled in the margins: "It does not."[82] In a more optimistic tone, Mrs. Roosevelt wrote: "I think things will come through on the school. I have taken the liberty of saying that you would rather have the work given to the Homesteaders, even if some of the school buildings are not ready by September. I thought that you could pick out the most important ones and have them done first. The gymnasium, for instance, could wait until later."[83] Baruch offered his support but made it clear that his interest was due only to his desire to help Mrs. Roosevelt. Writing to the First Lady, he described her as a "rare combination of intelligence and great heart." But he went on to clarify his intentions: "I am still willing to help you, but I really do not know enough about the subject to do other than contribute a little money from time to time." Mrs. Roosevelt used the timely contribution that accompanied Baruch's letter to help pay for the community's medical needs and to support a summer project of Clapp's.[84]

As the night school endeavor made clear, the Arthurdale educational experiment attempted to include all members of the community. Building and living in a homestead community meant learning not only construction skills but also animal husbandry and farming. Homestead women were taught how to feed and raise the animals but also how to can, cook healthy meals, and maintain a sanitary household. The homesteaders often turned to the teachers for assistance when federal officials were not available. The community itself was a classroom and included the homes and gardens, the school kitchen, various club meetings, square dances, and any informal gatherings.[85]

The school was clearly seen by Clapp as a means to build and restore community. However, one of the problems confronted in the attempt to create community was the fact that only a few of the families had known each other prior to moving to Arthurdale, although many of the men who had participated in the early homestead construction had bonded with each other. This early bonding led to the formation of the Arthurdale Men's Club. The club was faced with a number of problems, one of the earliest being the lack of firefighting resources available in the community. At first, there was substantial interest in creating a fire department—until the men discovered that they would not be paid as they were when they worked as firemen in the coal mines. Nevertheless, fire services were still needed, so the club continued to deliberate. It was eventually decided that, for the sake of fire prevention, an inspection of each home was necessary, so several of the men created a checklist and inspected all the houses, when necessary mandating cleanup, repair, or alterations. The school participated by providing brochures educating the homesteaders about fire safety. The Fire Committee created a makeshift fire engine by attaching a large fire extinguisher to a government car, and it also divided the community into fire districts and trained the men in those districts how to respond to a fire call. During Clapp's tenure (1934–1936) there were no serious fires that required the assistance of others, and the Fire Committee felt justified in its efforts. "Furthermore," according to Clapp, "the Committee had not only learned much about ways and means of solving acute community problems, but had also developed in the process an esprit de corps which to them was very pleasing."[86] The committee also demonstrated a shared purpose in resolving an issue that potentially touched the lives of all the homesteaders. Working together, its members identified a problem before it arose and sought and shared the information and the means necessary to solve it.

Not to be outdone, the homesteader women organized as the Eleanor Roosevelt Farm Women's Association—an obvious tribute to the First Lady—by spring creating its own constitution and bylaws. While at first the club members were engaged only in social events, they too soon became attentive to problems in the community and began to take actions to solve them. For example, the women played an integral role in the preparation of school lunches, as we have seen.

The clubs served a democratic function in bringing "people together," Clapp surmised. "Matters of common interest were there considered, and through the Clubs the men and women made acquaintance with each other and with the needs for the community."[87] This sense of community extended to the teachers and their spouses. Even though many could not initially find housing in the community, they all became club members.

Following the departure of Bushrod Grimes, who was not immediately replaced, George Beecher, the high school principal and the only teacher with a background in farming (progressive educators being largely from urban backgrounds), made himself available for consultation should the homesteaders have farming problems. He and Adolph Ipcar helped the homesteaders keep track of their farm accounts and also advised them on how much to plant. With Beecher's assistance, several of the men volunteered to work in gardens on Beecher's and Clapp's homesteads that had been made available for their use, providing food for the school lunches. The school paid for the fertilizer, and the homesteaders provided the labor, even though they actually "needed the free time to work in their own gardens."[88]

Early childhood education was a prominent facet of the Arthurdale community. One of the most notable and influential divisions of the Arthurdale School was its nursery school, under the direction of Mary Elizabeth Sedman and designed by Jessie Stanton. Clapp and Stanton had, as we have seen, become close friends at the City and Country School. Both Lucy Sprague Mitchell, a member of the National Advisory Committee at Arthurdale, and Stanton greatly influenced Clapp and her understanding of early childhood education. Mitchell was well-known in progressive education circles at the time for her book *Here and Now Storybook*.[89] The Arthurdale Nursery School had precedents in the early 1920s when advocates such as Harriett

Johnson and Mitchell began to approach the study of preschool children in a more scientific manner through the Bureau of Educational Experiments in New York City. The bureau's nursery school attempted to link the work of child play to the realities of work. The teacher was to serve as a guide and, by continuous observation of the children, develop a "solid body of data to be used in constructing the school's learning environment."[90]

The Arthurdale Nursery School, which accepted children aged three to five, began in September 1934 with about thirty-six children in the first group. Typically, the children stayed from nine in the morning to midafternoon. When they arrived that first fall, most had, as we have seen, scabies or impetigo.[91] Along with Dr. Harry Timbres and the nurse, Kay Plummer, the nursery school staff taught the mothers about child care, including prenatal and postnatal care. This education was part of the well-baby clinic and helped bring about a broader understanding among the homesteaders of health and sickness.

Clapp considered the nursery school at Arthurdale to be the heart of the school program, and it was an obvious source of pride for the community. It provided custodial care for the community's preschool children, but it also viewed itself as having an educational mission, offering instruction in proper health care, diet, hygiene, and nutrition.[92] "Perhaps never before has a nursery school so actively served a community as a laboratory," Clapp declared. "It was the center of all the childcare in the community, with its baby clinics, health work, and parent education."[93] The parents realized that the health of their children was getting better and soon regularly sought the help and advice of the medical and nursery school staff.

Unfortunately, in September 1934 there was no facility for the nursery school, but soon a one-story white-frame building was built near the Town Hall. This temporary building consisted of four rooms, two of them bathrooms. Doors opened into a small yard surrounded by a white-picket fence and rhododendron bushes. With no school supplies or desks available when school opened, the nursery school teachers used crates from a local grocery store as desks, old newspapers from the local paper office so that the children could paint, chairs and other furniture donated from sources in New York, and sand for sandboxes donated by the local Greer Gravel Company. The Mountaineer Craftsmen's Cooperative made sawhorses and blocks, so in essence the entire community was involved in helping get the nursery school operational. "Miss Sedman's patience and her ability to see the other person's point of view," Clapp noted with appreciation, "together with her wisdom and skill, gained acceptance of the things she advocated for the children—an acceptance that grew into staunch belief as they began to gain in health and emotional stability."[94]

Clear progress was made the first year of the Arthurdale School and community, but there was much to be done. Some of the children still lacked adequate clothing, and many parents were too proud to accept charity. Clapp used a generous donation from Mrs. Roosevelt that in her own words "enabled [her] to meet the care of an acute appendicitis case, a truss that will enable one of our fathers to continue working, and care for a serious prenatal case": "We are so grateful."[95]

As the first year of school came to a close, George Beecher continued to assist in the farm cooperative and the planting of gardens for the school lunch program. By June, the Arthur mansion was no longer used as a school facility, and in the fall of 1935 the children were moved into the new buildings. Carlton Saunders continued to direct athletics, engaging the children and the adults of the community. "Somehow on these summer evenings," Clapp recalled, "we all felt that this village was ours to be enjoyed, a place of pleasant and comfortable living."[96]

Dr. Timbres and Nurse Plummer continued their work in health care, pushing through the inoculation of recently arrived homesteaders and their families. The final event of this eventful year was a music festival held on 7 July under the direction of Fletcher Collins. Collins nurtured his deep love of folklore and folk music and with the homesteader Charles Stearns drove around the region to find musicians willing to take part in the festival. Only amateurs were allowed to participate, and ribbons were awarded for best performance. Collins viewed the festival as an opportunity for building community, bringing people together.

On the evening of the festival, the Assembly Hall at the Town Center was "packed with homesteaders and their neighbors," and "space was reserved for a group of guests from Washington, including Mrs. Roosevelt." The festival consisted of a fiddle contest, jig dancing, ballad singing, mouth harping, and square dancing. As Collins described it: "The musical culture latent in the people of Arthurdale and the region was encouraged and dignified by the emphasis of the festival. The music and dancing were the people's own, and they knew it."[97] Collins believed that, through the festival, the homesteaders gained a sense of ownership in their community, something they had not felt in the coal camps. Through music and dance they could find a sense of identity with their culture, their world. The Arthurdale folk music festival was one of the first in the United States and was recorded by Charles Seeger, "then the technical advisor for the Special Skills Division of the Resettlement Administration from 1935–1938."[98]

Regardless of its educational success, politics continued to threaten Arthurdale's existence. On 8 July 1935, Mrs. Roosevelt cautioned Clapp to be attentive to and respectful of the chain of command. "There is one thing I want to suggest to you," she wrote, "namely, Mr. Tugwell has the complete responsibility and when we are with him, I think you should make it a point to make him feel that we recognize his responsibility and do not even suggest that I do anything except stand ready to help in an unofficial way on educational and health questions." She continued that Clapp should recognize that the homesteaders are "his people" and not "[her] people."[99] This letter was stimulated by Clapp's expressed dissatisfaction with the government's failure to help the homesteaders become homeowners rather than renters or lessees and her attempts to work through Mrs. Roosevelt, whom she knew could move agencies to act. Most likely Clapp believed that home ownership gave the people a sense of pride and investment in the community, a sense that the community was theirs and that they were not just part of a relief project. Baruch, who supported Clapp, was constantly concerned about this problem and the lack of readily available employment and thus the lack of opportunity for the homesteaders to afford to pay for their homes.[100]

Regardless of the political climate, there was hope in the future as the homesteaders watched the community being constructed around them. They could see the new school buildings being built across the road from the community center that in large measure would be ready by the next school term, even though the physical plant budget for the school itself had been reduced to $125,000. The school roads, parking spaces, and athletic field were to be completed with FERA labor. Oscar Chapman, an assistant secretary in the Department of the Interior, had conferred with Clapp about the construction of the last of the sixty-five houses. The homestead community was coming alive.[101]

The educational experiment at Arthurdale was part of that energy and attempted to embody several principles of community school education. Clapp and her progressive contingent of teachers envisioned the teacher as a guide, not a taskmaster. There was, as we have seen, clear attention paid to the health of the children and to the design of the school buildings—"clean and well-ventilated buildings, with easy access to the out of doors," as Patricia Graham puts it— which were constructed in a way that maximized light and fresh air. Clearly, there was an attempt to link the school and the community, undergirded by "intelligent cooperation between parents and teachers."[102]

In reporting to Lucy Sprague Mitchell on that first year at Arthurdale, Clapp wrote: "Preoccupation with community problems has now largely replaced the former jealousies and feuds: habits of working, idleness and apathy, increased security and reborn hope, fear and bleak despair." Clapp believed that, in its first year, the school had served to unite the people in a common cause and a shared purpose and helped alleviate the previous "feeling of insecurity and suspicion" experienced in the early fall of 1934. "They slowly grew out of their bickering and attitude of distrust," she noted, and by the spring of 1935 were "beginning to think in terms of common welfare and the feeling of security and belief as their better fortune increased."[103] When asked about her new home and surroundings, one homesteading mother replied: "It is paradise for us."[104]

A West Virginia coal miner. (Courtesy Special Collections Research Center, Elsie Ripley Clapp Collection 38, Morris Library, Southern Illinois University)

A typical West Virginia mining community. (Courtesy Special Collections Research Center, Elsie Ripley Clapp Collection 38, Morris Library, Southern Illinois University)

The Scotts Run mining community. (Courtesy Special Collections Research Center, Elsie Ripley Clapp Collection 38, Morris Library, Southern Illinois University)

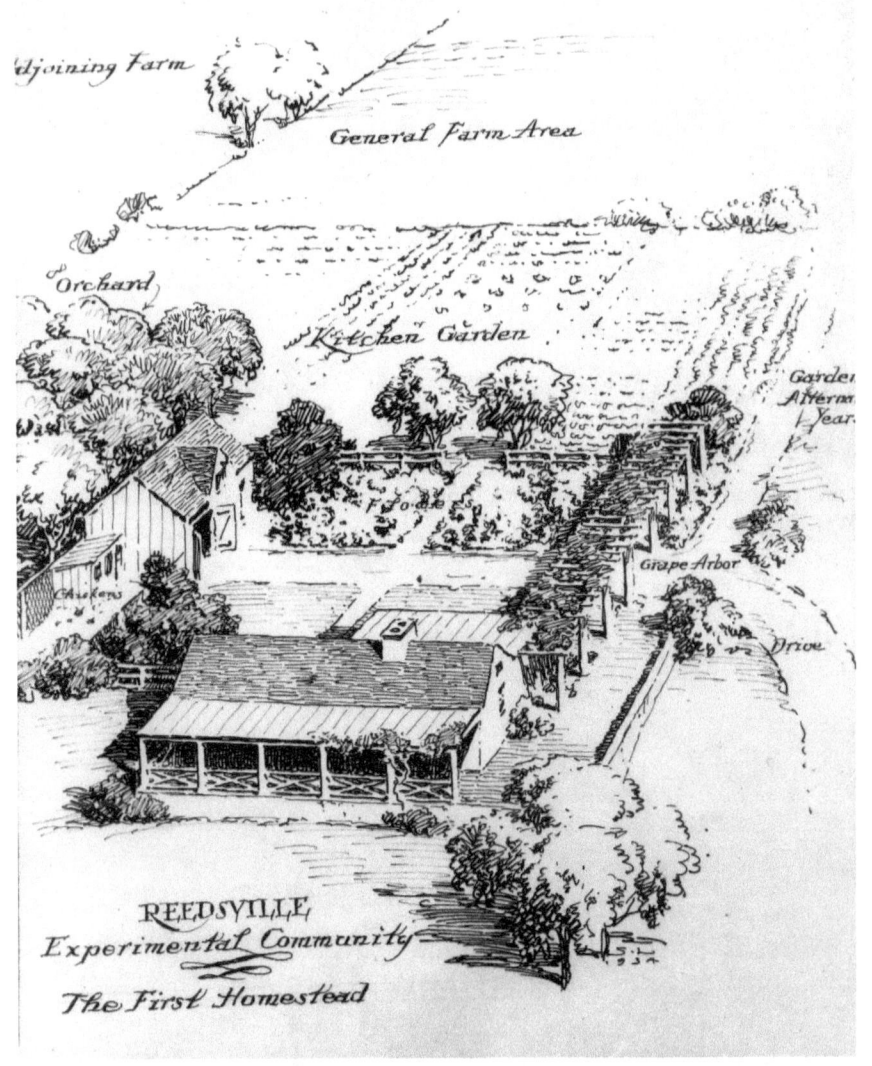

Plans for the homesteads at Arthurdale. (Courtesy West Virginia Regional History Center, West Virginia University Libraries)

One of the early Arthurdale homesteads. (Courtesy West Virginia Regional History Center, West Virginia University Libraries)

A log cabin on the property used for school activities in pioneer life. (Courtesy Special Collections Research Center, Elsie Ripley Clapp Collection 38, Morris Library, Southern Illinois University)

Elsie Ripley Clapp, who was living in Exeter, New Hampshire, at the time this photo was taken. (Author's collection)

Eunice Jones's second graders building their own village of Arthurdale. (Courtesy Special Collections Research Center, Elsie Ripley Clapp Collection 38, Morris Library, Southern Illinois University)

Elisabeth Sheffield's fourth graders participating in pioneer life activities. (Courtesy Special Collections Research Center, Elsie Ripley Clapp Collection 38, Morris Library, Southern Illinois University)

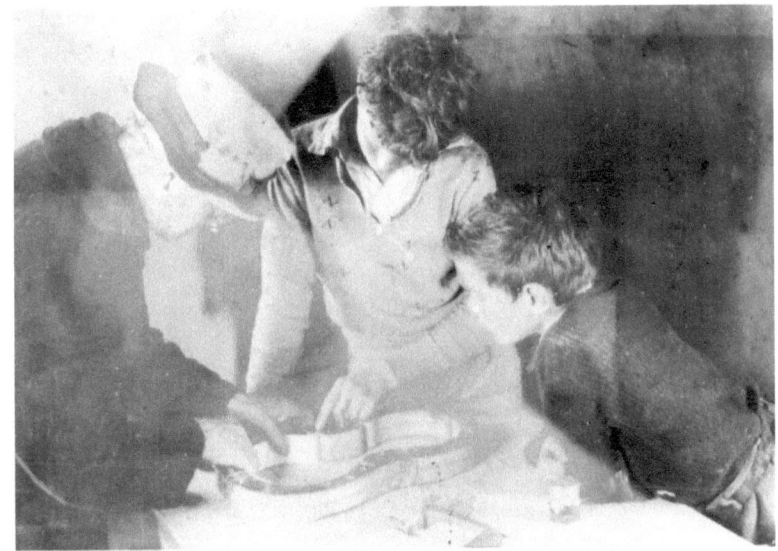

Bert Nicholson, a local craftsman, teaching Arthurdale boys how to make a fiddle. (Courtesy Special Collections Research Center, Elsie Ripley Clapp Collection 38, Morris Library, Southern Illinois University)

Eleanor Roosevelt square dancing at Arthurdale. (Courtesy West Virginia Regional History Center, West Virginia University Libraries)

Schoolchildren building sets for a play. Arthurdale also had an outdoor amphitheater for school and community plays. (Courtesy Special Collections Research Center, Elsie Ripley Clapp Collection 38, Morris Library, Southern Illinois University)

Elsie Ripley Clapp and Lucy Sprague Mitchell shaking hands on the steps of the Arthur mansion. Mitchell was a member of the National Advisory Committee and had brought Bank Street students to Arthurdale as part of a larger tour. (Courtesy Special Collections Research Center, Elsie Ripley Clapp Collection 38, Morris Library, Southern Illinois University)

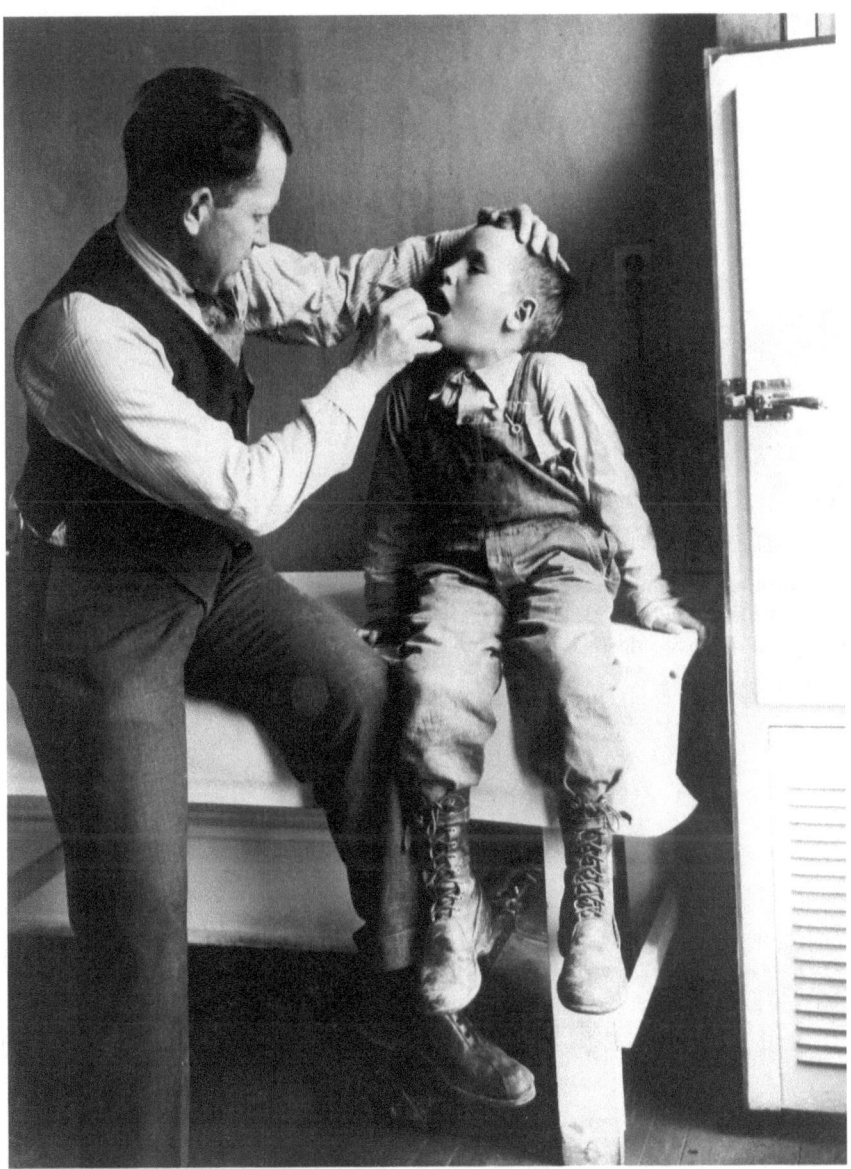

Dr. Harry Timbres gives an Arthurdale boy a checkup. (Courtesy Special Collections Research Center, Elsie Ripley Clapp Collection 38, Morris Library, Southern Illinois University)

The Arthurdale School complex looking past the nursery school to the school center building on the far left (1935–1936). (Courtesy Special Collections Research Center, Elsie Ripley Clapp Collection 38, Morris Library, Southern Illinois University)

A rear view of the nursery school building showing the sleeping porches and the underneath play areas for use during inclement weather (1935–1936). (Courtesy Special Collections Research Center, Elsie Ripley Clapp Collection 38, Morris Library, Southern Illinois University)

The Arthurdale high school with the greenhouse on the right (1935–1936). (Courtesy Special Collections Research Center, Elsie Ripley Clapp Collection 38, Morris Library, Southern Illinois University)

The school and community recreation building used for athletic events, plays, square dancing, and the music festival (1935–1936). (Courtesy Special Collections Research Center, Elsie Ripley Clapp Collection 38, Morris Library, Southern Illinois University)

The Arthurdale elementary school (1935–1936). (Courtesy West Virginia Regional History Center, West Virginia University Libraries)

FDR preparing to give the commencement address for the 1938 high school graduation. (Courtesy West Virginia Regional History Center, West Virginia University Libraries)

5

The Struggle to Survive

In August 1935, prior to the beginning of the second school year at Arthurdale, the National Youth Administration (NYA) director, Aubrey Williams, sent a memo to Eleanor Roosevelt detailing the current situation of young people aged sixteen to twenty-four in the United States. For starters, 2.9 million of them were receiving some form of relief. "Approximately 1,700,000 of these youths lived in urban areas," Williams declared, "and more than 1,200,000 lived in rural areas. About 200,000 were estimated to be in Civilian Conservation Camps and about 68,000 were actual transients receiving aid through various camps throughout the country." Williams advocated for the continual education of young people because "more than half of the youth on relief in the United States had not gone beyond the eighth grade."[1] With unemployment still rampant and 1.8 million youths looking for employment, he called for more apprenticeships and vocational training. Later that fall, he published an article in the journal *Progressive Education* further articulating his concerns about unemployed youths and the role government could play in assisting them through proper education and training. He saw the NYA not as a relief agency but as an agency that provided assistance to students and the institutions they worked for. He concluded that for many of the unemployed traditional schooling was not the solution. "The solution of the problems," he wrote, "lies rather through jobs and training." He realized that industry could not absorb most of those thus trained and that the NYA therefore needed to create job opportunities through work projects. "Despite all efforts," he noted, "too many young people are still wasting in idleness. Too many are so rapidly losing their morale. . . . The ultimate solution for our economic problems undoubtedly rests upon a further reorganization of industry with an end to creating greater opportunities for both young and old."[2]

The most nagging problem plaguing Arthurdale was the lack of employment or the inconsistent employment of the homesteaders and high school students of working age. Gradually, the educators were able to help the high school students through the NYA's program for older high school boys and girls. Under the Works Progress Administration (WPA), the NYA supported high school aid programs to keep students in school.[3] At Arthurdale, such programs took the form of a traveling library project, practical nursing clinics, and training in home economics.[4]

While one might expect the second school year to be less challenging, such an expectation was premature. Clapp described the homesteaders as "uneasy and unsatisfied, beset by middle class ambition and harassed by economic problems."[5] One homesteader raised two disconcerting questions: "Are we paying for our homes or are we just paying rent and may be sent away at any time? Is our school the right kind of school for our children? Well, our school is a progressive school—that is what they call it. I don't know why we are so anxious for our children to have the same of kind of schools we had."[6] When the school year began in September 1935, the last groups of homesteaders arrived in the community, the last set of homes was being constructed, keeping the men working, and crops were being harvested. While the homesteaders were employed or engaged in homestead activities, the uneasiness Clapp described typically abated; however, she felt that the homesteaders still lacked an understanding of community. Reiterating the progressive concern that the time in the mining camps had fostered a survival-of-the-fittest attitude, she believed that the issue of community building needed to be addressed to eliminate or at least stem the doom-and-gloom attitude of many homesteaders. Nevertheless, in her description of the work of the school during what turned out to be her final year as its supervisor, she desired to show it as a bright spot and an institution that was influential in the community.

Even though the physical plant was finished by the start of the second school year, most of the facilities were still without equipment. Regardless, one homesteader noted in her diary: "What a good place for our children to go to school. . . . Some people say our school isn't any good. They want to take our children out of it and send them to the county schools. We won't. The children are happy and learning." Pressure was also placed on the facilities and the teachers by the constant arrival of new children owing to the gradual completion of the homes and the movement of families into the community.[7] By November 1935, the total enrollment in the grade school, nursery school, and high school was 336. By June 1936, that figure had increased to 400. Three West Virginia teachers were added to the first-year cohort along with science teacher Carson Ryan and the eighth-grade teacher Nell Rider from Morgantown.

Relying on reports submitted by the teachers, Clapp described the progress and activities of the 1935/1936 school year. The first grade took an interest in the subsistence agriculture of the homestead, visiting gardens of the students' families and observing the threshing of buckwheat to be made into flour. Exposure to block play in the nursery school the previous year fostered creativity and cooperation, according to first-grade teacher Ethel Carlisle. The children's block play often mimicked the construction in the community, as we have seen, and Clapp and Carlisle believed that it led to an improved understanding of math owing to the counting and measuring required. Through storytelling, the first graders worked on sounds and word recognition, which were believed to enhance reading and writing. There was some observation of the children of new arrivals, who were perceived to be less active, but Clapp believed that their gradual exposure to better conditions would result in improvement and that they would soon be part of the group, enjoying both its activities and "companionship with other children."[8]

The second-grade teacher, Eunice Jones, noticed a marked improvement in the students from the first year. They were now better clothed and healthier, although a few students still lacked shoes. These needs were often met through private contributions, such as those from the philanthropist Bernard Baruch. Mrs. Roosevelt noted in a letter to Baruch her contribution (amount unspecified) to Clapp's salary (which totaled $6,000) and told Baruch that the money he had provided the previous year for medical care helped save the lives of three homestead women.[9] The second graders had also followed their predecessors in wishing to construct a miniature version of Arthurdale. They split themselves into groups and began to work on the makeshift village store and post office, hospital, two houses, and a farm. Harry Carlson's shop students helped clear a spot for the village replica, and construction soon began. The students learned to measure, level, frame, and cut lumber for their village structures. They took field trips to observe the construction taking place throughout the community. The construction of their village's post office inspired them to start their own postal service and write letters. This activity stimulated their interest in writing, and by midyear they had, Jones believed, made decided gains in reading and also "becom[e] more facile in adding and subtracting numbers." By the spring, the second graders were actively reading and ready once again to pursue their work on the village, slowed down by the inclement winter weather. Through the construction of the village, the teachers believed, the children learned to work together toward a common goal. The teachers paid attention to what the children were interested in and used that information to enhance their basic skills. The previous year, Clapp had described these children as "depleted and languished"; now they were well fed, well clothed, confident, and competent, "for they were able and had the will to work."[10]

The fourth graders under Sara Liston, a native West Virginia teacher, were now entering their second year at Arthurdale. Liston discovered that education in the coal camps was sporadic and that many of the children could not read or write. The other fourth-grade teacher, Elisabeth Sheffield, began to build on her students' previous accomplishments. She described the children as "hand minded," meaning that they learned best by doing, "what they themselves made and did."[11] Following the discovery of an arrowhead, she led the children in a discussion of pioneer life and how settlers had crossed the mountains into what was then western Virginia. The old cabin on the Arthur farm became a classroom once again. The students cleaned it up and brought items from their homes to be placed in it. Sheffield realized that her students were still having difficulty with reading, writing, and math skills and sought to use their interest in the cabin to enhance those skills. The children had relatives who actually lived in log cabin–like structures, and they began to collect and write down stories of their experiences. As another part of the study of pioneer life, the fourth graders worked and carded wool, made soap, dipped candles, popped corn, cast bullets, used a spinning wheel to make thread, and made looms in the shop so they could weave the thread they had made. Later in the spring, they began a study of flax. They kept track of their progress and studied how the pioneers had used the material. The study of flax was popular in progressive schools and began in the Dewey Lab School at the University of Chicago. Dewey wrote in *School and Society* (lectures originally given to the lab school parents): "You can concentrate the history of all mankind into the evolution of the flax, cotton, and wool fibres into clothing. I do not mean that this is the only, or the best, centre. But it is true that certain very real and important avenues to the consideration of the history of the race are thus opened—that the mind is introduced to much more fundamental and controlling influences than appear in the political and chronological records that usually pass for history." Dewey envisioned the study of the historical evolution of flax as a form of scientific inquiry.[12]

Sheffield shared a play written by Ballard students with her Arthurdale students. Not surprisingly, the fourth graders wanted to write their own plays. Sheffield noted: "I never saw a class do such focused composing of a play, and the way they used the facts they have learned was surprising too." As part of their science instruction, the students began to talk about collecting bugs, fish, butterflies, tadpoles, etc. The science teachers George Beecher and Carson Ryan found books for them to use as resources. Fletcher Collins, the art and music teacher, helped them incorporate music in their flax play. As part of the process of learning about flax, cotton, and wool, the students took a field trip to the Engelhardt Woolen Mill, during which they observed the complete textile-production process, from dying, carding, rolling, and spinning to weaving. They did not just observe the process, however; more importantly, they participated in it. As Clapp noted: "It is, I think, interesting that this group, who found it hard to tell in words facts they had learned, were able to write this account of what they had seen in the Woolen Mill. It was, of course, because the children had themselves washed wool and carded it, had dyed wool and woven it on looms they had made, that they understand what the machines in the mill were doing; and because the descriptions they had written of the wool processes, and the flax play too, probably, accustomed them to using words, that they could report what they observed." Sheffield believed that her fourth graders had made remarkable progress, that their activities stimulated their curiosities and interests.[13]

As for the high school, the first year it was open the students were taught in two sheds and the community center. Students and teachers lacked books, supplies, and equipment, and classes generally met in groups rather than by grade level. Still, Clapp reported that the students were "eager and curious, liked to investigate and explore, and as their teachers discovered, functioned best when they had more than enough work to do."[14] At the beginning of the 1935/1936 school year, the high school students moved into their new building, which contained the school/community library, a science room and a greenhouse, a photography room, and a garage for vehicle maintenance.[15] George Beecher, the high school principal as well as a science teacher, described the ninth grade's study as centered on the medieval period. He believed that life at Arthurdale held much in common with the Middle Ages. "Studying medieval life," he surmised, "broadened [the students'] understanding of their families' immediate economic problems and cultural understanding." This connection to Arthurdale included "division and use of land, industrial labor organization, and community control of marketing and consumption, folk drama and music." The ninth graders delved into a study of the language and history of the period and the lifestyles of the people and evidently prepared for presentation during the Christmas season a play written by the crafts guilds of Towneley and Coventry in fourteenth-century England. As part of the preparation, musical instruments were constructed. The ninth graders also studied Roman numerals and developed an abacus of the type used "in Europe throughout the Middle Ages." Instrument making, popular in Arthurdale owing to its square dances, reinforced the importance of math. This included attention to the string length, materials for tone and tension, and even the playing of music. One example was the construction of mandolins. "The problem of constructing mandolin fingering boards," Collins wrote, "is pressing enough to engage all our attention until everyone understands how to locate frets mathematically. This involves reviewing the mathematics of the musical scale we did in October, and discussing metric rulings and measurements that will aid in making the fingering boards for the mandolins." The high school newspaper, *The News,* reported that the ninth graders had become miniature craftsmen.[16]

The ninth-grade science curriculum also took advantage of the new greenhouse. Since agriculture was central to the homestead community, the students undertook a study of plant life in the area, drawing samples of ferns, mosses, herbs, and leaves. A collection of the drawings was then printed, all class members as well as the school/community library receiving a copy. Clapp believed that the ninth graders showed energy to learn even though their schooling in the mining camps was "erratic and irregular." "It is clearly," she concluded, "an instance of what boys and girls eager to investigate and discover, and teachers informed and able to guide and focus their efforts, together can accomplish."[17]

The tenth grade consisted of fifteen students, seven who had attended the year before, three who had just moved to Arthurdale, and five boys who had previously attended night school. The tenth graders began the year studying the late medieval and early Renaissance periods, constructing a hand printing press, hand carving pieces of type, and also learning about printmaking and engraving. Beecher found them, however, less enthusiastic than other students in the high school, perhaps owing to their previous school experience and lack of opportunity. He attempted to stimulate their interest in education through the study of botany and animal and insect life in the Arthurdale community. While most of the class took part, some of the boys did on occasion become disruptive, and Beecher sought a solution to the problem by teaching them beekeeping, a potential economic resource not just for them but for the community at large. Similarly, and in the spirit of the Arthurdale planners, who encouraged the community's self-sufficiency, he also covered human and domestic hygiene, including testing water and soil for bacteria.[18] The tenth graders were also in charge of the student-run school bookstore, which offered basic school supplies but was created mainly to promote an understanding of math in general and bookkeeping in particular, skills that would be helpful to the various economic cooperatives being developed in the community.

Because there were so few of them—only nine—the eleventh and twelfth graders were combined. American industrial history was the theme of their study, which took on a mostly manual nature owing to their lack of experience with formal schooling. Their activities included setting up a printing press and building a cotton gin. Carlson wrote: "Both the press and the cotton gin gave substance and veracity to their economic history studies." The students kept notebooks tracking their progress and had written to officials in various states to compile information on labor, commerce, agriculture, geology, and mines. The class also studied child labor laws, the concept of a minimum wage, and safety and health regulations for industry as well as "biographies of scientists, statesmen, crusaders and journalists covering the past seventy-five years of American life." This focus on American industrial development was partly aimed at helping them understand the changing nature of labor and how that change "affected the lives and welfare of all workers so vitally that laws had been enacted to regulate them."[19]

Central to the work in mathematics of the eleventh and twelfth graders was their operation of the school's bank, to which thirty-two of the Arthurdale children had, in September 1935, contributed. The bank's high school managers produced weekly reports, through which they learned about the concept of interest and the importance of accurate record keeping and regular auditing. To enhance their study of science, the eleventh and twelfth grades also focused on inorganic chemistry and glassmaking. They began by constructing a furnace and through a process of trial and error arrived at a reasonable and cost-efficient method for melting the glass into liquid form, thus increasing their working knowledge of chemistry and putting that knowledge to use. As Clapp described the experience: "The groups emerged from their years of work knowing that research, experiment, and a spirit that does not admit defeat are needed in solving science problems."[20] She fully realized that such a spirit was necessary to nurture and build community.

As Arthurdale grew, sharing information with the community was vital to continued growth, and it became clear that the publication of a "local newspaper was highly desirable." George Beecher, Adolph Ipcar, and Harry Carlson worked together to write, edit, and produce the paper, assisted by the eleventh- and twelfth-grade students. "By the end of the regular school year, *The News* was an out-and-out community newspaper," Clapp reported, "appearing in three pages every Friday and circulating through a fairly large subscription list."[21] Assisted by George Beecher and Fletcher Collins, the students also used the printing press to print event tickets, programs, and bulletins.

Dramatic productions were always popular in the Arthurdale community, and the school was often the center of those efforts. Under the direction of Fletcher Collins, the students worked on Thomas Hardy's *The Three Strangers* and a Christmas pantomime called *The Cherry Tree Carol*. The production of *The Three Strangers* took place on the stage of the new recreation building, which also served as the school/community gym. Other stagings of interest included a variation on Edgar Allan Poe's *The Masque of the Red Death* and an incident from Stephen Vincent Benet's *John Brown's Body* entitled *Spade*. The latter was, as Collins described it, "a portrayal in a chiaroscuro of the fortunes and misfortunes of the Negro Spade, who searches for freedom and found in a northern industry much the same slaveries he had fled from in the South."[22] One of the teachers most sensitive to the issues of class and race, Collins seemed more interested in the students' performances than in an in-depth analysis of the subject of race. The argument that northern industrial wage labor was the same as southern chattel slavery had been one of the tenets of the proslavery forces in America in the antebellum era.

The Arthurdale School carried on its innovative curriculum with experienced teachers largely, as we have seen, through private funding. On 25 October 1935, Clapp reported to Eleanor Roosevelt on a visit to the school by the donor Bernard Baruch: "I hope he got from it what he wanted," she wrote. "No one who has visited brought to bear such penetrating intelligence, a more deeply sympathetic insight. I got a great deal from his questions and comments. I am eager to learn what conclusions he will reach. He spoke of sending back a report." Clapp felt that Baruch had a good sense of what the progressive school was trying to accomplish and was a strong supporter of her attempt to build a community school.[23]

Clapp believed that she and her teachers had achieved some success with the high school students, many of whom had had previous negative school experiences. She noted witnessing in them since their arrival at Arthurdale "this zest for new knowledge and new experience, their quickness in laying hold of essential facts, their power to address themselves to a task, and the patient and unflagging efforts they put forth day after day." Yet there was a great concern about their future. Clapp was working with the placement section of the NYA in the fall of 1935 collecting data. "For some time part of the staff and I have been developing plans," she wrote, "many of which are already started, for work with the older high school students that will investigate and develop and study out, possibilities of the development later by older individuals in the community of small businesses. These students can test out and study into markets for various commodities such as honey, tree nurseries, cheese, chickens, and eggs, quilts, clay, berries, etc." With suggestions from Aubrey Williams, Clapp had developed a few projects for both boys and girls in the project. Boys studied carpentry, plumbing, electricity, and mechanics along with forestry and agriculture, while girls studied practical nursing, home keeping, store keeping, and dairy apprenticeships.[24]

Clapp also wrote Mrs. Roosevelt prior to Thanksgiving 1935, telling her about a gift the homesteaders had sent her: "The people took great joy in giving something to you—to express their love and gratitude."[25] Always a champion of Arthurdale, the First Lady, accompanied by a small entourage—Clarence Pickett, Nancy Cook, Dr. Homer P. Rainey, president of the American Youth Council, Dr. W. D. Woodward of Richmond, Indiana, and Mr. and Mrs. Allie Freed of New York—made a surprise visit to the school complex on 11 December 1935. Apparently the trip was made in secret to avoid interruption of school activities and to facilitate inspection of the new physical plant, suggesting that Mrs. Roosevelt had not seen the newly completed buildings.[26]

At the heart of the educational activities at Arthurdale was the nursery school's early childhood education or "new education" program, a popular site for visitors. One journalist described the program as follows: "Here the children of Arthurdale receive their education, but the arrangement of the educational system of Arthurdale is much different from the regularly ordered school districts of counties in the state which has caused the experiment to be watched with great a deal of interest among educators in West Virginia. Children begin their schooling, not with first grade, but in the kindergarten classes."[27] The nursery school also instructed parents on child care and served to teach and support high school girls through the NYA. In the fall of 1935, the new nursery building was complete, with each of five classrooms having access to a covered playground area and their own toilets. The nursery school contained a conference room, an isolation room for health inspections, and one-way observation screens that "made it possible for parents and visitors to watch the children without disturbing them."[28] Elisabeth Sedman, the director of the nursery school, noted that the health of the children was better than it had been the previous year. Following Sedman's departure,[29] the work was carried on by Ethel Wadsworth. Wadsworth worked actively with student teachers, some sponsored by the WPA and others by the NYA. Clapp wrote of her: "She seemed always to have time, however, to take care of all the details that fostered the children's' growth and welfare, to keep in close touch with their families, and to help new children and those returning after absence adjust to school life and routines."[30] Wadsworth was actively involved in the teaching of mothers about the connection between diet and health, trying to move them away from a diet heavy on fat, salt, meat, and carbohydrates.

Visitors to the nursery school were constant—even though it was positioned as far as possible from the center of the community to avoid disruption—and during some weeks ran as high as 150. And it was not just local teachers and officials who toured the facilities but also representatives of normal schools, universities, and high schools from other states. Clapp noted: "We realized . . . that one of the services the school could render was to show the kind of work which might be carried on in a rural public school with simple equipment."[31]

One of the most important components of the Arthurdale School philosophy was making the school central to the life of the community. As far as the nursery school was concerned, this meant offering well-baby clinics. These educational forums were run by the community nurse Kay Plummer and the high school girls taking Plummer's practical nursing course. As Clapp represented their function: "In promoting the children's growth and learning and in teaching the mothers and older girls about child care, the Nursery School was developing a resource which seemed to them and to us too, their chief asset."[32] While the nursery school served as one cornerstone for linking the school and the community, educating young mothers and girls, adult education was also a component of the educational philosophy of Arthurdale.

Describing the school the second year, Kathryn Carlson, the wife of the shop teacher Harry Carlson, wrote: "The school, as a school for the children, really seems to be doing an excellent job this second year. Miss Clapp and most of her staff, however, came to Arthurdale because they felt that here much more than that could and should be done, that the chief significance of their job lay in really educating the entire community, not merely the children, and not only in the school itself but in all the aspects of living and working here." Kathryn Carlson noted the difficulty involved in educating adults who lack a sense of community: "Social ideals do not come uppermost. There is a terrific lack of cooperation and of intelligent and forceful public opinion. The activities of the men's club resolve themselves most often into petty rivalry, jealously and suspicion of the other fellow. They seem unable to handle their own dances or other social affairs and yet they feel themselves too closely regulated by an arbitrary authority, for the only handling of this problem so far attempted has been the imposition of what seem to the homesteaders to be severe and arbitrary regulations." She continued: "The possibilities of educating these adults is a much more difficult one than that of the education of their children but the possibilities it offers are too challenging either to ignore or to postpone. The parents now trust the members of the staff enough to ask for their help. That in itself, is a sign of a certain amount of progress but it is even more a sign of greater need which must be met."[33]

The challenges of building community were still great, yet the spring of 1936 brought with it hope and a sense of energy and optimism. A new factory planned to employ up to sixty homesteaders. Edmund deS. Brunner, a faculty member at Teachers College, was planning a visit to assist community school efforts in Aurora, West Virginia, "a thrifty, independent farm community in Preston County." The Arthurdale School was presenting several plays to benefit the community medical fund, and a free baby clinic was being offered. Clapp did show some concern that the winter season might result in a "midwinter depression" because when "under pressures [the homesteaders] revert to the old pattern of jealousies and complaints."[34] Bernard Baruch expressed to Clapp some of his concerns. "I am fearful of the disappointed hopes of these homesteaders," he wrote. "Since my last visit there I have stressed to those who asked me to do two things. 1. The success of the school and your work generally to be used as a model in other places. 2. The bad planning of earning a subsistence. The need of a cheaper rent which I understand has been reduced to less that $15 a month. I was promised it was less than $10 a month. That is all these people can stand. We must set them on their feet and on sound feet or they can never stand."[35]

Clapp must have been elated at Baruch's assessment of her work and his appraisal of the school as a model for community schools with the potential to be used elsewhere. Baruch was not so positive about the agricultural and economic aspects of the community, however. He seemed almost angered that the government had given the homesteaders a sense of false hope and shared his concerns with Mrs. Roosevelt. He felt not only that the rent was too high but also that the community should not be enlarged until another factory could be built, thus ensuring adequate employment. While the building of the homes provided the men some employment, it was not enough, and, furthermore, the homesteaders were given less-than-fertile land on which to grow their own food. "The one bright spot in this is Miss Clapp's school," Baruch informed Mrs. Roosevelt. "It has cost somewhat more than we had expected, but I do not regret that as far as I am concerned. It is the one thing the government had nothing to do with, and is the one bright shining spot." Baruch credited the First Lady. "This is due to you more than anyone else. However, some arrangements will have to be made for its further continuance, and even then it will not be of value unless Arthurdale, or some place nearby, will have the pupils to send to it."[36]

Mrs. Roosevelt was a constant presence at Arthurdale, and, on 28 January 1936, a cold and snowy day, she led a group of fifteen on a visit, including Dr. E. E. Agger of the Resettlement Administration, Nancy Cook, and Clarence Pickett. Some members of the party were from the Department of Commerce, intending to study and suggest possibilities for homesteader employment, a constant problem. On her arrival, Clapp took the First Lady to the school kitchen, where three volunteer mothers were preparing lunch, which consisted, Mrs. Roosevelt recalled, of "mashed potatoes and beans and whole bread and milk." They also visited the Mountaineer Craftsmen's Cooperative and the forge and attended a meeting of the Women's Club. Seeing the First Lady as sympathetic to their problems, some homesteaders voiced complaints. According to Mrs. Roosevelt: "[The women] feared that work was being given to people not on the project to the detriment of their own husbands and finally there were some questions of difficulty in attitude between them and their neighbors in the nearby villages. It was finally agreed that it would be best to forget disagreeable things and to keep in mind that the objective of living is to get on with your neighbors."[37] Although sympathetic to the concerns of the homesteaders and a champion for them, the First Lady was also determined to make Arthurdale a success and thus was inclined to see dissent as a problem rather than as a part of the solution.

On 8 April 1936, the Arthurdale School National Advisory Committee visited the community and held a meeting there. Prior to the meeting, Mrs. Roosevelt, Clapp, and occasionally Baruch had been involved in ongoing negotiations with the Rosenwald Fund and the American Youth Commission of the American Council of Education to fully fund the educational project at Arthurdale. Baruch could not attend the meeting of the National Advisory Committee, but he did offer some of his thoughts to Mrs. Roosevelt: "Let us not put these people on their feet unless it is humanly possible for them to stand by themselves when the hand is removed. If we can't do it here, we can in some places nearer markets and work I am sure." He reiterated his concern that the government should not make promises it could not keep. He ended, however, on a positive note: "Miss Clapp's school has been worth all of the time and money expended on it."[38]

The National Advisory Committee consisted of Mrs. Roosevelt, E. E. Agger of the Resettlement Administration, representing Rexford Tugwell, Fred Kelly of the Office of Education, Clarence Pickett of the American Friends Service Committee (AFSC), John Dewey, W. Carson Ryan, and Lucy Sprague Mitchell. Dean William Russell from Teachers College, Columbia University, was also present. As a former student of his and now a practitioner of his thought, Clapp was thrilled to have Dewey make his first visit to Arthurdale. He spent several days at Arthurdale visiting the homestead and the schools. He also requested a tour of the small rural schools in the area. One teacher recalled of the experience: "Looking up from my desk I saw John Dewey walking in the door. I still can't believe that it was our school he came to see."[39]

Dewey reported his thoughts on the visit to his son Sabino in a letter shortly following the visit. "I was much struck with what I saw in Arthurdale," he recalled. "The school as a whole is the best I've seen and there is an unusually fine lot of teachers and their wives. Science and machine shop are closely connected." Thinking of a potential job for Sabino, he continued: "I thought of you when I was there but there was a machine shop man so I saw no chance. Yesterday, Mr. Beecher, the head of the school came in to see me about them. He mentioned the shop man had resigned and did I know anybody for the science. I said I did, meaning you." Dewey envisioned

Sabino coming to Arthurdale as a shop teacher and developing some ideas with the local craftsmen, probably the furniture craftsmen. He noted how hard the teachers worked and that he believed their pay to be low, although the project did furnish their housing. "As far as the school is concerned," he continued, "I have never seen one where the teachers work out their plans together and work is adapted to the needs of the community; in science they study their surroundings and the industrial possibilities." He described Principal George Beecher as a fine man who "knows science and farming and English." Sabino Dewey never worked at Arthurdale, owing perhaps to health issues or the departure of the larger progressive education contingent in the months to come.[40]

On this trip to Arthurdale Mrs. Roosevelt made a special visit to Scotts Run, where many of the Arthurdale families had originated. She visited the University Demonstration High School, the teaching lab school for West Virginia University. She addressed the student body at the high school and praised their initiative and creativity. Before leaving Arthurdale for Washington, she attended a square dance, one of her favorite activities, and a dinner party for the National Advisory Committee at Clapp's home. The guests included John Dewey, Clarence Pickett, Nancy Cook, Alice Fayweather, George Colebank, L. B. Hill, Justus Deahl, H. B. Allen, Robert Clark, Walter Riddle, James Marland, and Edith Glenn. Some teachers were also present.[41]

Many of the activities begun during the first year of settlement were continued into the second to meet the needs of and enhance the quality of life in the community. One of the attempts was the formation of cooperative businesses. On approval by Washington, the first cooperative established was the Arthurdale Store. Another committee was formed to help build the science laboratory tables that were necessary if the high school was to achieve science accreditation. Clapp also formed a parent advisory committee to help with another school accreditation issue—the feeling among the homesteaders that, because the high school was not accredited, it must not be good. "However fantastic and unfounded," Clapp remembered, "the fear was wreaking havoc, for in their minds the schools and the hopes the homestead held for them were interwoven, and with a poor school their prospects for a new and better life at Arthurdale seemed dark and uncertain." The committee requested that the West Virginia Advisory Committee come inspect the school, giving both advice and criticism. Clapp seemed pleased and relieved when the committee, which was composed of public school teachers and administrators and university faculty, commended the activities of the school. The chairman of the committee, state superintendent W. W. Trent, stated that he believed he spoke for all the committee members when he said that "the Arthurdale School had more than fulfilled the hopes and plans they had for it."[42] While the immediate crisis seemed to be over, the Arthurdale high school did not receive state accreditation until 1938, two years after the departure of Clapp and her contingent of progressive educators.

In attempting to alleviate concerns about the school, "the staff quickened its pace in initiating and developing adult activities," particularly focusing on the winter months. Drama and other recreational activities provided what Clapp claimed were "good winter diversions." The home economics teacher organized cooking classes for women in the homestead and also continued to enlist their support in the preparation of the school lunches. Much of the food for the school lunches came from the homesteads, and, to alleviate future shortages, the teachers recommended that "each homestead family raise in its own garden a proportionate amount of the vegetables used in the hot lunch at school."[43] The canning of the food was to take place in the school community canning kitchen housed in the school center building.

One of the more difficult groups to reach remained the older high school students and young adults. Traditional educational experiences had alienated them, and most saw education as at best preparing them for jobs. But even that practical end seemed fruitless owing to the lack of employment in the area. Fortunately, Arthurdale was aided by the NYA, which provided funding for work projects for a group of about thirty of the community's boys and girls. Projects for the boys included shop work and mechanics under the direction of Harry Carlson, Carson Ryan, and George Beecher. Both boys and girls had the opportunity to take typing and library classes. Girls worked in the nursery school studying practical nursing and housekeeping, including nutrition and child care. During the Depression, women tended to remain on relief longer than men, largely because their employment outside the home remained socially unacceptable, and what work they were offered was often of a domestic nature.[44]

On 11 May 1936, a concerned Baruch made it clear that he had fulfilled his promise of financial contributions to the school, having given a total of $23,755 for the 1935/1936 school year. As he expressed his frustration to Mrs. Roosevelt: "It is too bad that the government could not do as you have done with this school. I do not know how we can go ahead while the government is making promises and holding out hopes that cannot be fulfilled."[45]

One of the activities that brought the school and the community together was music. On 21 May 1936, one local newspaper reported that twenty musicians from Arthurdale were traveling to Washington to entertain at a garden party and picnic lunch for disabled veterans given by Mrs. Roosevelt. The president was also in attendance. The cadre of musicians consisted of a harmonica player, singers, a quartet, and a caller for a square dance. The art and drama teacher Fletcher Collins was to direct the performance, and prior to leaving for the capital the group performed for the community.[46] Within a month of this performance came the Arthurdale Music Festival and preparation for the Arthurdale School's graduation ceremonies. Invitations to participate in the music festival were distributed throughout the area. Entrants included ballad singers, mouth harpers, jig dancers, square dancers, orchestras, and choirs. The festival also featured musical instruments made by Arthurdale students, typically mandolins and violins. It was held in the new recreational building with over one thousand people in attendance.

The community school at Arthurdale continued its activity during the summer of 1936, although changes were clearly on the horizon. On 28 June, Mrs. Roosevelt returned once more to receive the first vacuum cleaner produced by a new plant in Arthurdale. This plant was originally announced in April 1936 and was designed to employ some sixty homesteaders. West Virginia senator Jennings Randolph made the initial announcement of a ten-year lease signed by the Electric Vacuum Cleaner Company. At the ceremony at which the First Lady was presented with her vacuum, Randolph praised her contribution to Arthurdale: "We are all mindful of the debt owed to Mrs. Roosevelt for her part in this great homesteader project."[47] Rexford Tugwell, who was also present at the ceremony, discussed the future of the project, optimistically forecasting that the Resettlement Administration would have two more plants to employ the homesteaders up and running within a year. A social worker accompanying Mrs. Roosevelt spoke on the need for projects like Arthurdale. The First Lady spent a relaxing evening at the Arthurdale gym handing out ribbons to the winners of the music festival contests before retiring for the night at Clapp's homestead. She described the event in her "My Day" column: "There was an audience of some eight hundred men, women, and children, and their approval of the program was attested by the quiet in the hall as each contestant played his contribution. . . . One boy showed me his instrument with pride and I recalled the day when I saw him holding up the piece of wood through which he had just made a hole, which meant that he had to begin all over again the slow process of shaving down which is not only a question of skill but of self control and patience. So do we learn many things in the process of doing one thing well!"[48] She spent the next day visiting the well-baby clinic, the women's garden project, and the Four-H projects in the community.

The onset of summer brought on more "feelings of insecurity." Clapp believed that much of this was brought on by the confusion of home ownership and fueled by the homesteaders' inconsistent unemployment. This insecurity led to criticism of the school. On returning from a June 1936 trip, Clapp noted: "The community's feeling of insecurity had suddenly become located in the school. The fact that the high school has not been classified by the state as an accredited school emerged as a cause of panic. I saw the county superintendent of schools, who was extremely cooperative and somewhat amused at the situation. He said he thought the Arthurdale School was growing faster than any school he had ever seen. He told me to tell the people that Arthurdale had applied for classification and would undoubtedly receive it just as soon as it met the various points on which classification rests." She blamed the recent panic on Earl Riley, a homesteader who, she noted, had not met his financial obligations in the community and had sent his child to Masontown High School.[49]

In her role as director of community affairs, Clapp spent much of her time seeking the commitment of factories to build at Arthurdale. The lack of suitable employment for the homesteaders had led to funding failures with the Carnegie Foundation and the General Education Board. Baruch wrote Mrs. Roosevelt: "Now to the real gist of this matter. I do not think it would be fair to keep the school open, or Reedsville [i.e., Arthurdale] going unless the people there are assured of a living. So far as I have been able to see, and after running down all the hopes and promises, that is not in sight." He continued: "Miss Clapp is troubled in her mind as to what she ought to do more perhaps because of her feelings for you than about herself. If the school proceeds for another year, I do not see that it would be any better off unless we can get factories that will employ approximately two hundred men."[50]

Regardless of the confusion about the future of the project, the summer school offered several educational activities. The teachers taught weaving, gardening, nature study, soil testing, cooking, canning, quilt making, singing, printing, and pottery making, and Clapp taught art.[51] However, by mid-June, it was clear that the Arthurdale School was about to change. The First Lady asked Clapp to provide for her some estimates as to what it would cost to keep the school running, but without the progressive education contingent.

(Of the progressive component she was willing to ask Baruch to continue to support only the early childhood education program at the nursery school and the health-care work being done in the community.) She did, however, try to end her letter on a positive note: "I enjoyed my visit very much as always and I think you are doing a wonderful job. No matter what happens your work has not been wasted."[52] Several days later, Clapp provided the First Lady with an estimate of a minimum of $10,000 and a maximum of $16,000. She explained that Preston County could not supply more teachers for the school even though the nursery school enrollment was increasing from 73 to 100. She noted that she wished to continue the health-care work and believed that the funding of a community doctor and nurse was absolutely necessary owing to the addition of four more families. She also still held out hope that some financial solution could be found to continue the progressive experiment.[53]

Two weeks later, Mrs. Roosevelt passed along the bad news that a grant from Dean William Russell of Teachers College and Edmund deS. Brunner that Clapp had been pursuing to underwrite the costs of the whole school would not be forthcoming but that it might be possible to supplement the cost of the nursery school, thus allowing Jessie Stanton to remain in charge. The First Lady did try to soften the blow, noting: "[Russell and Brunner] were interested in what we had done and distressed that the experiment was not going on this year as they felt it was so valuable but I explained that both Mr. Baruch and you felt that the economic condition was not secure enough to warrant it."[54] Mrs. Roosevelt returned to Arthurdale on 7 July and met the next day with the West Virginia advisory committee, Clapp, and some of the teachers in Fletcher Collins's home, reporting on the results in her "My Day" column. As she explained there: "It has become necessary from Miss Clapp's point of view and mine to make certain changes and we wanted to discuss them with the committee, set the machinery in motion for a transition period and have a meeting this afternoon with the homesteaders to tell them of our decision and discussion and get their suggestions."[55] While donors had agreed to continue to support the health-care programs, the nursery school, and a portion of teacher salaries for one year, it was decided to cede control of the Arthurdale School to the Preston County and West Virginia authorities.[56]

Mrs. Roosevelt wrote Baruch shortly thereafter: "I explained the entire change to [the homesteaders] of course, not telling them that we doubted their future economic situation but stressing that it was important to them to carry on the work on their own responsibility and to tie themselves in every possible way with the state, the committee, and the general neighborhood. . . . They will, of course not be as with Miss Clapp and her trained staff but I think they can with the two years opportunity they have had, and the grant which you are giving them, do much better than they would otherwise."[57] Clapp herself seemed finally resigned to the end of the progressive education experiment when shortly thereafter she wrote to Mrs. Roosevelt discussing some of the difficulties the county might face in its attempt to "find teachers and a principal able to carry on." She described a move by some of the homesteaders to have the current staff hired by Preston County. "As they see it," she explained, "the county could hire us better than teachers who don't know how. They want the school to go on as it was and 'just as good' they say, and they fear the strife and let down of our leaving. I do not see, however, how it can change the conditions (of which of course they do not know) that guided our discussion." Clapp planned to leave Arthurdale by 1 August and spend the next month in Robinhood, Maine. "What the fall will bring I cannot foresee," she wrote. "I shall do my best to place the teachers and to reinvest my efforts elsewhere."[58]

"For all of us," Clapp concluded in later years, "it seemed impossible to cease upon the instant, as it were, the many and interrelated school and community activities which had both immediate and long-range benefits in view. The children, we felt confident however, could and would now go forward in their learning. And the adults, whose hardihood had run them their chance to make a new start in life, would in all probability gradually gain stability and compromise as time brought healing and perspective. Certainly they, like the children and the girls and boys, had to an extent that did not two years ago seem possible regained lost energy and initiative and learned how to live and grow in the new conditions and surroundings."[59]

By mid-August, the progressive contingent had left Arthurdale. Clapp was working on the manuscript that would become *Community Schools in Action*. George Beecher and Carson Ryan sought opportunities to construct a science program for high schools in North Carolina. Ethel Carlisle was teaching at the Lincoln School in New York, and Elisabeth Sheffield was teaching at a progressive school in Connecticut. Clapp wrote Mrs. Roosevelt discussing her pursuits and aspirations. "I am hard at work here on the manuscript of the book on community education at Arthurdale and in Kentucky which Dewey urged us to write last spring. What I really want to do," she stressed, "is another school in a community. The need in the country is so urgent. I feel I should be used whether or not Mr. Baruch really wishes to sponsor such a piece of work. I do not know. At Dewey's urging I have been meaning to write you a note to tell you that we have all finally withdrawn from Arthurdale after endeavoring to give the homesteaders assurance of our continuing interest and concern." She noted that some of the homesteaders had created a petition to keep Clapp and some of the staff: "It was signed by a majority of the families and a number of the high school boys and girls, and based its request on the patience and understanding shown them, on ability to run the school, and on the fact that the children had learned and had been happy."[60]

There is no question that Clapp held out hope that she and her staff might in some way be able to continue the progressive experiment at Arthurdale. Yet she was realistic enough to know that, as long as the employment situation did not improve, the morale of the community would be in constant jeopardy. The lack of economic stability permeated the entire community, and children brought their own insecurity to the school, which certainly affected their learning. Clapp knew that government ineptness had created many of her problems as well as those of the community, but she never let that get in the way of her attempt to aid the homesteaders. She was in a difficult position, being the director of community affairs and the school's principal and thus forced to balance political realities with the social and economic needs of the children and their parents, all the while aware that what happened at Arthurdale reflected on the First Lady's and ultimately the president's policies. She must have been bolstered by the faith Mrs. Roosevelt, Bernard Baruch, John Dewey, her staff, and many of the homesteaders had in her efforts. This support encouraged her to pursue her work in rural community education elsewhere. It is unfortunate that Arthurdale was her last true experiment in community education. The Arthurdale School and the community carried on even though the community school experiment gradually came to an end.

6

From Community School to Traditional

There is no question that Elsie Clapp and her contingent of progressive educators expected the educational experiment at Arthurdale to last longer than two years. "To all of us it seemed almost impossible to cease upon the instant," Clapp wrote, "as it was the many and interrelated school and community activities which had both immediate and long range benefits in view. The children, we felt confident however, could and would now go forward in learning. And the adults, whose hardihood had won them the chance to make a new start in life, would in all probability gradually gain stability and composure as time brought healing and perspective."[1] For Clapp and her colleagues, the early departure engendered more resignation and resolution than anger. They had accomplished a great deal in two years, not even having adequate school facilities until the second year. "[Miss Clapp] did such a wonderful job at the Arthurdale, West Virginia, school," declared Mrs. Roosevelt, "not only in planning and starting it as a progressive school, but in helping to draw the community together and in making the school the center of almost every community activity." Commenting on Clapp's new role as the editor of *Progressive Education,* she continued: "I feel she can do a very great service to education through this magazine."[2]

Although not physically present in Arthurdale, Clapp continued to respond to Mrs. Roosevelt's queries. The First Lady asked her about the Arthurdale health fund, and she responded with receipts and expenditures as of 14 August 1936. She also included an update on the former Arthurdale teachers and her own present work:

> You will be glad to know that all the teachers but one are now settled—either teaching or studying. I think he will also find some-

thing. I am still at work on the account of a community school, using materials from both Arthurdale and the Kentucky experiences. The educational world is anxious to have this material. Everyone now is concerned with community education but few know just what it involves or how it is done. Teachers College wanted to subsidize the writing of the book, but was not able to arrange it. So I am going forward with it myself for Dr. Dewey wants me to do it. Beyond that I have no immediate plans. I hope to get the manuscript in shape by January. Then I would like to investigate the problem of education in remote rural areas, and determine how to further it.[3]

Unfortunately, little is known about the teachers following their departure from Arthurdale. Fletcher Collins and George Beecher found jobs at Elon College, which was located in Alamance County in rural North Carolina and supported by the Christian Congregational Church. Elon's predominate mission was the preparation of teachers, and it was accredited by the state. Beecher was in charge of practice teaching and gave extension courses preparing science materials for use in the county schools. Collins headed the English Department, worked in literature and drama, and continued his exploration of folk culture. Clapp wrote Mrs. Roosevelt about Elon's attempt to establish a better connection with the local public schools. She also raised the possibility of funding some of the projects at Elon, situated as it was in an area that she described as "agricultural and industrial" and dealing with unemployment and limited access to health care.[4]

Collins recalled that he had no prior knowledge of Elon College, becoming aware of the opening there only through the efforts of the Yale placement office. He found Elon to be in bad shape but nevertheless enjoyed his time there. "I'd have been on the faculty at Elon a long time but for the war," he later recalled. "Things were going very well there—really good kids that were interested in learning. They weren't all fouled up with the Wall Street ambitions—things that I'd been used to at Yale."[5] Collins continued to collect folklore, generally folk songs and ballads, a focus that had been nurtured at Arthurdale. Some of this work was supported by the Works Progress Administration (WPA) and eventually culminated in an extensive donation of material to the Library of Congress. Beecher went on to found Goddard College, but, while at Elon, he worked with the Alamance County schools and studied the science curriculum in local rural secondary schools. The former Arthurdale School secretary Alice Bowie assisted him in this project.[6]

Adolph Ipcar, the math and history teacher at Arthurdale, became a successful dairy farmer in Maine. He wrote of the response to the decision to turn the Arthurdale School over to the county: "Elsie was indignant at the sudden termination of the Arthurdale project, but I never sensed basic frustration. Her entire career was a historical education success. Elsie Clapp vigorously interpreted her school into the lives of the Arthurdale people; into their politics, economy, health, planning, and education. Her efforts and that of her staff met with general approval and expected resistance. It was tragic and traumatic for Elsie and all of her staff to be forced to abandon our unfinished work."[7] Ipcar later became involved in local politics, championing environmental issues and the arts. He married Dahlov Zorach, the daughter of the sculptor William Zorach, who had given Elsie Clapp art lessons.[8]

"So it all came to an end in June 1936," explained Margaret Collins, the wife of Fletcher Collins. "We had roamed around fixing up our little homestead to have Mrs. Roosevelt for lunch. Then I rode with her part of the way to Connecticut for my sister Martha's wedding. Mrs. Roosevelt talked for hours (she was working on her memoirs) while I just sat and listened. Maybe it was a good way to wind down the whole experience. It was while we were at the wedding that we found out they were turning over the schools to the county."[9]

Following the departure of the progressive education contingent, one might surmise that the progressive philosophy was abandoned as well. It was, but not immediately. Clarence Pickett noted: "When the time came to turn the school over to the county, certain aspects of the experimental program were kept for the time being: the health work and the nursery school were especially wanted and those who had been subsidizing the school continued to supplement the budget somewhat, on behalf of the special features that were retained."[10] E. Grant Nine became principal of the school following Clapp's departure. He was supportive of the "method and some of the organization" that had evolved at Arthurdale. "I don't believe," Nine explained, "in structuring education to a program dictated by the central office for all its schools. There used to be a time in this state when you were supposed to be on a certain page at a certain time of the year. To me, this was hogwash! That isn't the way to live life. So I've tried to use those kinds of methods and encourage my teachers to do that." Like Clapp's, Nine's salary was underwritten by the proceeds of Mrs. Roosevelt's "My Day" column and her radio talks and funneled through the American Friends Service Committee (AFSC). Nine noted that the private funds further helped Arthurdale fund the teaching of ceramics and painting, courses of study not offered by the local Preston County schools.[11]

Mrs. Roosevelt returned to Arthurdale one last time that year—on 3 December 1936—although Clapp and most of the progressive contingent of teachers had departed. Her party included Mrs. Harry Hopkins and Lorena Hickok. The First Lady left Washington by train around midnight, arriving in Fairmont, West Virginia, around 8:30 A.M. "I was very much interested to go through the school, meet the new principal and many of the teachers," she wrote, "and finally at luncheon to sit opposite two of the high school boys who are running the Arthurdale newspaper.... The president of the Arthurdale Association sat next to me and I was impressed by his cooperative spirit and his interest in all the questions affecting the welfare of the community." While she did not comment on her meeting with the school administrators and faculty, she seemed pleased that the poultry cooperative was "doing very well" and that the dairy cooperative was "about to start." The vacuum cleaner factory, which employed some of the homesteaders, appeared to be doing well. Encouraged by her visit, she commented: "On the whole, I think that Arthurdale is becoming a community, able to work out its own problems and to find a satisfactory solution for them which may be helpful in other parts of the country."[12] Mrs. Roosevelt had not given up on the experiment at Arthurdale, feeling that the community could serve as a model for community reform throughout the nation. As she wrote to Clapp about her visit:

> I found everything at Arthurdale quite encouraging. Mr. Nine is doing a good job in the school and, while of course it isn't as good a school, the people do seem able to go along on their own initiative. I was given some money for books which the school needed and do hope they will continue to be as interested. The nursery school is to continue and the only thing now for which money is needed is the medical end. The Women's Club handled the Christmas party and I think, on the whole, the people are happy and satisfied.[13]

Mrs. Roosevelt remained interested in Arthurdale. On 18 January 1937, she spent more time in the community, visiting the new "cottage hospital" ("three beds and one bassinet") there. "From there," she reported, "I went over to the nursery school and visited every grade through the high school."

She also attended a school committee meeting and a medical committee meeting and observed lunch in the nursery school.[14]

Clapp left no written record of her response to Mrs. Roosevelt's December visit, and one wonders what she must have thought about the First Lady's comments, which seem meant to reassure her that all was well despite the change in direction at Arthurdale. Clapp had plans to work in the Art Department at Ohio State, but they fell through owing to lack of funding. However, she was offered and accepted the editorship of the journal *Progressive Education* by Carson Ryan, the president of the Progressive Education Association (PEA), although she requested that the appointment be for one year only as she held out hope of involvement in another community education experiment. Still, she informed Mrs. Roosevelt of her goals for the journal: "We are to make an attempt to know more fully public education and social conditions significant for education—an effort that is needed if this younger educational association is to be really serviceable. I shall be free to move about to have contact with what is going on. If you care to send me word from time to time of work that needs recognition or conditions that invite fresh understanding as you meet them I shall be glad to look into them and bring them to attention." She also asked the First Lady to provide her with any information she might have "about friends at Arthurdale."[15]

On 1 August 1937, Mrs. Roosevelt had a visit from Fletcher Collins, after which she commented: "He did a wonderful piece of work in the field of English, Dramatics and Music in the Arthurdale, West Virginia school and is now working in a small college in North Carolina on a very interesting educational project."[16] Clapp too spent some time with the First Lady at Hyde Park in early August 1937 shortly after the death of her brother. She remarked: "I come away always with renewed courage and serenity and that day with you in the cottage I recaptured peace and a sense of beauty for the first time since his death."[17]

A few weeks earlier, Clapp had written to Mrs. Roosevelt about contributing to the first issue of *Progressive Education* that she was to edit—a special issue tied to the centennial of the birth of Francis Parker and titled "Where Is Education Going?" "It need not be long," Clapp noted, "five or six questions expressed as briefly or as lengthy as you please." Mrs. Roosevelt responded with the following list:

1. Should a different type of education be given in urban and rural schools?

2. Is education in our public schools today fitting young people to: a. earn a living?, b. to be intelligent and useful citizens?, c. to lead satisfying lives?, d. to enjoy their leisure periods?
3. Should nursery schools be part of our free public school education?
4. Are nursery schools as necessary for rural children as for city children?
5. The problems of citizenship today are more complicated and require a wider knowledge and a greater social understanding. Will our present day school teaching give this knowledge and understanding?
6. Is the training of teachers adequate in all of our states?
7. Is the fact that many of our states do not provided free textbooks for children a serious detriment to their education?[18]

When the school year began in September 1937, the employment situation at Arthurdale was less than rosy. Owing to changing product, the vacuum cleaner plant now employed no homesteaders, and a shirt factory employed only thirty homesteaders, mostly women and young girls; twenty homesteaders worked outside the Arthurdale community, and eighteen were employed making school furniture. Mrs. Roosevelt continued to seek private contributions to aid the school. As of 27 October 1937, disbursements for the year (January 1–October 15) were $15,999.59. These figures included the nursery school, salaries, transportation, food, administrative salaries, travel, and adult education. In her private discretionary fund, the First Lady still had a balance of $22,449.26 to support the school and other endeavors in which she was interested, much of the funding coming from radio talks for which she received financial compensation. Despite Mrs. Roosevelt's contributions, funding the school was still an issue, as is made evident by the proposed 1937/1938 budget. Total expenditures were expected to be around $24,500. This included the nursery school, the elementary school, and the high school. Of that figure, Preston County was to be responsible for $11,070, leaving $13,430 to be covered by private funds and the Resettlement Administration. There was also some discussion of shortening the nine-month school year to reduce costs.[19]

The new year at the Arthurdale School began with homesteader Daniel Houghton teaching adult classes in wood- and sheet metal–work and thirteen teachers from Doddridge County observing day-to-day operations. The school was also visited by "twenty persons from the Lincoln School, Columbia University," and five student teachers under the direction of Nina Richmond from Fairmont Teachers College. The high school glee club presented an operetta entitled *Ask the Professor*, with proceeds going to buy sheet music. By late January 1938, 158 homesteads were occupied, and seven more families were to be selected.[20] School lunches were being served to around 220 students. Several of the faculty attended the Middle Atlantic State Regional Conference of the PEA in Washington, DC. Teachers continued to assist in the distribution of clothing to children in the community, a project initially begun by Mrs. Roosevelt. Another difficult situation involving homesteader employment had also arisen. Both the shirt factory and the vacuum cleaner factory were shut down with no definite plans to reopen; however, by April, Glenn Work, the acting Arthurdale project manager, reported that twenty-one people had been reemployed by the shirt factory.[21]

By the spring of 1938, the Arthurdale School occupied six buildings under the supervision of the Preston County School Board with Paul Watson as superintendent. Under the recently passed Bankhead Act, the federal government still contributed to the school in lieu of taxes.[22] While the homesteaders continued to have problems securing employment, their homestead farming appeared to be successful, with families generally able to meet the goal of producing $200 worth of farm product annually. Most of the homesteads consisted of "a little more than three acres, some of them containing as much as five acres" and others as little as two acres. A combination of subsistence farming and industrial employment "seemed to be the logical solution," and "the homesteads were designed accordingly." The Arthurdale community also operated a general farm, a poultry farm, a dairy, and a grist mill along with the furnituremaking operation of the Mountaineer Craftsmen's Cooperative.[23]

Two summers after Clapp's departure, Eleanor offered in her "My Day" column a positive note about Arthurdale following a visit on 27 June 1938: "Everything went off well there. Mr. Baruch, who joined me on my arrival, voiced what I have been feeling for some time. Namely, that there is a greater sense of solidarity and security among the homesteaders than ever before. I only hope that the work which has been done in Arthurdale, in spite of all the mistakes and drawbacks, will give the 200 families there real security and will, therefore, give more courage to those in other homesteads all over the nation."[24] She continued to support the school, sending $300 for textbooks and $200 for the Women's Club to use for Christmas, and was especially concerned about meeting the social and educational needs of the children.[25]

Literacy remained a constant concern at Arthurdale, especially among the younger children, as Nine discovered when he took up his post as principal. Still, the high school received accreditation in the spring of 1938, which must have pleased many of the parents, alleviating some of their concerns about the curriculum. At the time of accreditation, the high school employed ten teachers and had enrolled 108 students.[26]

Shortly after the high school received its accreditation, Arthurdale learned that President Roosevelt would be making his first visit to the community. Mrs. Roosevelt had requested that Nine invite the president to give the high school commencement address (to nineteen students!), something she usually did. The presidential party included Eleanor, John Roosevelt, the Roosevelts' youngest son, Missy LeHand, Malvina Schneider, Mrs. Henry Morgenthau, and Mr. and Mrs. George Bye.[27] FDR used the 27 May 1938 address to attack the tax structure in the country, which he believed favored the wealthy and big corporations, and to point out the positive and negative aspects of a new tax bill then under consideration in Congress. (After all, what better place than Arthurdale to condemn social inequality?) He advocated for the continued use of federal funds to support projects like Arthurdale, suggesting: "We . . . are getting more practical results in the way of bettering the social conditions of the nation out of our taxes than ever before in our history." Clearly aware of the politically charged nature of Arthurdale, he admitted that among the "many different types of projects . . . undertaken . . . there were some failures—not a complete failure in the case of any given project, but partial failures due to bad guesses on economic subjects like new industries and lack of markets." Nevertheless, Americans had a right to expect their government to step in and help them when necessary: "Back in 1933 the whole Nation knew that it faced a crisis in economic conditions but the Nation did not realize that it also faced a crisis in its social conditions. If anyone were to ask me what is the outstanding contribution that has been made to American life in the past five years, I would say without hesitation that it is the awakening of the social conscience of America."[28]

Shortly after FDR's visit, the faculty of the high school published a report analyzing the current state of the community. The report began by addressing the historical roots of Arthurdale, strongly praising the integral role that Mrs. Roosevelt had played in attempting to help people make a living through subsistence farming. It touched on the most glaring problem for the homesteaders, that being the lack of employment and the resulting instability in a community that needed stability, an instability that affected the children as well as the adults. "This apparent uncertain state of affairs," the report emphasized, "has sometimes made the homesteaders feel up in the air since Washington seemed to have so much say about what happens here, but does not seem to know or understand very well just what is happening here."[29] The employment issue was exacerbated by a lack of wage equity among the homesteaders.

Furthermore, parents' concerns about the progressive philosophy of the school had constantly created problems. Although the homesteaders had in 1934 voted on the initial school philosophy paragraph by paragraph, ultimately they still understood education only in terms of their limited and traditional experience. For them education was strictly a teacher/text-centered affair. Clarence Pickett agreed with this assessment, asserting: "We learned that at least some of the parents, while acquiescing in what was happening, often had not really understood, and feared that their children might not be getting as good an education as children in regular schools. Doubtless the economic insecurity which had hounded them during the past few years intensified their desire to be like other communities and made them suspicious of experiments."[30] During the Depression, most Americans, including the Arthurdale homesteaders, viewed education as a means to the ends of stable employment, despite the current state of the job market, and social mobility.

Most of the parents of the Arthurdale schoolchildren had less than an eighth-grade education and no more than "a sprinkle of books and magazines" in their homes. And, while the homesteaders seemed to have accepted certain of their responsibilities, for example, growing sufficient food for their families, others were not necessarily embraced. "The things that seem most lacking in Arthurdale," noted the teachers' report, "are initiative, vision, value of human personality, and the acceptance of community responsibilities. . . . If Arthurdale is to develop into a truly cooperative community, it must do better than it has so far." Still, adhering to the earlier progressive school theme, the report held out hope that the school could serve as a means for the teachers to become partners with the community, "building and sharing the experiences and lessons of education and democracy."[31]

When the report was written, there were approximately 140 students in the Arthurdale high school, most from families that had experienced "economic hardship" before coming to the community. The report categorized the students in terms of good and bad characteristics. As for the good characteristics: "There are many fine, upright cooperative and appreciative students in A.H.S. who realize the opportunities and take advantage of them.... Practically all of the students will work at something until it is done, and enjoy displaying their handiwork." On the other hand: "Some of the students do not try to cooperate with one another or with the teachers." Other problems were enumerated: for example, "bad manners," disrespectful pupils, and "not [being] clean in appearance," even though "they all have excellent toilet facilities in their homes." Measured in terms of intelligence, the students had IQ scores mostly between 70 and 90, considerably below average, at least according to the report. The teachers also perceived a general lack of school spirit.[32]

The report concluded with certain recommendations. The lack of literacy skills led the teachers to believe that the students might learn best through "hands on activities" that might include training in vocational skills. The recommended fields of preparation included landscaping, pottery making, and (for girls) "kindergarten work." The faculty suggested further the integration of classes such as English and printing; art, social studies, and English; biology and English; and commerce, art, and shop. These combinations are far from traditional and imply that a progressive thread was still present in the curriculum, despite the growing vocational focus. Finally, in conclusion it was noted: "We need to include in this educational program some instruction so the pupils will have a wider knowledge of this present day work. If they could understand more clearly this age of machinery, perhaps they could become more easily adjusted to it socially and financially."[33]

Overall, the report suggested that the more progressive elements introduced by Clapp were not working and that there needed to be more of an effort made to prepare students for the work environment. Yes, there were some attempts to integrate subject matter, but this seems to be more a matter of logistics than a philosophical change. The high school curriculum was being less and less guided by Clapp's emphasis on community building.

By June 1938, the National Advisory Committee was recommending that the "program at Arthurdale School should become more and more the responsibility of local and state agencies and be made less dependent upon exceptional aid from the Farm Security Administration." The 1938/1939 school year was to be the transition year for the process to take place. The recommendations called for Preston County to "assume full responsibility for the employment of elementary school teachers in Arthurdale School for 1938/39." It was understood that "the distribution of state aid in West Virginia and the political responsibility of local state officials to apportion educational services equitably throughout the county limits the Arthurdale high school to a teaching staff inadequate for a functional and progressive program at the secondary school level." The remedy for this financial dilemma? "[The high school should] be required to serve a much larger area than the project. It should be required to furnish a practical and purposeful education for participation in the arts, crafts, trades, industries, and the community planning and development problems which will confront the youth of the area for many years." Confusion still reigned about the actual control of the Arthurdale School. This confusion had "permitted local school authorities to either stand apart from the Arthurdale School program or regard the recommendations of the Educational Advisory Committee [probably the National Advisory Committee] as administrative recommendations sometimes in conflict with the administrative problems of the county."[34]

The committee also made it clear that additional funds were needed for the maintenance and operation of the physical plant, a secretary for the principal, the operation of the nursery school, and travel funds for the principal. Personnel concerns included salary increases beyond the $2,150 budgeted and also funding for increasing the high school staff beyond four full-time and two part-time employees. The committee sought assurance from the Farm Security Administration (FSA) that federal money would continue to finance the physical plant in terms of fuel, electricity, and general operation and maintenance. The FSA was further requested to supply the secretary for the principal. The nursery school—which at the time was being financed by private funds and the WPA—could not legally be financed by Preston County or the state, so the committee recommended that, when private funds were no longer available, the program be discontinued. The proposed budget for the 1938/1939 operating year was $23,166, a figure that did not include FSA funding.[35] Before the end of the 1938/1939 school year, the Arthurdale faculty drew up a document outlining the school's philosophy. Grant Nine sent a copy of that document to Clapp, who then forwarded it to Mrs. Roosevelt. "The philosophy is quite reminiscent of the early original school plan as drafted by the West Virginia School Committee," Clapp noted. "On the whole," she continued, "I think that the portion which is called the Arthurdale School system is a very intelligent and singularly simple and direct statement. Quite evidently the work with the young children has been thought through more completely than the work in the high school. The best feature seems to me evident that it is an expression of their own convictions and thinking. I am sending it to you chiefly because it seems to me necessary on this point."[36] No doubt Clapp was pleased with what she read, although she felt that the high school was being moved away from its progressive origins. The educational philosophy emphasized the importance of "cooperative responsibility and democratic life" and the children learning to balance individual and group experiences and thus come to an understanding of responsibility and democracy. There was an attempt to provide "opportunities for the child to think in scientific manner in meeting his present problems so that as his responsibilities increase, his ability to meet them efficiently will have increased in proportion to his needs": "The school must be life and education and must grow out of life experiences."[37]

It was its philosophy of education that undergirded the curriculum principles and practices of the Arthurdale School. The curriculum was influenced by the characteristics of the homestead community, and Nine emphasized it was "not to be hampered by traditional and formal courses of study, nor by standardized grading and grouping of pupils." Teachers used themed units that were project based and often lasted throughout the year. "This type of work guides toward the development of an understanding of social relationship which is essential to character and citizenship, and at the same time, gives [students] command of knowledge and skills necessary to effective living in the world as it is." Those activities or units were based in the needs, interests, and abilities of the students. The role of the teacher was as a guide to direct their growth, "even as they watch for signs that the child is ready for this or that type of educational experience." The Arthurdale School as Nine envisioned it saw learning as "an active process and one based on the conviction that the most effective learning takes place when pupils are engaged in doing things that seem worthwhile to them." Clapp and Mrs. Roosevelt must have been pleased when he wrote: "In this project the school and community share and cooperate together for the common good. It provides one of the opportunities for the children, patrons, and the teachers to work together cooperatively. It also provides a channel for community adult education. It functions as a democratic process." The concept of community still guided the Arthurdale School as students took part in activities and traveled through the community developing, it was hoped, "a cultural appreciation [of] and a scientific attitude toward their surroundings." The school still made use of the study of pioneer life and coupled that with increased reading, writing, and weaving activities.[38]

The high school description, which seemed to disturb Clapp, claimed to provide experience in cooperation and citizenship, although it clearly acknowledged: "Our students will not attend college." Therefore: "We are attempting to offer courses that will fit them by work available in this resettlement community. We try to replace traditional subject matter with material they can use later." The curriculum was devised so that students would "learn how to adapt [themselves] to [their] surroundings." For the girls, emphasis was placed on becoming the efficient homesteader. They studied weaving, making clothes, preparing meals, appearance, child care, and some practical nursing. Boys studied nutrition, woodworking, sheet metal–working, and some furnituremaking. Adult classes were offered in weaving and needlework for women, woodworking for men, and pottery making for both.[39]

In May 1940, the faculty of the College of Education at West Virginia University issued a report that challenged this move to preparation for work and to a more traditional practice. This report was requested by the National Advisory Committee and financially supported by the AFSC under the direction of Clarence Pickett. The West Virginia Department of Education along with the Preston County Board of Education also supported it, knowing that state and county resources were not sufficient to continue to maintain all the educational programs of the Arthurdale School. The goal of the report was to explore the feasibility of the program in its current manifestation. The survey staff was composed of Miss Ruth Noer, M. C. Garr, and Dr. D. W. Parsons of the College of Agriculture, Home Economics, and Forestry and the College of Education; Dr. Lloyd Jones of the School of Physical Education and Athletics; and Drs. Rebecca Pollock, H. B. Allen, Robert Dodge Baldwin, Leonard B. Hill, Earl Hudelson, Forrest Stemple, and H. G. Wheat, also of the College of Education.[40]

The authors of the report believed that the original school philosophy had not changed but that "in many respects practice has been considerably modified." This was attributed to some pressure from those homesteaders who had called for a more traditional, textbook-based education for their children. Because of the general economic instability of the Arthurdale project, it became difficult to recruit teachers, particularly for the high school, the atmosphere of which was described as sober, lethargic, academic, and stifled. There was also the concern that the teachers recently hired did not have adequate training in or sympathy with the ideas of progressive education. "It was somewhat disquieting," the report noted, "to find the school at Arthurdale tending to lean away from its initially conceived functional curriculum for high school youth toward one more traditional and textbook dominated."[41] The committee recommended that the Arthurdale, Masontown, and Reedsville area be considered as a unit for providing broader services to the county, that the Meadowview and Triune schools be integrated or centralized into the Arthurdale School, that supplemental services be expanded and split between Masontown and Arthurdale, and that Arthurdale continue as a type of experimental school for teacher training, early childhood instruction and care, industrial arts, weaving, handicrafts, pottery, and art.

Dr. H. G. Wheat described the curriculum in 1940 as quite different from what it was in 1934 and noted that the Arthurdale high school was an activity school in appearance only. He discerned no attempt to mesh the school and the community. He favored an activity program that transformed the pupil into a viable community member. He explained:

> In theory, the activity program brings to a head in the consciousness of the pupils the problems of community life, and thus provides for pupils a purpose and a drive for learning the lessons which the activities determine the school shall teach. In practice and in theory, the activity program transforms the school into a community in miniature; it withdraws pupils from the community and sets them down at once into a reproduction or a representation of the community from which they have just come; and it enforces through the process of direct experience (that is participation) the learning of the same lesson (some of the better lessons and with better effect, it is hoped) which participation in actual community activities would otherwise teach them.[42]

Wheat held a master of arts degree from the University of Chicago, where he studied under Charles H. Judd, "who impressed upon his mind the internal consistencies of the school subjects, and set the pattern of his thinking along the lines of the way the school subjects are organized for teaching and learning."[43]

It was quite clear that the faculty of the College of Education, or at least those constituting the survey team, did not support the move to a more teacher/textbook-based approach. Robert Dodge Baldwin of the survey team also believed the stress on a more traditional type of education was largely due to the parents' unrealistic expectations that their children would enter college. (The fact that the high school was not accredited until 1938 also contributed to the parents' concerns about education and social mobility.) Baldwin argued that such expectations were not realistic because at that time only six of thirty-five high school graduates pursued advanced study and therefore that a traditional college prep curriculum did not meet the needs of most students. He concluded: "Thus of the 5 graduates who had entered higher institutions which tend to stress abstract, academic learning, one is doing excellent work; one withdrew because of lack of funds to continue; and we know nothing of this student's academic achievement; one is passing all work taken but is deficient in honor points; and the other two have failed in more than half of their first semester's work, and one of these had withdrawn from the college." Baldwin understood that this sounded elitist and attempted to explain himself:

> Unquestionably the homesteaders' child stands on par with any other in matters of educational opportunity. This is the glory and the promise of American democracy. And significant, democratic educational opportunity is being denied a child who pursues a course of study not adapted to his capacity, his needs, and his prospects. Hence, it must be said that, to the extent that the Arthurdale program of studies has yielded to the pressure of parents to emphasize the traditional and the college-preparatory, as over against the consumer-pointed and the vocational, it has tended to deprive most Arthurdale students of functional educational opportunity.[44]

The survey team strongly urged the Arthurdale School to get back to its original conception, "growing out of and yielding its fruitage into the community," helping the people become "good consumers of economic goods, of things esthetic and cultural," and emphasizing "those courses which might aid the individual to husband his resources, produce his subsistence and earn his way in a part-time individual pursuit." Along these lines, their report suggested that the school could serve as a type of "experimental laboratory school, for teacher preparation and improvement and as a center for (1) observation and participation in child care and training, (2) industrial arts, (3) weaving and handicrafts, (4) pottery, and (5) art be actually developed and extended to the county as widely as funds will permit."[45] It also made note of the classroom conditions and how they might affect learning when it was discovered that temperatures varied greatly—from sixty-eight to eighty degrees. Further, it indicated that there was a need for more consistent janitorial service, the janitor being hired without consultation with the school administration through the FSA.

Of course, the primary focus of the report was economic, how Arthurdale could continue its programs with declining private support. Over the years, the educational project at Arthurdale had been funded by the federal government (through the WPA, the Resettlement Administration, and the FSA), the state government (through Preston County), and private donors such as Mrs. Roosevelt, Bernard Baruch, and the AFSC. It was suggested in the report that the Arthurdale homesteaders paid less in property taxes than did their counterparts in Preston County, thus not contributing their fair share to the county schools. (Indeed, there was a concern in Preston County that the county would incur the extra costs when the Arthurdale School funding dried up.)[46] As the report noted, if public and private funding ceased, "the nursery school would cease entirely, the secondary school would have less than half as much with which to carry on, and the elementary school would have one-third less than at present." It was predicted that, on top of the economic instability of the community as a whole, such change would lead to even greater discouragement among the homesteaders and their children. While some of the homesteaders may have disagreed with the experimental approach to education at Arthurdale, none ever wavered in their belief in the inherent value of an education for their children and the opportunity that the school afforded them.[47]

While state and county monies could not be used to fund nursery school education per se, they could be used to fund certain other educational activities, thus keeping the building up and running. Baldwin clarified: "[State funding can be obtained for] home economics and social science classes of approved practice in the care and training of little children as demonstrated in a well-managed nursery school, and some actual participation in such care and training of children under expert supervision. One basic purpose of the nursery school movement, probably the basic purpose, is practical parent education." The nursery school could benefit the surrounding area rather than just the Arthurdale community, but it still needed to find an alternative funding source.[48]

Various other findings and recommendations made their way into the report. Because of their lack of previous educational experience and their families' poverty, the majority of the children of Arthurdale were performing below average academically but making progress owing to the school's emphasis on reading. The researchers were concerned, however, by the instability of the teaching force. They also recommended that attention continue to be paid to the specific needs of the homestead community and that the educators "should not be hampered by traditional and formal courses of study." They asserted: "Arthurdale was conceived as a community, a structure built on the principles of social sharing and economic cooperation and dedicated to the proposition that all men aspire to a life better than many of them, under the economic conditions imposed by modern industrial organization, unaided can achieve, and that, if given a reasonable opportunity, they will strive faithfully to realize such aspirations."[49]

The researchers argued that the curriculum should remain activity based and that textbooks should be used only as guides and resources. They believed that the goals of the progressive education programs were still viable, even if some modification was called for. They called for a return to the "close knit school-community program of education for home and family life" begun in 1934: "Thus the school, perhaps in a community conceived as Arthurdale was, would be expected to maintain a steady sensitiveness to and sympathy with the daily lives of the people and problems of its constituents and to exert a corresponding endeavor to make its work practical and functional at the levels to which they may reasonably hope currently, as well as ultimately, to attain."[50] The committee recommended hiring a project director who was also an educator, one with a background in sociology who could coordinate the work in home economics, vocational agriculture, farm security, industrial education, and extension units. M. C. Garr and D. W. Parsons favored emphasis on the subsistence agriculture theme and recommended that agriculture be included as part of the regular curriculum from the seventh grade through the twelfth for all students who planned on farming as a career. They also suggested that such instruction be made available to older students who wished to take up farming. Instruction was to be based on the agricultural "enterprise" found on the homestead project.[51]

H. B. Allen followed a similar lead, arguing that the Arthurdale School could serve to meet the industrial arts need of the entire county. He advocated using the nursery school as a laboratory but being attentive to the selection of the teachers and building on the nature of the subsistence homestead.[52] Lloyd Jones recognized the importance of health, physical education, and recreation, which had been emphasized since Arthurdale's conception. He recommended that "greater services should be given to the community through the recreation program sponsored by the schools" and that the community make better utilization of the "resources of the woods and hills" that surrounded Arthurdale. He also called for the physical education program to be separate from participation in the athletic teams and for elementary and secondary school students to participate in fifty and twenty minutes, respectively, of physical education each day.[53]

Allen, who had participated in the original process of selecting the homesteaders, recommended that trade instruction be available to all project residents and that a full-time instructor be hired. He contended that the research favored an approach that stressed continued outside financial assistance owing to the "enriched and expanded program at Arthurdale, including the extension of some service to the whole county," and that this "be widely and earnestly publicized." This was considered the most viable approach largely because of the local sentiment regarding Arthurdale and its lack of funding. By 1940, Preston County was still responsible for only 44 percent of the Arthurdale School budget, but the idea was to get people beyond the immediate homesteader community involved in the enriched Arthurdale program and thus keep it going.[54]

Shortly after the report was issued, the Pittsburgh journalist Milburn Rice published an article in *Harper's Magazine* on the problems and successes of the Arthurdale project. Rice criticized the project because the homesteaders were not in charge regardless of all the democratic rhetoric of the policymakers. Because of the political nature of Arthurdale and the top-down planning by "absentee planners," he saw no possibility that the project ever could have been successful. "In short," he concluded, "Arthurdale seeks to reaffirm a belief still strong that men must find their own place in life; must work out the solution of their own problems; must do this by a process of adjustment and readjustment rather than suddenly—with sympathetic help." "One senses an attitude of resignation to things as they are at Arthurdale," he continued. On interviewing the wife of a homesteader, he concluded: "There is a feeling on the part of many homesteaders that perhaps the other fellow is getting more than them; perhaps some pay or perhaps he gets some improvement to his homestead others do not receive." "I am afraid we are too jealous of one another now," claimed the wife of the homesteader.[55]

The community had problems other than jealousy, however. For example, a group of homesteaders being entertained by Mrs. Roosevelt at the White House met with the president and informed him that the tractor plant (another attempt to employ the homesteaders) had closed, resulting in numerous people "being thrown out of work."[56] Later that summer, an attempt was made to bring to town the Blue Bell Globe Manufacturing

Company, which could have employed some of the homesteaders in textile work. Negotiations fell through when company officials feared that the homesteaders might seek to unionize. A company official stated that his company would be entirely agreeable to negotiate so far as collective bargaining was concerned, but "he felt certain that no area of agreement could be reached on the question of a closed shop and check off."[57] Mrs. Roosevelt knew of the proposed plan and, as a strong supporter of worker's rights, believed that an arrangement with Blue Bell would prove too prone to failure owing to the company's reputation for fighting unionization. An attempt to establish a branch of the Quartermaster's Depot at Arthurdale also failed.

The community had other problems, however. Given its impending loss of funding the Arthurdale School continued to come under scrutiny. The National Advisory Committee met in July 1940 and considered several crucial questions. What was the Preston County Board of Education doing to accept responsibility for the complete control of the Arthurdale Schools? To what extent was the county board going to contribute to the financial support of the school? Was the school to be traditional in philosophy and practice or experimental? Could the county board accept control of the private contributions coming into the school? Should the school be considered "a consolidation center or be attended only by children living on the project?" Would the board accept the responsibility for the employment of teachers at Arthurdale previously paid with private and public funds? Was the board going to appoint only teachers approved by the principal?[58]

While the role of the school in this period of transition was not clear, it was even less clear what role in the life of the community was being played by the federal government, the project now under the jurisdiction of the FSA.[59] The National Advisory Committee wanted clarification as to the relationship between the school and the federal project manager. What financial responsibilities did the FSA have when it came to maintaining the school plant, for example, janitorial service, electricity, fuel, repairs, and general maintenance? The committee also voiced concern about how private contributions might be affected if the school chose a traditional over an experimental approach and whether those funds would even be available if the experimental approach were continued.

While the National Advisory Committee pondered these questions, Clapp informed Mrs. Roosevelt that she was still engaged in work involving her Arthurdale experience, "doing some writing on the educational use of resources which Dr. Dewey believes should follow the record of the two community schools just published"—referring to *Community Schools in Action*, which had appeared in 1939. "I am of course," she wrote, "[interested] to know if you approve of the record of the community school at Arthurdale. I tried to present a concrete, actual record, and hope I included nothing that could in any way hurt the homesteaders at Arthurdale." She concluded: "I want you to know, however, that I stand ready as always to be used in any place of work where my services could be useful for our country."[60] Clapp's fortunes seemed to parallel that of the Arthurdale community. On several occasions, she probed the First Lady in her search to find consistent work. For example: "I wonder if I could not perhaps be used in community organization, or community education in the more inclusive sense. If these suggestions are not relevant, I can of course be used in any kind of organization, job or work with people that need to be done, anywhere."[61] Mrs. Roosevelt did attempt to find Clapp consistent work and wrote a memo to Edgar Kaiser, noting: "Miss Elsie Clapp has tried to get in touch with you, as she would like to work for your organization. I have known Miss Clapp for many years, as a teacher and social worker and believe that you would be interested in talking with her."[62] There is no record that Clapp ever worked for Kaiser, but she did meet with his secretary in New York City.

While Clapp was seeking fulfilling employment, many of the homesteaders found economic relief by returning to the coal mines, whose operations had been stimulated by the war economy. Others found work in local munitions plants, and others joined the armed forces. The war-stimulated economy and the war itself drew attention away from the reformist zeal of the New Deal projects that included the subsistence homesteads and often drew unwanted attention. By the end of the war, the federal government clearly wanted to end its association with Arthurdale, and, by 1947, it had completely divested itself of its interest in the project, selling the homes to the homesteaders at a loss. In the process, the Arthurdale community and its school became much like any other rural community in America.

7

The End of a Dream?

Even before the Great Depression, the traditional notion of the yeoman's way of life was in decline, not only in Appalachia but nationwide as well. Yet, as the Appalachian historian Richard Drake points out, many farmers who ended up in the coal mines still often farmed on the side for basic food subsistence. They realized that farming alone could not sustain the family. With the collapse of the market, resulting in Appalachia in a move back to the farm for those who held land, New Deal policies such as the Subsistence Homestead Act sought to build on the perceived traditions and values of rural/agrarian life.[1] Regardless of the rural move, the economic conditions of these farms generally did not improve unless the farmer owned his own land. Although in reality the homesteaders at Arthurdale rented their land, the subsistence opportunity "allowed some of the original homesteaders to escape horrible conditions, to buy land and houses on attractive terms, and to make a better life for themselves and their families."[2] FDR suggested: "'Subsistence' does not connote the thought that any of us have in mind. It is not a question of keeping people from starvation. It is a matter that affects education, social contacts, and a chance to live. It is the thing that we have called 'the more abundant life,' and even if it costs a little more money to see that these communities have American facilities in them, this government is rich enough to provide the additional funds."[3]

The reformers who planned Arthurdale believed in an almost spiritual connection between man and the land he worked, a connection that had been broken by the Industrial Revolution. Man was no longer in control of his labor but worked for another who often determined where he lived, where his children went to school, where they played, and where the family worshipped. Foundational to the resulting spiritual loss was a concomitant loss of community and cultural identity that was only compounded by the economic disaster of the Great Depression. While the economic and political facets of the Arthurdale experiment are important, to think of it only in those terms, as scholars often do, misses a key facet that the community school seemed to understand, at least until the 1940s. While much of the focus on Arthurdale tended to be on tangible factors such as building the homes and structuring the community, the real essence of the project was building the spirit of community, and the school was deemed the best institution to accomplish that.

This chapter attempts to discuss the integral role that the Arthurdale School played in building—or, more precisely, rebuilding—community. There is no question that, like the progressive educators inspired by Dewey, the Depression-era federal planners saw the loss of community as a problem that urgently needed to be addressed. But why settle on a particular educational program as the means to do this? Because these progressive educators envisioned education not as a mere rite of passage but as a social process, a form of community life in which one learns the rights and responsibilities of belonging to a social group.

Clapp believed that, by and large, teachers were becoming more aware of their social responsibilities, working within the community to meet the needs of children. Education should, as Clapp noted in an article published after her departure from Arthurdale, be a "cooperative enterprise, a democratic process." In that article, she quoted Dewey's "My Pedagogic Creed" (1897): "Education being a social process, the school is simply that form of community life in which all those agencies are concentrated that will be most effective in bringing the child to share in the inherited resources of the race, and to use his own powers for social ends." For Clapp, this shared experience could strengthen community, gaining "wider and deeper social significance."[4]

Some social planners, like Rexford Tugwell, believed that the lost sense of community could be restored by cooperative economic—and often educational—enterprise.[5] Clarence Pickett believed such cooperative enterprise vital "to build community spirit and interdependence among the settlers as part of the process of the physical construction."[6] Partly, this meant allowing the homesteaders to build their own homes, which process gave them a wage but also gave them a sense of contribution and ownership. Pickett knew the heartbreak, alienation, and general suffering in the coal camps through his early relief work in Scotts Run and had also served as an assistant to Milburn Wilson. Clapp's plans for the Arthurdale School served "as a manifesto for community education, stressing lifelong learning, the acknowledgement of the fundamental importance of trusting and encouraging peoples' own initiative and resourcefulness; diversity and individual talent; and a curriculum based on the special needs of the community."[7]

To observers of the history of Arthurdale, the school is generally perceived positively. The educational experiment has been referred to as *notable*, and it has been suggested that Clapp's *Community Schools in Action* could serve as a loose blueprint for rural progressive education. Clapp noted that the book was "a tribute to John Dewey, whose philosophy and whose vision of the school as a social institution prompted our efforts to create a community school and to participate in community education." She further acknowledged the assistance of Eleanor Roosevelt, whose "special gifts of sympathy, insight, fairness, and courage in the face of obstacles held us true to the purposes of serviceableness to the people of the community and of helpfulness to other rural schools, for which the Arthurdale School was established."[8] However, one reviewer of her work at Arthurdale described it as more educational than sociological, as failing to address race, labor, unemployment, and the role of technology, as "lack[ing] a clear exposition of educational and social philosophy," and as "fail[ing] to develop a more progressive social education in the high school."[9] This critique is a fair one and similar to those offered by contemporary historians.

Harry Carlson, the shop teacher at the Arthurdale School from 1934 to 1936, attempted to get a grant to study Arthurdale from a more sociological perspective, arguing that Clapp's *Community Schools in Action* did not fully capture "the real picture of Arthurdale, its real implications" or attempt "to formulate, even though incompletely, the forces and adjustments that have made it the outstanding experiment of our day." "A study of Arthurdale, I feel," he wrote, "will reveal valuable materials for any group influential in revising our view of public housing, relief, and industrial relocation."[10] Carlson's request for funding failed to convince Mrs. Roosevelt or Clarence Pickett. But his criticisms and concerns were fair. Why did Clapp not include more social/political and philosophical analysis of her work? She certainly understood philosophy well enough to do so, but she seemed to wish the work to stand for itself, perhaps believing that her audience understood the philosophical underpinnings of her work. Of course, the obvious problem with this assumption is the intellectual diversity within the field of progressive education. The title *Community Schools in Action* implies that the school is closely integrated with the community, that it is of the community, not separated from it as far too many contemporary schools are. Even a critic of Clapp's work claimed: "Urban as well as rural educators may well read this book to gain new insight about the relation of vital education to community resources."[11] Others thought that Clapp's experiment in community education clearly embodied the philosophy of John Dewey. They praised the teachers at Arthurdale, one reviewer describing them as "a staff with a common philosophy of education who lives and works together, a staff which surveyed their communities by living in them and used the results": "This school begins in the home when parents are educated to the concept of the nursery school, the shop, the health program, recreation, traditions and culture, and handicrafts."[12] Eduard Lindeman referred to Clapp's community school as a handbook for project-based learning. He believed that the Arthurdale experimental school was driven by linking the needs of the people and community to the local resources; what was important to the community was important to the school. He wrote: "Merely to read this simple homely account is to share in the excitement of living in a genuinely progressive school."[13]

Clapp believed that Dewey's theory of education should serve as the basis for inquiry and for structuring democratic society. While Dewey's writings took on a more sociopolitical tone in the late 1920s and the 1930s, to suggest that his thoughts on community are not present in them is to miss an integral part of his philosophy. While the idea that the school was able to reform the social order had lost its appeal, the idea that it could nurture a sense of community was not lost. Dewey sought to "deconstruct theories of knowing and morality arising from earlier social arrangements that continue to obstruct the democratic ideal."[14] Owing to rapid social, political, and economic change in the late nineteenth century and the early twentieth, new social arrangements could be and needed to be constructed, and Dewey believed the school to be the best institution to create those arrangements. For Dewey, it was the school that could restore community life, community being grounded in shared experience—aims, beliefs, aspirations, and common understanding. As he noted: "Men live in a community in virtue of the things which they have in common; and communication is the way in which they come to possess things in common."[15] It was community that grounded democracy. "Regarded as an idea," Dewey wrote, "democracy is not [just] an attractive alternative to other principles of associated life. It is the idea of community life itself.... The clear consciousness of a communal life, in all its implications, constitutes the idea of democracy.... Fraternity, liberty, and equality isolated from communal life are hopeless abstractions."[16] Dewey felt, as did Clapp, that his vision of progressive education was in accord with the democratic ideal that ideally produced a better quality of life and human experience. Education, conceptualized by Dewey as growth, is a process by which we can grow morally and intellectually, and it is the role of the educator to create and nurture such an experience.[17]

One crucial characteristic of democratic community was sympathy, which Dewey described as "the bond of union between men": "It is to the social sphere what gravitation is to the physical." Dewey identified sympathy as the identification of our experiences with those of others. This attempt at identification brings sympathy within the social arena as it is a form of interaction. "In sympathy we take the feelings of another for our own," Dewey claimed. "In disgust or indignation, we say that we would not have such feeling for our own." Like community, sympathy implied a "spiritual unity" of sorts. "It constitutes society an organic whole, a whole permeated by a common life, where each individual still lives his own distinct life unabsorbed in that of the community. . . . Or is it possible to conceive such a development of sympathy that each should simply project himself outward, and lose his individual life in the life of the community, becoming more absorbed in it. . . . But, as matter of fact, the nature of sympathy is such that growth in individuality is a necessary accompaniment of growth of universality of feeling."[18] Sympathy formed the foundation for community.

There is little doubt that the philosophy of the Arthurdale School attempted to achieve the lofty goal of building community. The school sought through its curriculum to stem the traditional, individualistic, and competitive nature of contemporary education and build on the identity of the individual rather than fostering individualism. Community could be created only when individuals understood their identity in relation to others or at least lived in sympathy with them. However, such a development depended fundamentally on the nature of trust, and that was difficult, if not impossible, to achieve owing to the political nature and economic insecurity of the Arthurdale community. Fearing the failure of the homestead ideal—an outcome that the Roosevelt administration wished to avoid if it could—federal officials often refused to allow the homesteaders to make decisions for themselves, thus leading to a lack of trust. The climate fostered by those in charge of the project was often at odds with what the children were being taught and experiencing in the school. As director of community affairs and principal of the school, Clapp often found herself caught in the middle of this dilemma, trying to be responsible for preparing democratic citizens and at the same time limiting their freedom and decision-making ability if a proposed activity might bring unwanted attention to the community.[19]

Some have viewed the school as a form of "pervasive imposition," acting on both the parents and the children. C. J. Maloney writes sarcastically: "Education [at Arthurdale] was to be the pottery wheel upon which God's children would be remolded and improved, and the school system would for a short time become to them the most interesting and important component erected in the laboratory of Arthurdale."[20] One incident involved a beer and oyster party planned by some of the homesteader men that Clapp refused to allow. She had little choice in the matter, as regulations did not permit alcohol in Arthurdale. And, as it turned out, the party—which was relocated to a nearby tavern—almost led to a brawl. Imagine the headlines had Clapp allowed the party to occur on the homestead and a fight ensued. Still, Holly Cowan suggests that the members of the men's club could not get along and that it did not help that Clapp held the community reins tightly.[21] Kathryn Carlson, wife of Harry Carlson, commented on her concerns and on this particular event to her father:

> If the community is really to become socially competent its members must have training in managing their own affairs. It must be they who make whatever regulations are necessary. A skillful teacher should be able to guide without himself finally imposing an arbitrary set of rules upon them. They must become increasingly independent. There is a great danger that they are instead becoming increasingly dependent on a single external authority. Too many things must go through the sole authority of Miss Clapp even down to the final okay on which color we shall paint the bus or in what form the men's club ballot shall be set up. . . . Harry and I feel so disappointed in what is being done with the project that we shared this feeling with you when you were here. If an expression of this feeling can be of any help to others interested in the possibilities and opportunities which the project offers we shall be very glad.[22]

While generally supportive, opinions on the character of the Arthurdale School varied greatly. When asked in 1940 about his future, the student body president responded: "I would like to move around and see the world, we don't have any difficult problems in our community because everyone helps each other and one person knows what the rest are doing." A student observer noted: "While visiting the classes I noticed that instead of having group discussions that the boys and girls did a lot of written work." Another student, knowledgeable about the school's philosophy, concluded: "For me this did not seem very democratic because the boys and girls did not get to hear everybody's opinion and draw their own conclusions. Freedom with responsibility is not practiced as much as it should be."[23]

On the whole, however, the Arthurdale students seemed to tell a different story, even after Clapp's departure. One response to a 1941 survey suggests: "[The high school was a] good trainer of citizens. The teachers and the students seem much more understanding toward one another, thus making lessons more interesting and enjoyable. In this school there is no reason for one who will not cooperate with others, just as it is in the work we must do outside of school and the sooner one learns this the better." Another student stated: "Arthurdale high school is a progressive school and therefore the students should be good citizens. They are given every chance to learn to be cooperative, considerate, polite and to think for themselves also, they have a say in what they prefer in studying as well as the arrangement of schedule and rooms. When I graduated I felt as though I were leaving a place as familiar to me as my own room." Another considered the high school an "excellent trainer of citizenship":

> Not only did it give us the experience but it gave us enough freedom to use our own creative ability and initiative. Our teachers were friendly guides, not absolute rulers. They taught us to be proud of our community, to utilize the resources and to strive to make it the best community that we could. Our education was not divorced from life situations but was an integral part of our lives. They taught us to appreciate the beauty of nature, the honest effort of our fellowmen and to respect the work of our own hands and minds and yet realize its weaknesses. It seems to me that every citizen may be with other people under certain rules and regulations but if he is to be a good citizen he must be able to use his initiative and creative ability for the betterment of mankind and as an emotional outlet for himself.

The study concluded that the school program was well adapted to the community even though some graduates commented on the lack of vocational training and a few complained about the lack of traditional academic programs. Students often mentioned the cooperative spirit of the community and at the time they were surveyed were employed and generally showed a "decided inclination toward cooperativeness, adaptability, and independence."[24]

Whether Clapp ever saw the survey results is not known, but they would certainly have pleased her. Critics of Arthurdale often point out that the homesteaders were never allowed fully to govern themselves. There is some truth to this criticism, but to understand the lack of independence it is important to take into account the complex political nature of Arthurdale. Clearly, the school continued to articulate a democratic philosophy five years after Clapp's departure. Paternalism often seems to be a part of government policy, and the subsistence homestead projects were no exception. The federal reformers and educators associated with those projects believed that they understood the best way to create community—through literal and spiritual sharing and cooperation that would result in a sense of identity and belonging. Federal bureaucracy led to confusion as to who was in charge, however, and Mrs. Roosevelt's attempts to reduce red tape may have inadvertently created a dependency on her rather than building the self-reliance and responsibility that went along with being a homesteader and building community. Clarence Pickett expressed his disgust with the endless rules set up by the government: "There were interminable delays and never ending competition between local politicians, most of their efforts exerted for the genuine welfare of their communities, but sometimes for the sake of patronage and votes."[25] Still heralded to this day in Arthurdale, Eleanor Roosevelt has been seen as politically naive by critics who ignored the chain of command, resulting in Arthurdale becoming what Maloney characterized as a "public fiasco." Maloney's final judgment on the project was that "Eleanor Roosevelt's lack of concern about costs[,] . . . combined with FDR's willingness to grant her great leeway with taxpayer money, . . . allowed and encouraged a devil-may-care attitude toward what the cost of it all would be—waste and inefficiency pervaded the building of the town."[26]

It was often Mrs. Roosevelt who felt the brunt of attacks on Arthurdale that were in fact directed at FDR's policies and the Democratic Party. While her biographers have often been critical of her involvement in the Arthurdale project, it is impossible to deny that she held a deep, sincere compassion for the homesteaders and wished for them to have the chance to live like other Americans. She was aware that it was an experiment and hoped that it could serve as a model of community planning. "Every new movement must have a laboratory and experimental spot where things are tried and often found wanting," she explained. "Many people will think of this time and the extra money spent as wasted but I do not think that it will prove to be so in the long run."[27] As Paul Conkin notes: "[The First Lady] wanted Arthurdale to be an exhibit of a new way of life, visited by 50,000 to 100,000 people each year."[28] Through these visits, the ideas and ideals of building community could be spread. Stephen Haid writes: "[Mrs. Roosevelt] was Arthurdale's promoter, financier, and guiding spirit. Without her it would not have been possible."[29]

The continuing problem of unemployment kept the Arthurdale community from attaining economic stability, and without that stability the progressive school could not function after Clapp's departure as it had from 1934 to 1936. While the homesteaders met their end of the bargain when it came to subsistence farming, "adequate cash income was the first and most important key to the success of a homestead project."[30] Thus, the failure to attract enough industry to Arthurdale to provide the homesteaders with opportunities for reliable wage labor led to the downfall of the project. Only with the onset of World War II did the men of the community find consistent work, many returning to the rejuvenated mines, others joining the armed forces. Especially disturbing was the case of the excellent craftsmen of the Mountaineer Craftsmen's Cooperative. Clarence Picket noted that the fact that men "who found great joy in producing beautiful handmade furniture [would] abandon it for routine jobs that pay better causes one to ask pertinent questions about our civilization."[31]

The idealism that led to the idea of Arthurdale was clearly fading by the beginning of World War II. Rexford Tugwell and other federal reformers believed that the poor and homeless could be resettled on land they could improve and moved from land where the soil had been depleted. However, as Amity Shlaes notes: "In [Tugwell's] view the Roosevelts were being too romantic when they imagined successful little communities in the countryside. Where would the people work? Industry was more the future." Tugwell believed that building homes alone was not enough and that people needed to be "taught how to live" and work in the world. Like many progressive reformers, he worked to remake America, perhaps with a bit of nostalgia for a foregone golden age that most likely never existed.[32]

By the early years of World War II, Arthurdale was perceived by many as a "great blunder."[33] By 1942, the federal government was anxious to rid itself of the homesteads. Subsistence farming did not provide the economic relief measure earlier envisioned. As Lord and Johnstone write: "No quantity of vegetables, fruits, milk, eggs, and meat produced at home on a very small tract will pay rent, buy clothing, or supply any of the desires that have become entrenched in the mass of people for the industrial product of our highly developed modern technology."[34] In 1943, the Cooley Committee, headed by the North Carolina congressman Harold Cooley, attacked the Farm Security Administration (FSA), seeking among other things the elimination of the homesteads. At the time there were 165 homesteaders at Arthurdale, and, under pressure to distance itself from such projects, the government finally sold the homes to the homesteaders (who had previously been renting) for prices ranging from $750 to $1,249 even though many had been appraised at around $6,000.[35] (The total cost of the Arthurdale project alone is virtually impossible to determine, but FSA estimates put it at roughly $2.8 million.)[36] Furthermore, the FSA was soon barred from "using any appropriated funds for resettlement projects" unless they were devoted to speeding up the liquidation of the subsistence farms. By 1947, all the original Arthurdale homesteads had been sold, and the school facilities had been broken up between a shirt manufacturer and the Preston County School Board.[37]

At the onset of the Arthurdale experiment in 1933, the federal planners encouraged the movement from town to country to alleviate the growing relief problems in the cities. While the back-to-the-land movement offered hope to a few, most people just wanted "the security of employment and the adequacy of income which a properly functioning economy could offer them."[38] Even homesteaders did not abandon materialism entirely, desiring the things that others had, but the fulfillment of their dreams required the availability of wage labor. And it is generally accepted that it was World War II, not economic planning, that jump-started the American economy. Perhaps by its very nature economic planning entails a degree of paternalism—the attitude that we know what people need and will supply it for them. Whatever the cause, it was the perception of economic planning as socialist that left the Democrats, and the New Deal homestead subsistence projects in particular, vulnerable.

While the Arthurdale project has tended to be viewed as a blunder, a waste of money, even immoral, it did succeed in creating some sense of community, and, as Rexford Tugwell and others have suggested, through its curriculum and involvement with the community the school buoyed the morale of the homesteaders and instilled in them a sense of solidarity, as it sought to do. With its progressive orientation, the Arthurdale approach to learning was unique. It was not dictated by the rules or mandates of an accrediting body but developed with the culture and experiences of the children in mind. Stephen Haid believes that the community spirit was the "most impressive aspect of the Arthurdale experiment" and that the homesteaders worked together (despite the occasional conflict) because they knew that they were part of something special and wanted to make it a success. One must also consider the homesteaders' intense loyalty to and admiration for Mrs. Roosevelt and the resultant desire not to hurt or embarrass her.[39] She was their champion, and they knew it.

It can be suggested that, having agreed to the philosophy of the Arthurdale School, the homesteaders should have known what they were getting themselves into. But, given their background, they could never have envisioned how education could be so different from what they had experienced. During the progressive years, perhaps up until World War II, the children at Arthurdale explored their heritage, their culture, and their identity. They learned from experience, not just texts, and they were very fortunate to have a highly educated, caring, and creative teaching staff who believed in the philosophy of progressive education. The Arthurdale School saw its greatest success with its younger students, as did experiments in progressive education across the country. This is because the nature of secondary education in the United States has traditionally been dictated by the needs of the higher education system, leading to a more structured curriculum, more traditional forms of assessment, and the training of teachers in specific disciplines. The Arthurdale School was no exception and, by the late 1930s, had adopted a more traditional curriculum notwithstanding the progressive discourse in which it continued to envelop itself.

Following his only visit to Arthurdale—in April 1936—John Dewey claimed the school to be among the best public schools in the country. He did not elaborate as to why.[40] He was certainly aware of the politically charged atmosphere of Arthurdale, as he served along with Mrs. Roosevelt on the Arthurdale School National Advisory Committee. He was sympathetic to the goals of the progressive reformers and their concerns about growing materialism and individualism in American society. Although he did feel that the politics of the New Deal failed to adequately address the most pressing problems of American capitalism, he appreciated Clapp's work at the Arthurdale School. He wrote: "Democracy will be a farce unless individuals are trained to think for themselves, to judge independently, to be critical, to be able to detect subtle propaganda and the motives which inspire it. Mass production and uniform regimentation have been growing in the degree in which individual opportunity has waned. The current must be reversed. The motto must be: 'Learn to *act* with and for others while you learn to *think* and judge for yourself.'"[41] Dewey is describing here the very essence of community, the key concept undergirding the Arthurdale community and its school. He believed that the Arthurdale School met this social function, and "has done it by creating a school to which Lincoln's words about democratic government apply: a school not only for, but of and by the community; the teachers being leaders in the movement, since they are themselves so identified with the community." "From the viewpoint of genuine community education," he continued, "country districts provide the greatest opportunity as well as exhibit the most crying need—the most vocal even if not in fact the deepest." Dewey envisioned the example of the Arthurdale School as an excellent demonstration where the school was central to the community and which grasped the "place of education in building a democratic life."[42]

The historian James Kloppenberg concludes: "The New Deal was designed to mitigate the effects of an unregulated economy that seemed stuck in a downward spiral, but its shape was so clearly determined by what was politically feasible that many commentators hence doubted there was any coherence at all to Roosevelt's policies."[43] This lack of coherence led to confusion and often bungled planning—and low morale owing to economic insecurity—at the Arthurdale homestead. Nevertheless, the project of creating a community school largely succeeded. Still, Mrs. Roosevelt, Clapp, and other progressive planners believed that the notion of community needed firmer grounding than just a school, and FDR agreed, outlining some of his ideas in his 1944 State of the Union address.

In this message to Congress and the nation, the president reiterated many of the themes of the early 1930s campaign that led to the establishment of the homestead projects. He chastised those who he believed had financially benefited during the war and compared their greed to the excesses of the "wild twenties when this Nation went for a joy ride on a roller coaster which ended in a tragic crash." Recalling the Depression era and perhaps even the homestead experiments, he called for economic security, social security, and moral security. The nation should commit itself to the common good as it had committed itself to the national by good protecting democracy and ending fascism. The president emphasized that the freedom America had been fighting for could not exist without economic security and independence. In what some historians have termed the New Bill of Rights, Roosevelt called for the right of every American to a useful job and a just wage, the right to a decent standard of living. He feared that selfish interest could undermine the lessons learned from the Depression and World War II and felt that the nation needed to be more concerned about the common good than about flagrant individualism and materialism.[44]

FDR failed to accomplish his larger political goals, but within the community of Arthurdale a sense of identity, purpose, and hope had been engendered. Arthurdale, like most communities, was not without problems and was certainly never a utopia. But what its school did during its progressive heyday was to bring people together in a common purpose with common goals.

Michael Johanek and John Puckett write: "The Depression era called forth powerful social forces that galvanized a small but hardy band of progressive educators to keep the reformist vision of community-centered schooling alive in the 1930s and early 1940s. Working in disparate locales and circumstances, their projects often unbeknownst to one another, these reformers [including those at Arthurdale] built community schools and educational programs designed to improve the quality of local community life."[45] Although the nature of these schools varied, they tended to have several traits in common. They tied curriculum to local issues and experiences, believing that all life, and not just formal schooling, was educative. They emphasized active participation over passive acceptance and were attentive to the needs of both adults and children. And they concentrated on the general improvement of community life overall. This latter often included cooperation with community health, recreational, cultural, civic, and religious agencies, with the view of having pupils utilize the services of these agencies to carry out and extend activities initiated in classrooms and extracurricular pupil affairs.[46] These extracurricular affairs could include public safety, civic beauty, community health, agricultural and industrial improvement, civic arts, and local history.[47]

A successful school was perceived as one that was integrated with the community, not detached from it, and in which achievement was much more than the acquisition of book knowledge, emphasizing "flexibility to provide for a wide-range of unpredictable needs and interests."[48] Success depended on the teachers, and, according to the community school advocate and founder of the Highlander Folk School Myles Horton, teachers needed to be more than subject matter specialists and also "have an understanding of individual personalities and their relationships to the community and to society as a whole": "Learning must not be meager, but supplemental practical experience. Teachers must live in the community and take active part in community life. They should seek to coordinate the most advanced thinking and become identified with progressive influences."[49]

There was a strong social justice component in the community schools of the 1930s, although this component was implemented in different ways. There was a sense that the traditions and customs of the past had failed and that that failure had led to poverty, unemployment, and alienation. For many progressive reformers, including the subsistence homestead planners at Arthurdale, the community school was the answer, the one institution that could improve the lives of many and provide services to the community with "educational, civic, social, and social welfare activities—the school as the center of neighborhood life." The Arthurdale School sought to attain this goal. However, because it was being developed in the first federal subsistence homestead community and in a highly charged political atmosphere, its uniqueness led to less engagement with the community and less attention paid to civic preparation. For example, it was not as successful as the Benjamin Franklin High School, a community school in New York City, in preparing citizens for participatory democracy.[50]

The conception of Arthurdale as a community declined in the late 1930s, and this affected the school. This change seemed to parallel the gradual change in the national conception of the community school and progressive education in general. The community school discourse in the 1940s rings similar to that of the 1930s, but seemed more about what the community school should do than about the necessity of being a community school. Johanek and Puckett point out that at this time the community school idea was being affected by the life adjustment movement, which "emphasized adolescents' personal growth needs, as opposed to intellectual development."[51] William Wraga argues that most educational historians and critics of progressive education have accorded the life adjustment movement a disproportionate significance.[52] Regardless, the post-Depression community school certainly seemed to have lost its concern for social justice and the creation of a thoughtful and engaged democratic citizen. There was still discussion about meeting the needs and interests of the people, building curriculum around community problems, enhancing group living, and encouraging cooperation among children and adults. The noted community school educator Lloyd Cook wrote in 1941: "Any school is a community school to the extent that it seeks to realize some such objectives as the following: a. educates youth by and for participating in the full range of basic life activities such as human needs, areas of living, persistent problems; b. seeks increasingly to democratize life in school and outside; c. uses community resources in all aspects of its program, and d. actively cooperates with other social agencies and groups in improving community life functions as a service center for youth and adult groups."[53] Summarizing the community school literature in the 1940s, Milosh Muntyan noted two primary goals: "to bring various activities of community life into the school, making these activities the heart of the school program and to take the school out into the community, centering the school program around their activities, as they operate in the community situation."[54] By the end of the 1940s, the community school paid more attention to programmatic change than to social and political change.

By the early 1950s, Edward Olsen, who was employed by the Washington State Department of Education, could write: "The community school idea has come to involve the most promising ideas and practices in education. The needs-centered curriculum, cooperative planning, interpersonal relations, group processes, problem solving, world-citizenship—are all part of the community school concept now. One early emphasis which seems to have gone is the matter of improving the social order."[55] Olsen commented on the passing of the emphasis on improving the social order in the context of the early Cold War years, which were a time of renewed prosperity for many Americans. Apparently, for many community school educators, the social order seemed to have stabilized, and, although the language or rhetoric of democracy was still present in community school discourse, it lacked the substance it had the 1930s. Democracy in the 1950s often meant cooperation in the form of patriotism, that we must all stand together against a common enemy, communism, activities associated with democratic cooperation often taking the form of civil defense preparation. But it was not true democracy. "The community-school program," noted the community educator Maurice Seay, "in a very real sense represents the essence of democracy. It is in part a return to an older practice wherein the adults of the community worked together to improve their school . . . for the 'added benefits to the community.'"[56]

There was an attempt to engage the community in creating and eventually evaluating the programs of the community school. By the 1950s, community school programs were conceptualized as "classroom studies; school-life as student activities; school coordinated work-experience; such resources as school camps, libraries, and recreation centers; assembly-type programs featuring speakers, concerts, plays and discussion; and guidance or counseling services."[57] While there was growing interest in community schools in the 1950s, there also seemed to be growing confusion as to what actually characterized a community school. While Olsen had noted a change of focus, Paul Hanna and Robert Naslund reiterated many of the concerns addressed by community school educators in the 1930s. Their definition is as follows: "A community school is a school which has concerns beyond the training of literate 'right minded' and economically efficient citizens who reflect the values and processes of a particular social, economic, or political setting. In addition to these basic educational tasks, it is directly concerned with improving all aspects of living in the community in all the broad meaning of that concept in the local, state, regional, national or international community." Hanna and Naslund cited Clapp's *Community Schools in Action*, calling it an "interesting account of the process of organization of a community school in a rural setting . . . a significant milestone in the development of the community-school concept in that it details possible steps whereby such educational endeavors can be carried on and the interest and cooperation of citizens secured." They also noted the important contribution of Dewey's *Democracy and Education* as the key to "the establishment and organization of the community school."[58] By the end of the 1950s, the journal *Progressive Education* and the Progressive Education Association had ceased to exist.

Regardless of the disagreements among them, community school educators believed that it was the school that could reach "into the greatest number of homes and in which every family can feel ownership and freedom in participation" and that "for this reason it is a peculiarly advantageous position to play a leading role in community welfare programs."[59] It is clear that the 1950s were characterized by a great deal of interest in the community school, although that interest was more pragmatic and less social activist. Johanek and Puckett refer to this change in the community school tradition as a move from being "citizen centered" to being "service centered." They also note that, beginning in the mid-1940s and continuing into the 1950s, "community education was swept up in an attack mounted by influential critics who charged that life adjustment education, by now the dominant version of progressive education, was diverting schools from teaching the liberal arts curriculum and depriving the nation of scientists, mathematicians, engineers, and linguists it needed to win the Cold War."[60]

The most influential critics included Hyman Rickover, Arthur Bestor, and Robert Hutchins.[61]

Dewey's *School and Society* is often cited as the source of his concept of the community school. In it he claims: "A society is a number of people held together because they are working along common lines, in a common spirit, and with references to common aims. The common needs and aims demand a growing interchange of thoughtful and growing unity of sympathetic feeling."[62] A "growing unity of sympathetic feeling" does not develop overnight and must be nurtured and embodied in both caring and trust. This "unity of sympathetic feeling" is more difficult to attain in a culture defined by "growing cynicism, distrust of institutions, and political disengagement that threatens not only the classroom but also democratic society."[63]

Since its onset, the community school concept has come to mean many things, those different things often reflecting the times and places in which different community schools originated. The Depression era, accompanied as it was by social, economic, and political upheaval, led to the unique experiment of the Arthurdale community and its community school. The Arthurdale School was concerned with what William H. Kilpatrick during the Depression referred to as an "antisocial and selfish individualism." He continued: "In an economy of interdependence, the common welfare comes first as the necessary, prerequisite means to the welfare of the individual. Democracy, then, in order to be itself, must henceforth stress cooperative efforts for the prerequisite common good."[64] Similar concerns can be found expressed from the Depression era to the present day. The most fundamental mission of the community school is to prepare citizens to take part in a participatory democratic society, a citizen-centered rather than a service-centered conception. It is the service-centered model that seems to have dominated the community school movement after the 1930s.[65] Yet, in reality, the true community school must integrate both citizen-centered and service-centered components since to be a good citizen is to serve the common good, embracing both individual responsibility and social responsibility. Community schools must nurture intellectual inquiry as part of their preparation. While in designing a curriculum attention should be paid to the local culture, it should always be kept in mind that the ethical core of democracy is social justice.

Paul Conkin writes: "In the fall of 1933 Arthurdale was a great dream, which somehow never became a complete reality. The dream involved a transition from hell to heaven for a group of stranded miners. From the huts clinging to a hillside above Scotts Run, from their lack of sanitary facilities, from the midst of malnutrition, disease, alcoholism, crime, delinquency, and high mortality, a fortunate few to escape from poverty. White homes situated on small plots of farm land, surrounded by lawns, flowers, orchards and fields. They were to enjoy regular meals, not through the bitter bread of charity but through the food produced by their own hands. They were to have cows, poultry, root cellars, preserve closets and plenty of air and sunshine."[66] Yet there was more to this dream for the homesteaders than owning a home. There was a better education and thus a better life for their children. It was through the community spirit engendered by the Arthurdale School that these children realized their hopes and dreams for generations to come.

Perhaps Joseph Hart, a community school advocate and student of the Danish Folk High School, said it best, offering a lesson for today: "The democratic problem in education is not primarily a problem of training children; it is the problem of making a community with which children cannot help growing up to be democratic, intelligent, disciplined to freedom, reverent of the goods of life, and eager to share in the tasks of the age." For Hart, as for Mrs. Roosevelt, Clapp, and Dewey, a school cannot produce this result; nothing but a community can do so. Consequently: "We can never be satisfied that we have met the educational problem of our day when we have good schools. We must have good communities."[67]

Acknowledgments

This study began on exposure to Lawrence Cremin's history of progressive education, *The Transformation of the School,* as a graduate student at the University of South Carolina under the tutelage of Alan Wieder. Though that was some time ago, I have not forgotten the compassion and caring of Alan's approach to scholarship, which I hope my work also embodies. I also acknowledge and thank Craig Kridel, who nurtured my interest in biography and helped me channel that passion into educational biography. Most of all I owe a great debt to Tim Bergen, who took me on as a graduate assistant, who mentored me, handled my southern accent with tact (he was from Brooklyn), and taught me as best as he could how to be a member of the academy. I have had the opportunity to work with some of the outstanding scholars in the history of progressive education, including Susan Semel, Alan Sadovnik, and Daniel Perlstein. I have learned much from their insight and collaboration. Barbara and Sheldon Rahn, Elsie Clapp's niece and her husband, shared with me Elsie's memoirs years ago, before they were available to scholars. Without their trust and support, an understanding of Clapp and her work would not be possible. They showed kindness and hospitality to a stranger who did his best to share and assess Elsie's contributions to progressive education. I also owe a debt of gratitude to Barbara Howe, a professor of history at West Virginia University (WVU), who introduced me to the Arthurdale story and community on my arrival at WVU.

Over the years I have received generous support from the West Virginia Humanities Council, the most recent grant allowing me to travel to the Franklin Delano Roosevelt Library in Hyde Park, New York, to study the Anna Eleanor Roosevelt Papers. A work of this sort is not possible without the assistance and support of archivists and librarians. I received excellent assistance at the Roosevelt Library; the National Archives, College Park, Maryland; Special Collections–Morris Library, Southern Illinois University; the Center of Dewey Studies, Southern Illinois University; the West Virginia Regional History Collection, West Virginia University; Arthurdale Heritage

Inc.; and the interlibrary loan department at West Virginia University, which located every obscure text I needed to complete the work.

Over the years I have received intellectual support from friends and colleagues, including Clint Allison, David Snelgrove, Karen McKellips, Charles Fazarro, and Dalton Curtis. Doug Simpson has served as a mentor and a collaborator and shared his knowledge and insight into the application of John Dewey's pedagogy, guided by a democratic purpose and undergirded by community. I thank several anonymous reviewers solicited by the University Press of Kentucky to evaluate the manuscript who made the work better. Any errors and weaknesses are my own. In seeking a publisher, I wanted one intimately familiar with Appalachian history and culture, and I could do no better than the University Press of Kentucky. Ashley Runyon, my editor, has been supportive of the project and showed great patience in answering my questions as I prepared the manuscript.

Finally, I wish to thank Cathy Falvey and Barbara Rocovich from the College of Education and Human Services, West Virginia University, who helped format the document, and also Kathy Fletcher from Academic Computing/Advanced Support, who provided me with templates for maneuvering through Microsoft Word.

Much of chapter 3 was previously published in Sam Stack, "Elsie Ripley Clapp and the Arthurdale Schools," in *Founding Mothers and Others: Women Educational Leaders during the Progressive Era,* ed. Alan R. Sadovnik and Susan F. Semel (New York: Palgrave, 2002), 93–110.

Notes

The following abbreviations are used throughout the notes:

AERP	Anna Eleanor Roosevelt Papers, FDRL
ERCM	Elsie Ripley Clapp Memoirs, Morris Library, Southern Illinois University, Carbondale
ERCP	Elsie Ripley Clapp Papers, Morris Library, Southern Illinois University, Carbondale (items in the Clapp Papers are designated by, respectively, collection, series, and item numbers, e.g., "21/1/1")
EW	John Dewey, *The Early Works, 1882–1898*, ed. Jo Ann Boydston, 5 vols. (Carbondale: Southern Illinois University Press, 1969–1991)
FDRL	Franklin Delano Roosevelt Library, Hyde Park, NY
FDRP	Franklin Delano Roosevelt Papers, FDRL
LW	John Dewey, *The Later Works, 1925–1953*, ed. Jo Ann Boydston, 17 vols. (Carbondale: Southern Illinois University Press, 1969–1991)
MW	John Dewey, *The Middle Works, 1899–1924*, ed. Jo Ann Boydston, 15 vols. (Carbondale: Southern Illinois University Press, 1969–1991)
NARG	National Archives Record Group, National Archives and Records Administration, Washington, DC
WVRC	West Virginia Regional Collection, West Virginia University, Morgantown

Introduction

1. Matthew C. Flamm, "The Demanding Community: Politicization of the Individual after Dewey," *Education and Culture* 22, no. 1 (2006): 35–54, 48. The establishment of community in Dewey's terms is described by Flamm as a "successful working out of the appropriate democratic relation between individuals and groups." Ibid., 47.

2. David Tyack, Robert Lowe, and Elisabeth Hansot, *Public Schools in Hard Times: The Great Depression and Recent Years* (Cambridge, MA: Harvard University Press, 1984), 3.

3. Arthur Zilversmit, *Changing Schools: Progressive Education Theory and Practice, 1930–1960* (Chicago: University of Chicago Press, 1993), xii.

4. Michael Johanek and John L. Puckett, *Leonard Covello and the Making of Benjamin Franklin High School: Education as If Citizenship Mattered* (Philadelphia: Temple University Press, 2007), 10. Johanek and Puckett chronicle the history of another community school, the Benjamin Franklin High School for boys in East Harlem, New York, which opened ten years after construction began on Arthurdale.

5. Douglas J. Simpson and Sam F. Stack Jr., eds., *Teachers, Leaders, and Schools: Essays by John Dewey* (Carbondale: Southern Illinois University Press, 2010), 2.

6. The year 1859 saw the publication of Charles Darwin's *The Origin of Species*, John Stuart Mill's *Essay on Liberty*, and the death of Horace Mann as well as the birth of John Dewey. It was also the year of the attack on the federal arsenal in Harper's Ferry, Virginia, by the abolitionist John Brown that set the American Civil War in motion.

7. Robert Church, *Education in the United States: An Interpretative History* (New York: Free Press, 1976), 253. See also Wayne Urban and Jennings Wagoner, *American Education: A History* (New York: Routledge, 2009), 186.

8. Lawrence Cremin, *The Transformation of the School: Progressivism in American Education, 1876-1957* (New York: Vintage, 1964), 88; John Dewey, *School and Society* (Chicago: University of Chicago Press, 1899), 23-24.

9. Darnell Rucker, *The Chicago Pragmatists* (Minneapolis: University of Minnesota Press, 1969), 92.

10. George Herbert Mead, *Mind, Self and Society* (Chicago: University of Chicago Press, 1934), 423.

11. Feodor Cruz, *John Dewey's Theory of Community* (New York: Peter Lang, 1987), 117; James Campbell, *Understanding John Dewey* (Chicago: Open Court, 1995), 175 (quote). See also James Campbell, ed., *Dewey's Conception of Community* (Bloomington: Indiana University Press, 1998).

12. *LW*, 2:332; Campbell, *Understanding John Dewey*, 172. Dewey used examples of child art in *The School and Society*. See *MW*, 1:27, 28.

13. Campbell, *Understanding John Dewey*, 266.

14. Susan F. Semel and Alan R. Sadovnik, "The Contemporary Small-School Movement: Lessons from the History of Progressive Education," *Teachers College Record* 110, no. 9 (September 2008): 1744–71, 1765, 1755–56.

15. Kathleen Weiler, "What Can We Learn from Progressive Education?" *Radical Teacher* 69 (January 2004): 4–9, 9. Weiler is discussing John Dewey and Evelyn Dewey, *Schools of Tomorrow* (New York: Dutton, 1959), which is critical of Dewey's "contradictory discourses on individualism and collectivism." Ibid., 7. For progressive education's neglect of race, see also Daniel Perlstein, "Minds Stayed on Freedom: Politics and Pedagogy in the African American Freedom Struggle," *American Educational Research Journal* 39, no. 2 (2002): 249–77, and "Community and Democracy in American Schools: Arthurdale and the Fate of Progressive Education," *Teachers College Record* 97, no. 4 (1996): 625–50.

1. Progressive Education and the Depression

1. Reuben Palm, "The Origins of Progressive Education," *Elementary School Journal* 40, no. 6 (February 1940): 442–49, 443 (first quote), 446 (on British periodicals), 447 (last two quotes). John and Evelyn Dewey's *Schools of Tomorrow* was the first book to chronicle the characteristics of progressive schools, which could vary widely. See also "Progressive Education," *Nature* 59 (January 1899): 235–38; "Progressive Education," *School World* 4 (April 1902): 140–41; and Samuel Parker, *A Textbook in the History of Modern Elementary Education* (Boston: Ginn, 1912), 471.

2. Cremin, *The Transformation of the School*, viii. Attention to the health, recreational, and vocational needs of students is a recurring theme throughout community school education and still present today.

3. Church, *Education in the United States*, 269. Robert Crunden argues that Dewey substitutes the school for the church. See Robert Crunden, *Ministers of Reform: The Progressives' Achievement in American Civilization, 1889–1920* (New York: Basic, 1982), 57–58.

4. William Reese, "The Origins of Progressive Education," *History of Education Quarterly* 41, no. 1 (Spring 2001): 1–24, 2.

5. Harold Alberty, "The Progressive Education Movement," *Educational Research Bulletin* 8, no. 8 (April 1929): 163–69, 164; Philip Olgin, "Let's Re-examine Progressive Education," *Phi Delta Kappan* 38, no. 8 (May 1957): 309–13, 309. Harold Alberty was a professor of education at the Ohio State University with an interest in teacher education, curriculum, school administration, and democratic pedagogy. He was also later associated with the Eight-Year Study. (The Eight-Year Study, sponsored by the Progressive Education Association, examined whether students in progressive education schools could succeed in college. See Cremin, *The Transformation of the School*, 251.) For a comparison of traditional and progressive schools by Helen Heyl, see also Tyack, Lowe, and Hansot, *Public Schools in Hard Times*, 151.

6. Cremin, *The Transformation of the School*, viii–xi.

7. W. H. Kilpatrick, *Education for a Changing Civilization* (New York: Macmillan, 1926), 75, 113. See also W. H. Kilpatrick, *A Reconstructed Theory of the Educative Process* (New York: Teachers College Press, 1931), 19, and "The Project Method: The Use of the Purposeful Act in the Educative Process," *Teachers College Record* 19 (September 1918): 318–35, 323. Kilpatrick's project method is thoroughly discussed in John Beineke, *And There Were Giants in the Land* (New York: Peter Lang, 1998), 99–116. It is further addressed in Herbert Kliebard, *The Struggle for the American Curriculum, 1893–1958* (Boston: Routledge & Kegan Paul, 1986), 161–65. See also David Tanner and Laurel Tanner, *History of the School Curriculum* (New York: Macmillan, 1990), 157.

8. Patricia Graham, *Progressive Education: From Arcady to Academe (1919–1955)* (New York: Teachers College Press, 1967), 29–30.

9. Ibid., 12–13.

10. Zilversmit, *Changing Schools*, 18.

11. Margaret Naumburg, "The Crux of Progressive Education," *New Republic* 63, no. 812 (June 1930): 145–46, 145. See Kilpatrick, "The Project Method." For further information on Naumburg, see Blythe Hinitz, "Margaret Naumburg and the Walden School," in *Founding Mothers and Others: Women Educational Leaders during the Progressive Era*, ed. Alan R. Sadovnik and Susan F. Semel (New York: Palgrave, 2002), 37–60.

12. This view is most clearly expressed in John Dewey, *Experience and Education* (New York: Macmillan, 1938).

13. George Counts, *Dare the School Build a New Social Order?* (1932; Carbondale: Southern Illinois University Press, 1978). See also P. S. Hlebowitsh and William Wraga, "Social Class Analysis in the Early Progressive Tradition," *Curriculum Inquiry* 25, no. 7 (Spring 1995): 7–21.

14. C. A. Bowers, *The Progressive Educator and the Depression* (New York: Random House, 1969), 75.

15. David B. Tyack, *The One Best System: A History of American Urban Education* (Cambridge, MA: Harvard University, 1974), 127, 29. See also Ronald Cohen and Raymond A. Mohl, *The Paradox of Progressive Education: The Gary Plan and Urban Schooling* (Port Washington, NY: Kennikat, 1979), 8; and Lynn Olson, "Tugging at Tradition," *Education Week* 18 (1999): 25, and "Dewey: The Progressive Era's Misunderstood Giant," *Education Week* 18 (1999): 29. David Labaree argues that both schools of education and child-centered progressives "were losers in their respective arenas: child-centered progressivism lost out in the struggle for control of American schools, and the education school lost out in the struggle for respect in American higher education." He suggests the administrative progressives won the struggle. See David Labaree, "Progressivism, Schools and Schools of Education: An American Romance," *Paedagogica Historica* 41, nos. 1–2 (February 2005): 275–88, 275.

16. For information on Caroline Pratt, see Susan F. Semel, "The City and Country School: A Progressive Paradigm," in *"Schools of Tomorrow," Schools of Today: What Happened to Progressive Education*, ed. Susan F. Semel and Alan R. Sadovnik (New York: Peter Lang, 1999), 121–40; and Mary Hauser, "Caroline Pratt and the City and Country School," in Sadovnik and Semel, eds., *Founding Mothers and Others*, 61–76.

17. Lawrence Cremin, *Popular Education and Its Discontents* (New York: Harper & Row, 1989), 118. See also the excerpt from Dewey's *School and Society* in James Fraser, *The School in the United States* (New York: Routledge, 2010), 238. Clapp knew personally the fragility of the capitalist system, her upper-middle-class family having lost their fortune in the depression of 1893. See Sam F. Stack Jr., *Elsie Ripley Clapp (1879–1965): Her Life and the Community School* (New York: Peter Lang, 2004), 91.

18. Ferdinand Tönnies, *Community and Society* (New York: Harper & Row, 1957), 33, 263; Cremin, *The Transformation of the School*, 88; and Church, *Education in the United States*, 269. *Gemeinschaft* is often translated as *community*, where individuals interact for a larger interest than their own, what some might term the *common good*.

This is grounded in a common value system, including appropriate behavior and individual responsibility. There is a collective sense of loyalty to the social group. In contrast, *Gesellschaft* is often translated *society* and is guided more by individual self-interest that commonality. It is associated with the formation of industrial relations. In *Gesellschaft*, relations are secondary rather than primary, and societies guided by it are much more susceptible to class conflict. These concepts also compare with Emile Durkheim's mechanical and organic solidarity. See Emile Durkheim, *The Division of Labor in Society* (New York: Free Press, 1997), 60–61, 85, 96, 297.

19. Alan Ryan, *John Dewey and the High Tide of American Liberalism* (New York: Norton, 1995), 148.

20. *MW*, 13:334.

21. Graham, *Progressive Education*, 145.

22. Zilversmit, *Changing Schools*, 16.

23. Burton Fowler, "President's Message," *Progressive Education* 7, no. 4 (May 1930): 159.

24. *Progressive Education* 7, no. 1 (February 1930): 2.

25. William Heard Kilpatrick, "A Theory of Progressive Education to Fit the Times," *Progressive Education* 8, no. 4 (April 1931): 287–93, 288, 291, 293.

26. Bowers, *The Progressive Educator and the Depression*, 5, 9.

27. Alex Baskin, "Education and the Great Depression: An Inquiry into the Social Ideas and Activities of Radical American Educators during the Economic Crisis of the 1930's" (Ph.D. diss., Wayne State University, 1966), 402.

28. Laura Zirbes, "The Status of Progressive Schools," *Progressive Education* 8, no. 3 (May 1931): 359–66, 359, 356. Zirbes began her educational career as an elementary school teacher, eventually earning a doctoral degree from Columbia University. She spent most of her academic career at Ohio State University, where she founded the university lab school.

29. Boyd H. Bode, "Education at the Crossroads: What Principles Should Determine the Curriculum?" *Progressive Education* 8, no. 7 (November 1931): 543–49, 546, 549. At the time he wrote "Education at the Crossroads," Bode was a faculty member at the Ohio State University, which, Cremin argues, was the intellectual rival of Teachers College, Columbia University, in the realm of philosophy of education. Bode noted the influence of John Dewey, *Democracy and Education* (New York: Macmillan, 1916). For a discussion of Bode's position, see William Heard Kilpatrick, "Bode's Philosophic Position," *Teachers College Record* 49, no. 4 (January 1948): 268–76, 271. See also Cremin, *The Transformation of the School*, 221–24.

30. Stanwood Cobb, "Progressive Education Today," *Progressive Education* 9, no. 4 (April 1932): 224–26, 226. Cobb is quoting John Dewey, "Excerpt from Philosophy and Civilization," *Progressive Education* 9, no. 4 (April 1932): 256. Cobb was later critical of the PEA, charging that it had been taken over by the Dewey supporters from Teachers College, Columbia University. See Baskin, "Education and the Great Depression," 402.

31. George S. Counts, "Dare Progressive Education Be Progressive?" *Progressive Education* 9, no. 4 (April 1932): 257–63, 258, 259.

32. Elsie Ripley Clapp, "Learning and Indoctrinating," *Progressive Education* 9, no. 4 (April 1932): 269–72, 269, 271.

33. Clapp's connection with social welfare and using education as part of social reform can be clearly seen in her work in the Paterson Silk Workers strike of 1913. During the strike Clapp worked with Margaret Sanger and met many leaders of the International Workers of the World, including John Reed, Carlo Tresca, Elizabeth Gurley Flynn, and Bill Haywood. These activities are documented in Stack, *Elsie Ripley Clapp*, 92–96. She was certainly aware of social welfare issues and concerns.

34. Bowers, *The Progressive Educator and the Depression*, 16, 132.

35. Baskin, "Education and the Great Depression," 403.

36. Harold Rugg, "Social Reconstruction through Education," *Progressive Education* 10, no. 1 (December 1932): 11–18, 16, 18.

37. John W. Herring and Ethel C. Phillips, "A Reference List on Economic Problems," *Progressive Education* 11, nos. 1–2 (January–February 1934): 145.

38. Willard W. Beatty, "Let Us Act to Save Our Schools," *Progressive Education* 11, nos. 1–2 (January–February 1934): 3.

39. Harold Rugg, "The Educator and the Scientific Study of Society," *Progressive Education* 11, nos. 1–2 (January–February 1934): 3–5, 3, 4.

40. Norman Woelfel, "The Educator, the New Deal, and Revolution," *Progressive Education* 11, nos. 1–2 (January–February 1934): 7–12, 12. At the time of writing, Woelfel was a graduate student at Teachers College. He sought a journal for social reconstructionist thought that eventually appeared as the *Social Frontier*, the most radical journal in education during the Depression era. George Counts, Mordecai Grossman, and Woelfel composed the editorials. Owing to the "extreme radicalism of the editorials," the *Social Frontier* gradually lost subscribers. Some Civilian Conservation Corps camps even banned it. See Bowers, *The Progressive Educator and the Depression*, 44, 162.

41. Merle Curti, "The Social Ideas of American Educators," *Progressive Education* 11, nos. 1–2 (January–February 1934): 26–31, 30, 31.

42. Helen Hefferan, "The Chicago Situation," *Progressive Education* 10, no. 1 (October 1933): 318–20, 319. See also Jeffrey Mirel, *The Rise and Fall of an Urban School System (1907–1981)* (Ann Arbor: University of Michigan Press, 1993).

43. Quoted in Baskin, "Education and the Great Depression," 117.

44. National Education Association, "Current Conditions in the Nation's Schools," *Research Bulletin of the National Education Association*, November 1933, 100; Dixon Wecter, *The Age of the Great Depression* (New York: Macmillan, 1948). See also Baskin, "Education and the Great Depression," 68. Total immigration from 1921 to 1930 was 4,107,206. From 1931 to 1940 it was 528,431.

2. Back to the Land and the Arthurdale School

1. Tyack, Lowe, and Hansot, *Public Schools in Hard Times*, 6. See also US Bureau of the Census, *Historical Statistics of the United States: Colonial Times to 1970* (Washington, DC: US Government Printing Office, 1975).

2. Carl Zimmerman, "The Place of Homesteads in Our National Economy: A Discussion," *Journal of Farm Economics* 16, no. 1 (1934): 84–87.

3. Baskin, "Education and the Great Depression," 69.

4. Studs Terkel, *Hard Times: An Oral History of the Great Depression* (New York: Pocket, 1978), 487–88.

5. Tyack, Lowe, and Hansot, *Public Schools in Hard Times*, 13. See also Robert Lynd and Helen Lynd, *Middletown in Transition: A Study in Cultural Conflicts* (New York: Harcourt, Brace, 1937), 145.

6. Arthur Schlesinger Jr., *The Crisis of the Old Order: The Age of Roosevelt, 1919–1933* (New York: Houghton Mifflin, 2002), 160, 249.

7. Anthony Badger, *The New Deal: The Depression Years, 1933–1940* (New York: Farrar Straus Giroux, 1989), 12.

8. Jerry Bruce Thomas, *An Appalachian New Deal: West Virginia in the Great Depression* (Morgantown: West Virginia University Press, 2010), 9.

9. Phil Ross, "The Scotts Run Coalfield from the Great War to the Great Depression: A Study in Overdevelopment," *West Virginia History* 53 (1994): 21–42, 34–35 (quote); and C. J. Maloney, *Back to the Land: Arthurdale, FDR's New Deal, and the Costs of Economic Planning* (New York: Wiley, 2011), 28.

10. Schlesinger, *The Crisis of the Old Order*, 112.

11. Badger, *The New Deal*, 19, 27 (quote).

12. Schlesinger, *The Crisis of the Old Order*, 185, 82. See also Clarence Pickett, *For More Than Bread* (Boston: Little, Brown, 1953).

13. Amity Shlaes, *The Forgotten Man: A New History of the Great Depression* (New York: Harper Perennial, 2007).

14. Schlesinger, *The Crisis of the Old Order*, 7.

15. Transcript of National Industrial Recovery Act (1933), sec. 1, http://www.ourdocuments.gov/doc.php?flash=true&doc=66&page=transcript.

16. Gary Dean Best, *Pride, Prejudice, and Politics: Roosevelt versus Recovery, 1933–1938* (New York: Praeger, 1991). The NIRA was declared unconstitutional in *Schechter Poultry v. United States*, 295 U.S. 495 (1935), the court deciding that it infringed on the power of the states. See also Badger, *The New Deal*, 80. Regardless of some capitalist support, Henry Ford and the National Association of Manufacturers did not support the NIRA. Eleanor Roosevelt later wrote of the act: "The basic importance of the NRA [i.e., NIRA] was that it made it easier for the industrialist who wanted to do the right thing. The chiseler and the man who was willing to profit by beating down his labor could no longer compete unfairly with the man who wanted to earn a decent profit but

to treat his employees fairly." Eleanor Roosevelt, *The Autobiography of Eleanor Roosevelt* (1961; New York: Da Capo, 1992), 182.

17. Dickens also attacks the education system of his day.

18. Jan Marsh, *Back to the Land: The Pastoral Impulse in England from 1880 to 1914* (London: Quartet, 1982), 5.

19. Russell Lord and P. H. Johnstone, *A Place on Earth: A Critical Appraisal of Subsistence Homesteads* (Washington, DC: US Department of Agriculture, 1942), 5.

20. Cremin, *The Transformation of the School,* 76 (first quote); Liberty Hyde Bailey, *The Country Life Movement in the United States* (New York: Macmillan, 1913), 27. Cremin credits Bailey with significant influence.

21. L. L. Bernard, "The Values of Farm Life," in *Farm Income and Farm Life: A Symposium on the Relation of the Social and Economic Factors in Rural Progress,* ed. Dwight Sanderson, John Kolb, and M. L. Wilson (Chicago: University of Chicago Press, 1927), 27–33, 30, 33.

22. Lord and Johnstone, *A Place on Earth,* 14.

23. Henry Ford and Samuel Crowther, *Today and Tomorrow* (1926; New York: Productivity, 1988). See also Paul Conkin, *Tomorrow a New World: A New Deal Community Program* (Ithaca, NY: Cornell University Press, 1959), 24.

24. Conkin, *Tomorrow a New World,* 25, 26; Shlaes, *The Forgotten Man,* 106; Lord and Johnstone, *A Place on Earth,* 17. For information on the Catholic rural movement, see Hilaire Beloc, *The Servile State* (New York: Henry Holt, 1946). For Borsodi's view, see Ralph Borsodi, *This Ugly Civilization* (New York: Simon & Schuster, 1929), and "Subsistence Homesteads, President Roosevelt's New Land and Population Policy," *Survey Graphic* 23 (January 1934): 11–14. See also Twelve Southerners, *I'll Take My Stand: The South and the Agrarian Tradition* (1930; Baton Rouge: Louisiana State University Press, 1977).

25. Conkin, *Tomorrow a New World,* 45. See also Elwood Mead, *Helping Men Own Farms* (New York: Macmillan, 1920).

26. Lord and Johnstone, *A Place on Earth,* 27.

27. Ibid., 35.

28. Federal Emergency Relief Administration, Document on Community Organization, n.d., 3, A&M 1646, WVRC.

29. Stephen Haid, "Arthurdale: An Experiment in Community Planning" (Ph.D. diss., West Virginia University, 1975), 56. For a brief description of the NIRA, see *Monthly Labor Review* 37 (December 1933): 1327–28.

30. National Industrial Recovery Act, http://www.ourdocuments.gov/doc.php?flash=true&doc=66.

31. Paul Conkin, "Arthurdale Revisited: When Subsistence Farming Made Sense," in *A New Deal for America: Proceedings from a National Conference on New Deal Communities,* ed. Bryan Ward (Arthurdale, WV: Arthurdale Heritage, 1995), 45–64, 46.

32. Executive Order on Homestead Authority, 21 July 1933, box 499 (1-277), NARG

48. For Ickes's description of the NIRA, see Harold L. Ickes, *The Secret Diary of Harold L. Ickes: The First Thousand Days (1933-1936)* (New York: Simon & Schuster, 1953), 53.

33. Certificate of Incorporation—Subsistence Homestead Corporation, box 501 (1-277), NARG 48.

34. Lord and Johnstone, *A Place on Earth*, 39.

35. Conkin, "Arthurdale Revisited," 56.

36. See M. L. Wilson, *Reminiscences of Milburn Lincoln Wilson*, Oral History Collection (1956; New York: Columbia University, 1973), 1186, and "The Place of Subsistence Homesteads in Our National Economy," abstract of an address, 27 December 1933, pp. 1-2 (quotes), folder 3, A&M 2178, WVRC.

37. Haid, "Arthurdale," 45; Conkin, *Tomorrow a New World*, 28; Maloney, *Back to the Land*, 63; Benjamin Rader, *The Academic Mind and Reform* (Lexington: University of Kentucky Press, 1966), 192-92. Richard Ely was educated at Columbia University and held a Ph.D. in economics from the University of Heidelberg. He taught political economy at Johns Hopkins from 1881 to 1892 and sought a balance between regulation and state intervention. See Sidney Fine, "Richard Ely, Forerunner of Progressivism, 1880-1901," *Mississippi Valley Historical Review* 37 (March 1951): 599-624.

38. Milburn L. Wilson and Oscar B. Jesness, *Farm Relief and the Domestic Allotment Plan*, Day and Hour Series of the University of Minnesota, no. 2 (Minneapolis: University of Minnesota Press, 1933), 50. See also Haid, "Arthurdale," 46.

39. Haid, "Arthurdale," 51-53.

40. Franklin D. Roosevelt, *The Public Papers and Addresses of Franklin D. Roosevelt*, ed. Samuel Rosenman, 13 vols. (New York: Random House, 1938-1950), 2:117 (see also 2:291). Lord and Johnstone, *A Place on Earth*, 3; Rexford Tugwell, "The Place of Government in a National Land Program," *Journal of Farm Economics* 16, no. 1 (January 1934): 55-69, 64; and Russell Lord, *The Wallaces of Iowa* (Boston: Houghton Mifflin, 1947), 323.

41. Quoted in Rexford Tugwell, "The Sources of New Deal Reformism," *Ethics* 64, no. 4 (1954): 249-76, 266. Also discussed in Conkin, *Tomorrow a New World*, 34.

42. Franklin D. Roosevelt, "Actualities of Agricultural Planning," in *America Faces the Future*, ed. Charles A. Beard (Boston: Houghton-Mifflin, 1932), 332.

43. See Ralph Borsodi, *Flight from the City: The Story of a New Way to Family Security* (New York: Harper & Bros., 1933), and *This Ugly Civilization*. The former discusses Borsodi's experiment in Dayton, Ohio.

44. Conkin, *Tomorrow a New World*, 96. See also John Dewey, *Individualism Old and New* (1930; Carbondale: Southern Illinois University Press, 1999), throughout which concerns about individualism in capitalist society featuring a challenge to participatory democracy and a loss of community are discussed.

45. M. L. Wilson, "How New Deal Agencies Are Affecting Family Life," *Journal of Home Economics* 27, no. 5 (1935): 274-80, 275. See also Lord and Johnstone, *A Place on Earth*, 22; Conkin, *Tomorrow a New World*, 97; and Haid, "Arthurdale," 47.

46. Conkin, *Tomorrow a New World*, 131.

47. M. L. Wilson, "The Place of Subsistence Homestead in Our National Economy," *Journal of Farm Economics* 16, no. 1 (January 1934): 73–84, 80.

48. Tugwell, "The Place of Government in a National Land Program," 58.

49. John Pratt Whitman to Harold Ickes, Report of the Committee on Administration of Subsistence Homesteads, n.d., 3, box 500 (1-277), NARG 48.

50. Quoted in James Brooks, "Arthurdale: An Experiment in Homesteading," *Atlantic Monthly* 155 (February 1935): 196–204, 204. See also Thomas Jefferson, *Notes on the State of Virginia*, ed. William Peden (Chapel Hill: University of North Carolina Press, 1955), 164–65; Walter LaFeber, "Jefferson and an American Foreign Policy," in *Jeffersonian Legacies*, ed. Peter S. Onuf (Charlottesville: University Press of Virginia, 1993), 370–91, 376; and Nobel Cunningham, *In Pursuit of Reason: The Life of Thomas Jefferson* (Baton Rouge: Louisiana State University Press, 1987), 329.

51. General Information on Subsistence Homesteads, box 1, entry 9, NARG 96.

52. Milburn Wilson to Harold Ickes, 14 October 1933, box 522, NARG 48.

53. Nathan Margold to Harold Ickes, 15 August 1934, box 500 (1-277), NARG 48.

54. On both Mrs. Roosevelt's and Pickett's roles in the AFSC, see "AFSC and the Eleanor Roosevelt Connection," 30 March 2010, http://www.afsc.org/story/afsc-and-eleanor-roosevelt-connection.

55. Ronald D Eller, *Miners, Millhands and Mountaineers: Industrialization of the Appalachian South (1880–1930)* (Knoxville: University of Tennessee Press, 1989), 183.

56. Lorena Hickok, *Reluctant First Lady* (New York: Dodd, Mead, 1962), 137.

57. William E. Brooks, "Arthurdale—a New Chance," *Atlantic Monthly* 155 (February 1935): 196–208, 198–99.

58. Ross, "The Scotts Run Coalfield," 35.

59. Ron Lewis, "Scotts Run: An Introduction," *West Virginia History* 53 (1994): 1–6, 4.

60. Matthew Yeager, "Scotts Run: A Community in Transition," *West Virginia History* 53 (1994): 7–20, 14.

61. Brooks, "Arthurdale," 199. See also Doris Faber, *The Life of Lorena Hickok* (New York: William Morrow, 1980), 143–44; and Hickok, *Reluctant First Lady*. For a description of the deplorable conditions in terms of health and sanitation in Scotts Run, see Sandra Barney, "You Get What You Pay For," in Ward, ed., *A New Deal for America*, 25–44.

62. Roosevelt, *The Autobiography of Eleanor Roosevelt*, 177.

63. Eleanor Roosevelt, *This I Remember* (New York: Harper & Bros., 1949), 127.

64. Harold Ickes to Senator James Couzens, 4 December 1933, box 503 (1-277), NARG 48. This letter was written in defense of a plan for the homesteaders at Arthurdale to build furniture for the US Postal Service that never came to fruition.

65. Eller, *Miners, Millhands and Mountaineers*, 156, 158 (quote), 176. Maloney reports that by 1932 annual coal production in Monongalia County (which included Scotts Run) had dropped drastically, with roughly 41 percent of the population on

some form of relief. Maloney, *Back to the Land*, 37. See also Haid, "Arthurdale," 4; and Malcolm Ross, "When Depression Blights a Great Area," *New York Times*, 31 January 1932, sec. 5, p. 6.

66. Tugwell, "The Place of Government in a National Land Program," 65. Tugwell clearly had the ear of Eleanor Roosevelt, and they both felt a similar understanding of community. See Shlaes, *The Forgotten Man*, 256.

67. US Department of the Interior, Memorandum for the Press, 12 October 1933, A&M 2178, WVRC; Harold Ickes, "Press Release," 12 October 1933 (quotes), box 13, entry 9, NARG 96.

68. Bushrod Grimes estimated the cost of the Arthur mansion as $35,000. Bushrod Grimes Document, 1–5, A&M 2178, WVRC. M. L. Wilson indicates that the costs were $35,000 for the Arthur farm, $12,000 for the land of William Watkins, and $1,500 to the Kingwood Building and Loan Association. Richard Arthur had originally requested $60,000 for his farm. See M. L. Wilson to Bushrod Grimes, n.d., folder 1, A&M 2178, WVRC.

69. Description of Arthurdale: Project Descriptions, n.d., box 4, entry 9, Records of the Farmers Home Administration (1933–1935), NARG 96.

70. Eleanor Roosevelt, Subsistence Farm Steads—Reedsville Project, n.d., box 503 (1-277), NARG 48.

71. Eller, *Miners, Millhands and Mountaineers*, 187.

72. Homesteader Women to Eleanor Roosevelt, folder 1, A&M 2178, WVRC. The term *colony* was sometimes used to describe the community and *colonists* to describe the homesteaders.

73. Bushrod Grimes to M. L. Wilson, 23 November 1933, folder 1, A&M 2178, WVRC.

74. Monongahela Valley Self-Help Association Homestead Project, box 2, entry 9, NARG 96.

75. Howard B. Allen to Clarence Pickett, 18 December 1933, box 2, entry 9, NARG 96.

76. See Personnel Profile Report, A&M 1646, WVRC; Pickett, *For More Than Bread*, 54. Applicants were assigned a grade from A through E with A being the highest. See also Case Worker Questionnaire, 3, A&M 1646, WVRC; and H. B. Allen, "Suggestions for Procedures in Organizing Forces to Recruit Prospects for Extended Projects," A&M 1646, WVRC. C. J. Maloney argues that Bushrod Grimes and Alice Davis were the initial members of the selection committee, with the final group consisting of Eleanor Roosevelt, Grimes, and Silliman Evans, an assistant postmaster general. H. B. Allen also appears to have been heavily involved in the selection process. See Maloney, *Back to the Land*, 102. See also Haid, "Arthurdale," 78; and Holly Cowan, "Arthurdale" (Ph.D. diss., Columbia University, 1968), 35. In what appears to be a court transcription found in folder 6, A&M 2178, WVRC, Grimes lists himself, Alice Davis, O. B. Smart, and Silliman Evans as the selection group.

77. Howard B. Allen, "Industrial Rehabilitation through Farm Placement of the Unemployed," paper submitted to Clarence Pickett, Division of Subsistence Homesteads, September 1933, A&M 1646, WVRC. Federal officials believed that six to seven hundred people had actually applied. See Milburn Wilson to Bushrod Grimes, 23 November 1933, folder 1, A&M 2178, WVRC. Grimes was the local representative at Arthurdale of the US Department of the Interior. For biographical information on Allen, see Kermit A. Cook, *Distinctive Leaders in Teacher Education in West Virginia University (1892-1963)* (Morgantown: West Virginia University, 1968), 76-80.

78. H. B. Allen to Clarence Pickett, 18 December 1933, box 2, entry 9, NARG 96.

79. For examples of letters from others displaced by the Depression and seeking homesteads or federal loans, see box 1, entry 9, NARG 96.

80. Haid, "Arthurdale," 76. See also Arthurdale Homestead Project, "The Selection of Families to Live in the Community," A&M 2178, WVRC.

81. Deposition of Bushrod Grimes, 2, folder 6, A&M 2178, WVRC. Grimes had surveyed the inhabitants of the mining camps on their interest in the back-to-the-land movement and supplied Mrs. Roosevelt with the results.

82. Guy Numbers to Bushrod Grimes, 10 November 1933, folders 1 and 2, A&M 2178, WVRC.

83. Haid, "Arthurdale," 79 ("Foreign-born whites and Negroes were excluded from consideration from the beginning"); Dan Perlstein and Sam Stack, "Building a New Deal Community: Progressive Education at Arthurdale," in Semel and Sadovnik, eds., *"Schools of Tomorrow," Schools of Today,* 213-36, 230 ("Almost all [homesteaders] were Scotch-Irish or Pennsylvanian Germans in upbringing and social background, predisposing them to 'generosity and good humor'").

84. Claude Hitchcock to Eleanor Roosevelt, 11 February 1934, ser. 70, FDRL. See also Haid, "Arthurdale," 80.

85. Elsie Ripley Clapp, *Community Schools in Action* (New York: Viking, 1939), 116-17. See also John Davis to Walter White, 25 January 1939, NAACP Papers, Part 1, Microfilm.

86. Eller, *Miners, Millhands and Mountaineers,* 171.

87. Perlstein and Stack, "Building a New Deal Community," 231. See also W. E. B. DuBois, "The Board of Directors on Segregation," *Crisis,* May 1934, 149, and "Does the Negro Need Separate Schools?" *Journal of Negro Education* 4 (1935): 328-35. For further information on African American projects, see Stuart Patterson, "A New Pattern of Life: The Public Past and Present of Two New Deal Communities" (Ph.D. diss., Emory University, 2006), 131-237. Maloney argues that "it was Grimes who went on record with this policy [i.e., segregation] and who therefore unfairly gets singled out as the villain for this piece of Arthurdale's history." Maloney, *Back to the Land,* 102. Blanche Wiesen Cook argues that the refusal to admit African Americans to Arthurdale and the homestead movement generally moved ER to begin her quest for civil rights. See Blanche Wiesen Cook, *Eleanor Roosevelt: The Defining Years (1933-1938)* (New York: Penguin, 1999),

152. African American homesteads included Gee's Bend in Alabama, Roanoke Farms in North Carolina, Sabine Farms in Texas, and Aberdeen Gardens in Virginia. A restoration effort was begun at Sabine Farms in 2007. See "New Deal Programs: Volunteers Pitch in to Save a Slice of History," *Texas C-Bar Bulletin*, Spring 2007, 1-2.

88. Eleanor Roosevelt, "Subsistence Farmsteads," *Forum* 91 (April 1934): 199-201, http://www.gwu.edu/~erpapers/documents/articles/subsistencefarmsteads.cfm.

89. US Department of Interior Bulletin, Division of Subsistence Homesteads, Bulletin 1 (Washington, DC, 1934), 4.

90. Roosevelt, "Subsistence Farmsteads."

91. "First Home Ready at Arthurdale," *Dominion Post* (Morgantown, WV), 10 March 1934.

92. Roosevelt, *Public Papers and Addresses*, 2:294.

93. Tyack, Lowe, and Hansot, *Public Schools in Hard Times*, 114.

94. For concerns about the placement of the Arthurdale children in local schools, see "Educational Concerns—Circular, United States Department of the Interior, 1933," box 501, and "Minimum Budget Request to Complete 125 Homes—Subsistence Homestead Project, Reedsville, WV," box 503 (1-277), NARG 48.

95. List of Experimental Enterprises of National Significance Which Will Be Carried on at the Reedsville Experimental Project, n.d., box 503 (1-277), NARG 48.

96. John Pratt Whitman, "New Frontier Eager to Learn," *Christian Science Monitor*, n.d., 21/4/2, ERCP.

97. Quoted in Conkin, *Tomorrow a New World*, 96. See also Milburn Wilson, "Beyond Economics," in *Farmers in a Changing World: The Yearbook of Agriculture* (Washington, DC, 1940), 925-27.

98. "Miss Clapp to Be Principal," *Dominion News*, n.d., folder 8, A&M 2178, WVRC.

3. Elsie Ripley Clapp and the Community School

1. Elsie Ripley Clapp, "A Rural Community School in Kentucky," *Progressive Education* 10, no. 3 (March 1933): 123-28, 128.

2. See Cohen and Mohl, *The Paradox of Progressive Education*; and Tyack, *The One Best System*, 130-32.

3. US Department of Interior Application to Arthurdale, Employment and Biographical Data, n.d., 21/1/1, ERCP.

4. Elsie Ripley Clapp, *The Use of Resources in Education* (New York: Harper & Row, 1952), and *Community Schools in Action*. Clapp considered these two projects to be her best work and the culmination of a productive career as an educator.

5. Stack, *Elsie Ripley Clapp*.

6. ERCM, 54. The memoirs are autobiographical and end when Clapp began the Ballard work in 1929 even though a cover page suggests that they progressed through 1964. The last twenty years of her life are difficult to chronicle. This may have been due to declining health as well as the declining fortunes of progressive education. There is

a discrepancy in the Clapp Papers regarding the actual date of her birth. The correct date is 1879. Materials were in the possession of Barbara Rahn, Elsie's niece, and her husband, Sheldon Rahn, who donated them to Southern Illinois University.

7. Ibid., 46. Clapp seemed to identify more with her father, seeking his comfort and solace, and did not feel comfortable in the traditional Victorian female role, exemplified by her mother. This created a tense mother-daughter relationship that Clapp did not resolve until adulthood.

8. Ibid., 70.

9. For a brief biographical sketch of Clapp, see Barry Westfall, "Elsie Ripley Clapp and the Arthurdale School: 1934–1936," *Vitae Scholasticae* 12, no. 1 (Spring 1993): 53–64.

10. For more detail on Clapp's work with the *Journal of Philosophy, Psychology and Scientific Methods* and the impact Dewey had on her intellectual growth, see Stack, *Elsie Ripley Clapp*, 62–68.

11. See Kilpatrick, "The Project Method." For further information on Kilpatrick, see also Beineke, *And There Were Giants in the Land*, 22, 73, 77, 81. Clapp and Kilpatrick remained lifelong friends and colleagues. Kilpatrick strongly supported the publication of Clapp's last book, *The Use of Resources in Education*, for the John Dewey Society. For more detail, see Stack, *Elsie Ripley Clapp*, 226–27.

12. ERCM, 109.

13. Ibid., 111. This gives some insight into how pragmatism was not intellectually accepted in American philosophy departments. For a broader discussion of the Department of Philosophy at Columbia University, see George Dykhuizen, *The Life and Mind of John Dewey* (Carbondale: Southern Illinois University Press, 1973), 116–52.

14. ERCM, 114.

15. Fragment concerning the Dewey Lab School, n.d., 21/2/32, ERCP. This fragment also reveals Clapp's disgust on the demise of the Dewey Lab School at the University of Chicago: "Its end was precipitated by the President of the University who, anxious of the unprecedented acclaim the school received, contrived a merger with the Cook County Normal School, an outgrowth of the Chicago Institute headed by Colonel Parker." Ibid. For more detailed discussion of the Dewey Lab School and the politics surrounding it, see Robert Westbrook, *John Dewey and American Democracy* (New York: Cornell University Press, 1991), 111–13. John Dewey's "My Pedagogic Creed" (*School Journal* 54, no. 3 [16 January 1897]: 77–80, reprinted in *EW*, 5:86–96) is one of his more succinct statements of his philosophy of education at the time and clearly challenged the teacher/text-centered approach.

16. John Dewey to Elsie Ripley Clapp, 18 September 1911, 21/1/15, ERCP.

17. John Dewey to Elsie Ripley Clapp, 2 September 1911, 21/1/11, ERCP.

18. Fletcher Collins, interview with author, Arthurdale, WV, 18 August 1997. Collins was head of the Music and Drama Department at Arthurdale from 1934 to 1936 and a personal friend of Elsie Clapp's.

19. Notes regarding Theories of Experience, ca. 1911, 2, 21/1/22, ERCP.

20. See Report of Dewey's Lecture on Desire, 31 October 1911, 21/1/29, ERCP.

21. For more extensive discussion of these topics, see Typed Copy of Dewey's "Environment and Organism" (originally published in *Cyclopedia of Education* in 1913), n.d., 21/2/35, ERCP. See also John Dewey's Syllabus for the Course "Types of Philosophic Thought," Columbia University, 1922/1923, 21/2/25, ERCP. For the reference to Clapp and Kilpatrick, see Dewey, *Democracy and Education*, v.

22. Chapter Notes Outlining the Dewey Course "Philosophy of Education in Their Historic Relations," 4 October 1910–18 May 1911, 21/1/6, ERCP.

23. Stack, *Elsie Ripley Clapp*, 70–76.

24. Steve Golin, *The Fragile Bridge* (Philadelphia: Temple University Press, 1988), 67. See also Steve Golin, "Defeat Becomes Disaster: The Paterson Silk Workers Strike of 1913 and the Decline of the IWW," *Labor History* 24 (Spring 1983): 223–39; and Christopher Lasch, *The New Radicalism in America, 1889–1963: The Intellectual as a Social Type* (New York: Knopf, 1965).

25. ERCM, 137. Not noted in her memoirs, Clapp had made an ideological transition to the liberal Left.

26. While in Charleston, Clapp spent time exploring the city and interestingly sought out the socialist local. ERCM, 150.

27. ERCM, 162. For an account of the events, see "Wilson Evades Vast Crowd," *New York Times*, 4 March 1913, 2; and "Wilson Takes Office Today as 28th President," *New York Times*, 14 March 1913.

28. In 1916, Clapp once again began to experience health problems, this time diagnosed with a cataract. In 1917, feeling a need to make a contribution to the war effort, she took a job with the Red Cross Canteen, which had charge of all soldiers and sailors passing through the city on their way to and from Europe.

29. ECRM, 189, 193. Clapp spent the summer of 1922 assisting Dewey in a course entitled Special Problems in the Philosophy of Education and painting with the artist William Zorach.

30. See Cremin, *The Transformation of the School*, 204–5. The City and Country School is also discussed in John Dewey and Evelyn Dewey's *Schools of Tomorrow*. See *MW*, 8:285–90. For another discussion of the school, see Semel, "The City and Country School." For Clapp's personal experience at City and Country, see Stack, *Elsie Ripley Clapp*, 125–37.

31. Hauser, "Caroline Pratt and the City and Country School." For a history of varied progressive schools, see also Semel and Sadovnik, eds., *"Schools of Tomorrow," Schools of Today*. Joyce Antler's *Lucy Sprague Mitchell: The Making of a Modern Woman* (New Haven, CT: Yale University Press, 1987) is the definitive biography of Lucy Mitchell.

32. During her short stay at City and Country, Clapp became friends with Jessie Stanton and Harriet Johnson, who would assist her at Arthurdale, largely offering expertise in early childhood education. There was a close network of women educators in progressive schools, and they kept in contact.

33. Elsie Ripley Clapp, "Subject Matters in Experimental Education," *Progressive Education* 3, no. 5 (October–December 1926): 370–75, 370.

34. ERCM, 228–29, 242. Clapp knew these children because she had grown up much like them in Brooklyn Heights.

35. Clapp, "Subject Matters in Experimental Education," 373.

36. Elsie Ripley Clapp, "In How Far Shall the Curriculum Be Based on Children's Interest and in How Far on Teachers' Judgment," *Progressive Education* 7, no. 4 (May 1930): 181–82.

37. Elsie Ripley Clapp, "Children's Mathematics," *Progressive Education* 5, no. 5 (April–June 1928): 131–35, 132.

38. Elsie Ripley Clapp, "The Teacher in Social Education," *Progressive Education* 10, no. 5 (May 1933): 283–87, 287. Cremin reiterated this belief in the special talents of the progressive teacher. See Cremin, *The Transformation of the School*, 348.

39. Elsie Clapp's conception of the teacher was influenced by Dewey. See John Dewey, "To Those Who Aspire to the Profession of Teaching," in *LW*, 13:343–47, and "Professional Spirit among Teachers," in *MW*, 7:109–12.

40. Dewey, "Professional Spirit among Teachers."

41. Clapp, "Children's Mathematics," 132.

42. ERCM, 271. Clapp conveyed a concern among progressive educators that their success was limited largely to the private sector and lab schools and that there was a need to validate their work in larger settings. This is clearly indicated in the Eight-Year Study. Dewey was acutely aware of this limitation and pushed Clapp to explore this option in Kentucky and West Virginia. For work on the Eight-Year Study, see Craig Kridel, *Stories of the Eight-Year Study* (Albany: State University of New York Press, 2007).

43. Elsie Ripley Clapp, "Social Education in a Public Rural School," *Childhood Education* 9, no. 1 (October 1932): 24–26, 24.

44. Notebook-Manuscript on the Ballard School (1929–1930), 7, 21/4/2, ERCP.

45. Dewey, "My Pedagogic Creed," 87.

46. Notebook-Manuscript on the Ballard School (1929–1930), 6, 21/4/2, ERCP.

47. Clapp, *Community Schools in Action*, 4. Clapp's limited expertise is again evidence of progressive educators' lack of understanding of and experience with rural/public education.

48. Notebook-Manuscript on the Ballard School (1929–1930), 18, 21/4/2, ERCP.

49. Clapp, "The Teacher in Social Education," 283.

50. Clapp, *Community Schools in Action*, 3.

51. Clapp, "Social Education in a Public Rural School," 24, 26 (quote).

52. Clapp, *Community Schools in Action*, 12.

53. Notebook-Manuscript on the Ballard School (1929–1930), 25, 21/4/2, ERCP. As noted above, Clapp studied with William Zorach (1887–1966), and she seems years ahead of Dewey in terms of understanding "art as experience" and its communicative

capacity. See William Zorach, *Art Is My Life: The Autobiography of William Zorach* (Cleveland: World, 1967).

54. *LW,* 1:293 (*Experience and Nature*), 10:144 (*Art as Experience*).

55. Typed Copy of Christmas Experience of School and Community by George Beecher, n.d., 21/3/9, ERCP.

56. See John Dewey, *Art as Experience* (New York: Perigee, 1934).

57. Elsie Ripley Clapp, "Plays in a Country School," *Progressive Education* 8, no. 1 (January 1931): 35–39, 38.

58. Clapp, *Community Schools in Action,* 22. Studies in pioneer life were popular in most progressive schools, including those in urban settings.

59. Clapp, "A Rural Community School in Kentucky," 127.

60. Conkin, *Tomorrow a New World,* 246. See also Milburn L. Wilson to Harold Ickes, 27 January 1934, box 503 (1-277), NARG 48.

61. Estimated Financial Budget Reedsville School, 1934–1935, 11 June 1934, box 503 (1-277), NARG 48. Total expenditures, including private funds, were estimated at $265,808. Clapp's salary is not included in this figure, which also overestimates the costs of the teachers because West Virginia never paid for more than three teachers during Clapp's tenure, meaning that from 1934 to 1936 teacher salaries had to be funded privately. An audit performed by the Farm Security Administration (FSA) estimated that the total costs of the Arthurdale School were at least $217,912. See "Arthurdale Community, Region IV, Final Report of Records of the Farm Security Administration Including Analysis of Actual Construction Cost from Inception of Project to 30 June 1939," 30 June 1939, file 430, NARG 96. The project architect responsible for the physical plant, Eric Gugler, estimated the cost of the school plant at $130,000. See chapter 4.

It should be noted that it is virtually impossible to provide entirely accurate figures for the financing of the Arthurdale School. Department of the Interior records from June 1934 are only estimates and lack detail. Also, Mrs. Roosevelt did not keep records on the amount of private funding that she provided for the school. The final 1939 FSA figure of $217,912 does not include private funds.

62. Memorandum to Harold Ickes, 20 June 1934, box 503 (1-277), NARG 48. (The author of this memo is not known but might have been Milburn Wilson.) To assist Mrs. Roosevelt in the financing of the school, Bernard Baruch contributed at least $57,293 from 1934 to 1936. See Clarence Pickett to Eleanor Roosevelt, 12 September 1934, and Bernard Baruch to Eleanor Roosevelt, 6 April 1936, box 503 (1-277), NARG 48.

63. See C. E. Pynchon to Assistant Secretary of the Interior, 23 April 1935, box 503 (1-277), NARG 48.

64. Employment and Biographical Data, n.d., 21/1/2. ERCP. Clapp described herself as being fifty-four years old, standing five foot six, and weighing 147 pounds. She listed John Dewey, William Heard Kilpatrick, and George Arps as references.

65. Catherine Patricia Surdovel, "Community Education: 1890's to the Present" (Ed.D. thesis, Rutgers University, 1985), 63–64.

66. ERCM, 284. Dewey's papers are virtually silent on Arthurdale even though he served as an adviser to the project. The Center for Dewey Studies located a letter from Dewey that he wrote following his visit to Arthurdale in April 1936. He describes the Arthurdale School as one of the best public schools in the nation. John Dewey to J. A. Rice, 16 April 1936, Black Mountain College Papers, Center for Dewey Studies, Southern Illinois University, Carbondale.

67. Notes on the Arthurdale School, 1934–1935, 21/3/6, ERCP. Most of Clapp's staff at Ballard joined her at Arthurdale. For a list of these teachers, see Clapp, *Community Schools in Action*, 395–98.

68. Clapp, *The Use of Resources in Education*, 4.

69. Clapp, *Community Schools in Action*, 116, 122.

70. Gilbert Love, "Hand Picked Ex–Coal Miner Ripe for Industry to Make Federal Homestead Project Succeed," *Pittsburgh Press*, 6 June 1934, folder 8, A&M 2178, WVRC.

71. Ibid., 397. Clapp knew Lucy Mitchell from their work in Caroline Pratt's City and Country School.

72. Thomas, *An Appalachian New Deal*, 161.

4. Beginning a Community School

1. *Report of the Survey of Arthurdale School* (Morgantown: West Virginia University, 1940), 120.

2. Elsie Ripley Clapp, "Schools Socially Functioning," *Progressive Education* 15, no. 2 (February 1938): 89–90.

3. "Local Committee Sets Up Arthurdale School," *Dominion News*, 12 February 1934, 2. See also Clapp, *Community Schools in Action*, 387. Other sources include Joe Short, "First Lady Will Return Again to Farm on February 26," *Dominion News*, 12 February 1934, folder 8, A&M 2178, WVRC.

4. Pickett, *For More Than Bread*, 58.

5. "Local Committee Sets Up Arthurdale School," 2.

6. Graham, *Progressive Education*, 30, 67.

7. Ibid., 62.

8. For the influence of Dewey on Clapp, see Stack, *Elsie Ripley Clapp*, 77, 88

9. Bruce Beezer, "Arthurdale: An Experiment in Community Planning," *West Virginia History* 36, no. 1 (1974): 17–36, 27.

10. John Pratt Whitman, Misc. Material, n.d., 21/3/11, ERCP.

11. Clapp, *Community Schools in Action*, 72 (see also Clapp, *The Uses of Resources in Education*, 9).

12. Clapp, *The Use of Resources in Education*, 9 (see also Clapp, *Community Schools in Action*, 73).

13. Clapp, *The Use of Resources in Education*, 9.

14. Clapp, *Community Schools in Action*, 74 (see also Clapp, *The Use of Resources in Education*, 10).

15. Clapp, *Community Schools in Action*, 74. As Joe Short wrote, a progressive type of education could be "provided rural children without excessive costs," conducted in "plain buildings, to be erected largely by the homesteaders and furnished with the aid of the mothers and the children." Joe Short, "First Lady Will Return Again to Farm on February 26," *Dominion News*, 12 February 1934, 1, folder 4, A&M 2178, WVRC.

16. See Harold Ickes, "Report of Preliminary Budget," 12 March 1934, box 503 (1-277), NARG 48. Ickes compares the Danish folk high school to the educational environment of the homesteads, and it is clear here that federal officials saw the project as experimental. The folk high school would later serve as the model for the Highlander Folk School under the direction of Myles Horton, a noted community school advocate in the 1930s.

17. Cremin, *The Transformation of the School*, 54.

18. Ibid., 158.

19. "Wirt Will Give Facts," *Dominion Post*, 3 March 1934. See also "Alleged Red Plot Inquiry Will Be Held," *Dominion Post*, 27 March 1934.

20. See "Wirt Attacks Arthurdale and First Lady Answers," n.d., folder 8, A&M 2178, WVRC.

21. See "Wirt Inquiry Comes to an End," *Dominion Post*, 19 April 1934; and *Hearings Before the Select Committee to Investigate Charges Made by Dr. William A. Wirt, House of Representatives, 73rd Congress, Second Session on H. Res. 317, a Resolution to Create a Select Committee to Investigate Certain Statements Made by One Dr. William A. Wirt and for Other Purposes* (Washington, DC: US Government Printing Office, 1934). See also Sam Stack, "Guess Who Is Coming to Dinner? William Wirt and the New Deal," *Journal of the Philosophy and History of Education* 60, no. 1 (Fall 2010): 244–50. For a detailed history of the Gary School, see Cohen and Mohl, *The Paradox of Progressive Education*. There is no known response from Clapp regarding this incident.

22. Clapp, *Community Schools in Action*, 76.

23. Clapp, *The Use of Resources in Education*, 12.

24. See "Tentative Reedsville Experimental Village School Budget," 11 June 1934, and Memo to the Secretary of the Interior, 20 June 1934, box 503 (1-277), NARG 48.

25. Clapp, *The Use of Resources in Education*, 13.

26. Eller, *Miners, Millhands and Mountaineers*, 196.

27. Clapp, *The Use of Resources in Education*, 14.

28. See Benjamin Betts to Milburn L. Wilson, 28 November 1933, box 3, entry 9, NARG 96; and Summary of Arthurdale School Construction, 20 February 1934, box 503 (1-277), NARG 48.

29. Clapp, *The Use of Resources in Education*, 14.

30. Ibid.

31. Biography of Jessie Stanton, n.d., 21/3/11, ERCP. Later in her career, Stanton served as an adviser to the Manhasset Bay School and the Hanbridge School in New Jersey, prepared teachers for early childhood work for the Works Progress Administra-

tion, organized a nursery school in Harlem, and served as a consultant for the Bank Street College of Education. She also lectured at New York University. See Stack, *Elsie Ripley Clapp*, 131, 132, 136.

32. Clapp, *The Use of Resources in Education*, 15.

33. C. E. Pynchon to Harold Ickes, 20 June 1934, and Ickes to Pynchon, 23 June 1934, box 503 (1-277), NARG 48.

34. "Homesteaders to Move Soon," *Dominion Post*, 26 June 1934.

35. "First Lady's Reedsville School to Be the Community Centerpiece," 12 July 1934, Elsie Clapp Scrapbook, 1933–1934, 21/4/2/, ERCP.

36. "Reedsville Gets Handicraft School," *Dominion Post*, 30 June 1934.

37. The surviving evidence suggests that, in providing a personal history, Clapp glossed over her work (however limited) with the International Workers of the World (IWW) and her defense of Margaret Sanger's fight with the postal service. This is hardly surprising. Given the political nature of the Arthurdale project, any association with radical causes could have presented problems. Witness Wirt's attack on the project as socialist. C. E. Pynchon to Elsie Clapp, 26 July 1934, box 503 (1-277), NARG 48. For Clapp's work with the IWW and Margaret Sanger, see Stack, *Elsie Ripley Clapp*, 92–94, 96.

38. Construction had begun in April 1935. See Clapp, *The Use of Resources in Education*, 29.

39. Clapp, *Community Schools in Action*, 78, 79. Photographs of the benches show them to be similar to the type of bench often found in rural one-room schools, which is most likely what Clapp meant by "oldest American school patterns."

40. Ibid., 79.

41. Clapp, *The Use of Resources in Education*, 17. In response to the inadequacy of the facilities the first year, Pynchon met with Clapp and also sought the advice of Alfred Feldheimer of the Public Works Administration. See C. E. Pynchon to Harold Ickes, 1 September 1934, box 503 (1-277), NARG 48.

42. "Arthurdale School Plan Is Discussed," *Dominion News*, 5 September 1934. This article covered a meeting of officials from the state department of education, officials from the Preston County Board of Education, and federal officials to discuss the financing of and teacher employment at Arthurdale.

43. Memo from Bushrod Grimes to Homesteaders and Elsie Clapp, folder 3, A&M 2178, WVRC.

44. Clapp, *Community Schools in Action*, 397. The Ballard staff members who followed Clapp to Arthurdale were the teachers Ethel Carlisle, Elisabeth Sheffield, George Beecher, Carlton Saunders, and Harry Carlson and the secretary Alice Bowie. Clapp, *Community Schools in Action*, 395–98.

45. See Labor Inventory, 1 January 1934, box 67, AERP.

46. See C. E. Pynchon to Solicitor Nathan Margold, 13 October 1934, box 503 (1-277), NARG 48. As Pynchon explained the situation: "The children of such prospec-

tive homesteaders live a considerable distance from the project. It is a desire to enter in a contract for the transportation of these children to and from the school on the project. Approximately one hundred and twenty children will have to be transported each day."

47. Clapp, *The Use of Resources in Education*, 25.

48. Ibid., 26.

49. C. E. Pynchon to Louis Howe, 7 September 1934, and Pynchon to Harold Ickes, 20 September 1934, box 503 (1-277), NARG 48. The $175,000 figure, quoted in an August 1934 report, included the construction of the nursery school, the primary and elementary units, the high school, the administrative building, the gymnasium, and a home economics cottage, the purchase of school equipment, and fees for the architectural drawings and their preparation. It did not include teacher salaries or houses for the teachers. See Report on School Budget, 25 August 1934, box 308, AERP.

50. Charles Pynchon to Assistant Secretary of Interior, 23 April 1935, box 503 (1-277), NARG 48.

51. Eleanor Roosevelt to Elsie Clapp, 12 December 1934, box 1401, AERP. Baruch wrote of the homesteaders: "There is no doubt about their earnestness. They are not the ordinary folks who will be helped by the Government and call it a day. You felt their sense of responsibility—they weren't going to let Mrs. Roosevelt down. They were interested; wanted to make good." Unidentified newspaper clipping, folder 8, A&M 2178, WVRC.

52. Elsie Clapp to Eleanor Roosevelt, n.d. (ca. 1934), box 609, AERP.

53. Clapp, *Community Schools in Action*, 91.

54. Clapp, *The Use of Resources in Education*, 27. Timbres remained at Arthurdale through October 1936, when he accepted a research position at Johns Hopkins. He was succeeded by Dr. M. L. White, who was himself followed by a pediatrician named Dr. Wills. See Clapp, *Community Schools in Action*, 92. Elsie Clapp to Eleanor Roosevelt, 14 December 1934, box 608, AERP.

55. Clapp, *Community Schools in Action*, 93.

56. Elsie Clapp to Eleanor Roosevelt, 13 November 1934, box 605, and Eleanor Roosevelt to Elsie Clapp, 17 November 1934, box 1401, AERP. Eleanor planned to spend some time at Arthurdale during the Christmas holidays. See Eleanor Roosevelt to Elsie Clapp, 13 December 1934, box 608, AERP.

57. Clapp, *The Use of Resources in Education*, 28-29.

58. Elsie Clapp to Eleanor Roosevelt, 13 November 1934, box 608, AERP.

59. Steward Wagner, "School Buildings: Arthurdale, West Virginia," *Progressive Education* 15, no. 4 (1938): 304-19, 304.

60. Ibid., 313; Clapp, *Community Schools in Action*, 301 (quote).

61. Clapp, *The Use of Resources in Education*, 29-30.

62. See Friedrich Froebel, *The Education of Man* (1826), trans. W. N. Hailmann (New York: Appleton, 1887); Caroline Pratt, *I Learn from Children* (New York: Simon & Schuster, 1948); and Semel, "The City and Country School," 127.

63. Clapp, *The Uses of Resources in Education*, 35. This information is based on a

half-year report that Clapp used in writing *The Use of Resources in Education*. Carlisle, like the other teachers, submitted her report in January 1935.

64. Clapp, *The Uses of Resources in Education*, 40.

65. Ibid. There is no historical evidence for the local connection to Fairfax, so the story may be local folklore.

66. For more on the dissolution of community life and the role of the school in restoring it, see *MW,* 8:316.

67. Clapp, *The Uses of Resources in Education*, 50.

68. John Maxwell, "Learning by Doing: Teachers Remember Arthurdale School," *Goldenseal* 8 (Spring 1962): 65–71, 69, 67–68, 67, 51.

69. Ibid., 51.

70. Bette Collins, *Margaret and Fletch* (Staunton, VA, 1983), 7. While at Arthurdale, Collins met Charles Seeger, the father of the American folk singer Pete Seeger. Charles was working at the time in the Resettlement Administration and in the summer of 1935 recorded a folk festival directed by Collins (the first at Arthurdale). Collins's academic career included jobs at Montclair State Teachers College prior to his tenure at Arthurdale, Elon College in North Carolina from 1936 to 1942, and Mary Baldwin College from 1946 to 1976. He also worked for Fairchild Aircraft from 1942 to 1946. He is considered a major contributor to the American Folk Song Collection at the Library of Congress and was named cultural laureate of Virginia at age seventy-five. See Ann Hoog and Todd Harvey, "'Real People Talking': Conversations with Fletcher Collins," *Folklife Center News* 24, no. 3 (2002): 9–11; and *Mary Baldwin College News*, 6 May 2005.

71. Maxwell, "Learning by Doing," 52; Harry Carlson, oral history transcript, 1990, folder 2, box 2, A&M 3649, WVRC. The Beecher and Carlson families shared a duplex in Masontown their first year at Arthurdale.

72. Clapp, *Community Schools in Action*, 274–75. Beecher was a descendant of Henry Ward Beecher and a friend of Collins. Beecher also held an interest in drama and had toured with Fletcher and Margaret Collins prior to coming to Arthurdale. See Collins, *Margaret and Fletch*, 3.

73. Clapp, *The Use of Resources in Education*, 56.

74. Clapp, *Community Schools in Action*, 281.

75. Clapp, *The Use of Resources in Education*, 59.

76. Ipcar eventually married the well-known artist Dahlov Zorach, the daughter of William Zorach, an artist who instructed Clapp in painting and also taught at the City and Country School under Caroline Pratt. Adolph Ipcar Obituary, http://www.exitfive.com/dahlov/Adolphobit.html.

77. Ibid., 61.

78. Elsie Clapp to Eleanor Roosevelt, 27 December 1934, box 609, AERP.

79. Clapp, *The Use of Resources in Education*, 63.

80. Ibid., 65.

81. Elsie Clapp to Malvina Schneider, 23 March 1935, box 609, AERP.

82. Oscar Chapman to Elsie Clapp, 5 April 1935, box 609, AERP. Eleanor Roosevelt, Clapp, and Bernard Baruch all were in favor of employing as many of the homesteaders as possible, not only so that they would have a source of income, but also so that they would build a connection with the community.

83. Eleanor Roosevelt to Elsie Clapp, 12 April 1936, box 609, AERP.

84. Bernard Baruch to Eleanor Roosevelt, 20 April 1935, and Eleanor Roosevelt to Bernard Baruch, 18 May 1935, box 307, AERP.

85. Clapp, *The Uses of Resources in Education*, 66.

86. Clapp, *Community Schools in Action*, 121.

87. Ibid., 122.

88. Clapp, *The Use of Resources in Education*, 74.

89. Lucy Sprague Mitchell, *Here and Now Storybook* (New York: E. P. Dutton, 1921).

90. Antler, *Lucy Sprague Mitchell*, 286. Stanton later worked at New York University and the Vassar Institute and assisted Dr. Benjamin Spock on his radio program. See Stack, *Elsie Ripley Clapp*, 131; and Bank Street College Library, *Bank Street College History*, 2011, https://www.bankstreet.edu/archives/guide-archives/record-group-10/subgroup-13.

91. Fragment of Newspaper Article by Dewey Fleming, n.d., 21/3/11, ERCP.

92. Haid, "Arthurdale," 289–90.

93. Clapp, *Community Schools in Action*, 172.

94. Clapp, *The Use of Resources in Education*, 74.

95. Elsie Clapp to Eleanor Roosevelt, n.d., box 608, AERP.

96. Clapp, *The Use of Resources in Education*, 78.

97. Ibid., 79, 80.

98. Hoog and Harvey, "Real People Talking." Years later, Margaret Collins recalled Pete Seeger, Charles Seeger's son, often contacting Fletcher Collins during World War II to come and "do something for People's Songs." Collins, *Margaret and Fletch*, 15.

99. Eleanor Roosevelt to Elsie Clapp, 8 July 1935 (quotes), and Eleanor Roosevelt to Elsie Clapp, 23 August 1935, box 609, AERP.

100. See Eleanor Roosevelt to Bernard Baruch, 9 August 1935, and Bernard Baruch to Eleanor Roosevelt, 14 August 1935, box 307, AERP.

101. Memorandum to the Assistant Secretary of Labor from Charles Pynchon, 23 April 1935, box 503 (1-277), NARG 48. See also Oscar Chapman to Elsie Clapp, 3 April 1935, box 503 (1-277), NARG 48.

102. Graham, *Progressive Education*, 29, 30.

103. Report of the Arthurdale School, 1934–1935, 3, 6, 21/3/5, ERCP.

104. Eleanor Roosevelt, "Reedsville and Faith," speech, 9 October 1934, box 1401, AERP.

5. The Struggle to Survive

1. Aubrey Williams to Eleanor Roosevelt, 20 August 1935, Aubrey Williams file, box 292, FDRL. Eleanor Roosevelt was a strong supporter of the NYA and had convinced

FDR to launch the organization, which he did by executive order on 26 June 1935. See Cook, *Eleanor Roosevelt: The Defining Years,* 270; and Aubrey Williams, "Rural Youth and the Government," *Rural Sociology* 3, no. 1 (March 1938): 3–10.

2. Aubrey Williams, "Youth and Government," *Progressive Education* 12, no. 1 (December 1935): 506. Williams sent a copy of the article to Eleanor Roosevelt. See Aubrey Williams to Eleanor Roosevelt, 19 December 1935, box 292, AERP.

3. Badger, *The New Deal,* 207.

4. Clapp, *Community Schools in Action,* 370–71.

5. Clapp, *The Use of Resources in Education,* 82.

6. "Diary of a Homesteader's Wife," 14 July 1935, 11, box 308, AERP.

7. Ibid.

8. Clapp, *The Use of Resources in Education,* 88, 90.

9. Eleanor Roosevelt to Bernard Baruch, 26 September 1935, box 307, AERP.

10. Clapp, *The Use of Resources in Education,* 90, 93, 96.

11. Ibid., 97.

12. For Dewey's use of flax in the curriculum, see *MW,* 1:15 (*School and Society*); *LW,* 1:106 (*Experience and Nature*); and *EW,* 5:243 (course syllabus).

13. Clapp, *The Use of Resources in Education,* 105.

14. Ibid., 106.

15. Wagner, "School Buildings," 316.

16. Clapp, *The Use of Resources in Education,* 106, 110.

17. Ibid., 112–13.

18. Ibid., 116.

19. Ibid., 119–20.

20. Ibid., 128.

21. Ibid., 125.

22. Ibid., 126.

23. Elsie Clapp to Eleanor Roosevelt, 25 October 1935, box 609, AERP.

24. Clapp, *The Use of Resources in Education,* 157.

25. Elsie Clapp to Eleanor Roosevelt, 22 November 1935, box 609, AERP.

26. "ER Makes Surprise Visit," 11 December 1935, Misc. Material, 21/2/11, ERCP. Freed was the owner of the Paramount Cab Co. and an ardent supporter of FDR. He may have been visiting Arthurdale to set up some sort of factory operation to help employ some of the homesteaders. Mrs. Roosevelt spent time at the home of Mr. Glen Work from Fairmont and also at Clapp's home in Arthurdale. Homer Rainey later served as president of the University of Texas from 1939 to 1944 but lost his job protecting academic freedom. See George N. Green, "Rainey, Homer Price," 15 June 2010, Handbook of Texas Online, https://tshaonline.org/handbook/online/articles/fra54. His *How Fare American Youth?* (New York: Appleton-Century, 1937) was based on his work with the American Youth Council.

27. "New Education at Arthurdale," *Dominion News,* 3 April 1936.

28. Clapp, *The Use of Resources in Education*, 127, 128.
29. Sedman left the project in January 1936, and there is no documentation as to why.
30. Clapp, *The Use of Resources in Education*, 134.
31. Ibid., 138–39.
32. Ibid., 142, 144 (quote).
33. Kathryn Ash Carlson to Charles Ash, 3 December 1935, folder 4, box 2, A&M 3649, WVRC. This letter seems to have been prompted by a request by Mrs. Roosevelt—who knew Kathryn Carlson's father, a New York dentist—for unofficial information about Arthurdale from an inside source.
34. Elsie Clapp to Eleanor Roosevelt, 10 January 1936, box 627, AERP.
35. Bernard Baruch to Elsie Clapp, 15 January 1936, box 627, AERP.
36. Bernard Baruch to Eleanor Roosevelt, 27 January 1936, box 625, AERP. Baruch constantly made it clear that he did not wish to disappoint the homesteaders and continually voiced his dismay at the poor planning of government officials. See Eleanor Roosevelt to Bernard Baruch, 29 January 1936, and Bernard Baruch to Eleanor Roosevelt, 31 January 1936, box 625, AERP.
37. Eleanor Roosevelt, "My Day," 28 January 1936, http://www.gwu.edu/~erpapers/myday/displaydoc.cfm?_y=1936&_f=md054244.
38. Bernard Baruch to Eleanor Roosevelt, 6 April 1936, box 625, AERP. See also Eleanor Roosevelt to Bernard Baruch, 2 April 1936, box 625, AERP, which discusses the various funding opportunities being pursued. John Dewey also wrote a letter of support for Clapp. See John Dewey to the American Youth Commission, 13 January 1936, box 627, AERP.
39. Clapp, *Community Schools in Action*, 397. See also Eleanor Roosevelt, "My Day," 8 April 1936, http://www.gwu.edu/~erpapers/myday/displaydoc.cfm?_y=1936&_f=md054300b.
40. John Dewey to Sabino Dewey, 8 May 1936, in *The Correspondence of John Dewey, 1871–1952*, ed. Larry Hickman, 4 vols. (Charlottesville, VA: Inteler, 1992), vol. 2.
41. See "ER Makes a Second Visit to Arthurdale," *Dominion Post*, 7 April 1936, Misc. Material, 21/3/11, ERCP.
42. Clapp, *The Use of Resources in Education*, 146–47.
43. Ibid., 148–50.
44. Badger, *The New Deal*, 206–7. Badger argues that the WPA "helped educational institutions to weather the strain of the Depression" through adult education, literacy, preschool, and after-school programs. He also notes that 20–30 percent of young people aged sixteen to twenty-six were unemployed during the Depression and that by the end of 1935 over two hundred thousand high school students throughout the country received some money to keep them in school "in return for doing jobs round the campus." The NYA was one of the more popular New Deal programs and also worked to "ensure fair treatment of blacks." Ibid., 207. The WPA also supported some of the work at the Arthurdale Nursery School.

45. Bernard Baruch to Eleanor Roosevelt, 11 May 1936, box 625, AERP. Baruch mentions that he had given the AFSC 150 shares of a stock that it could sell for around $12,000 to support the school.

46. "Arthurdale Musicians Get Invitation to White House," *Dominion News*, 21 May 1936. The visit was also recorded by Eleanor Roosevelt in her "My Day" column of 22 May 1936. See http://www.gwu.edu/~erpapers/myday/displaydoc.cfm?_y=1936&_f=md054337.

47. "Mrs. Roosevelt Presented First Vacuum," *Dominion News*, 24 June 1936.

48. Eleanor Roosevelt, "My Day," 25 June 1936, http://www.gwu.edu/~erpapers/myday/displaydoc.cfm?_y=1936&_f=md054366.

49. Elsie Clapp to Eleanor Roosevelt, 10 June 1936, box 627, AERP. Clapp included in her letter information about Earl Riley and his family. She viewed him as a troublemaker and listed his financial obligations.

50. Bernard Baruch to Eleanor Roosevelt, 22 June 1936, box 627, AERP. At the time Clapp was attempting to get support for the school from Dean William Russell of Teachers College and Edmund deS. Brunner. She was, as we will see, not successful.

51. Summer School Bulletin, Summer 1936, box 627, AERP.

52. Eleanor Roosevelt to Elsie Clapp, 27 June 1936, box 627, AERP.

53. Elsie Clapp to Eleanor Roosevelt, 30 June 1936, box 627, AERP.

54. Eleanor Roosevelt to Elsie Clapp, 12 July 1936, box 625, AERP.

55. Eleanor Roosevelt, "My Day," 8 April 1936, http://www.gwu.edu/~erpapers/myday/displaydoc.cfm?_y=1936&_f=md054377.

56. Clapp, *Community Schools in Action*, 319.

57. Eleanor Roosevelt to Bernard Baruch, 12 July 1936, box 625, AERP.

58. Elsie Clapp to Eleanor Roosevelt, 13 July 1936, box 627, AERP.

59. Clapp, *The Use of Resources in Education*, 164.

60. Elsie Clapp to Eleanor Roosevelt, 16 August 1936, box 627, AERP.

6. From Community School to Traditional

1. Clapp, *The Use of Resources in Education*, 139.

2. Eleanor Roosevelt, "My Day," 3 August 1937, http://www.gwu.edu/~erpapers/myday/displaydoc.cfm?_y=1937&_f=md054710.

3. Elsie Clapp to Eleanor Roosevelt, 4 October 1936, box 625, AERP. Clarence Pickett had suggested that Clapp contact Bernard Baruch about possible funding for her rural community education projects, but he was ill at the time.

4. Elsie Clapp to Eleanor Roosevelt, 6 June 1938, box 665, AERP.

5. Collins, *Margaret and Fletch*, 14. According to Collins, Elsie Clapp also spent some time at Elon, but Clapp did not write about her experiences there, and Collins is the only source.

6. See George Beecher, *Science Studies in Alamance County Schools: A Cooperative Program in Studying the Science Curriculum for Rural Secondary Schools by Elon College*

and Alamance County: 1938–1939 (Graham, NC: Superintendent of Public Instruction, Alamance County, 1939). See also Collins, *Margaret and Fletch*.

7. Adolph Ipcar to author, 9 October 1998.

8. See Adolph Ipcar, Obituary@TimesRecord.com, 24 October 2003, http://www.exitfive.com/dahlov/Adolphobit.html.

9. Collins, *Margaret and Fletch*, 7.

10. Pickett, *For More Than Bread*, 61. See also Haid, "Arthurdale," 283.

11. Maxwell, "Learning by Doing," 69 (quotes), 70.

12. Eleanor Roosevelt, "My Day," 3 December 1936, http://www.gwu.edu/~erpapers/myday/displaydoc.cfm?_y=1936&_f=md054504.

13. Eleanor Roosevelt to Elsie Clapp, 8 January 1937, box 648, AERP. Mrs. Roosevelt also congratulated Clapp on the potential of the project that would be published in 1939 as *Community Schools in Action*.

14. Eleanor Roosevelt, "My Day," 19 January 1937, http://www.gwu.edu/~erpapers/myday/displaydoc.cfm?_y=1937&_f=md054544.

15. Elsie Clapp to Eleanor Roosevelt, 24 June 1937, box 648, AERP.

16. Eleanor Roosevelt, "My Day," 2 August 1937, http://www.gwu.edu/~erpapers/myday/displaydoc.cfm?_y=1937&_f=md054709.

17. Elsie Clapp to Eleanor Roosevelt, 7 August 1937, box 648, AERP.

18. Elsie Clapp to Eleanor Roosevelt, 16 July 1937, and Eleanor Roosevelt to Clapp, 29 July 1937, both in box 648, AERP. See also Elsie Clapp to Eleanor Roosevelt, 27 July 1937, box 648, AERP; and *Progressive Education* 14, no. 6 (October 1937): 407. The centennial, celebrated on 28 October 1937 (Mrs. Roosevelt had been asked to speak but, owing to previous commitments, was unable to attend), marked the 1837 birth of Francis W. Parker, to whom Dewey referred as the father of progressive education. See Cremin, *The Transformation of the School*, 129.

19. Glenn Work to Eleanor Roosevelt, 18 September 1937, ER Transit Fund as of 27 October 1937, and Proposed Budget for Arthurdale School 1937–1938, box 308, AERP.

20. School Activities Monthly Report, 27 January 1938, box 317, AERP. These reports tend to repeat the contents of previous reports.

21. Glenn Work to Eleanor Roosevelt, 23 April 1938, box 317, AERP.

22. The Bankhead-Jones Farm Tenant Act (PL 75-210, 50 Stat. 522 [1937]) allowed farmers credit to purchase and rehabilitate damaged farmland and authorized the acquisition by the federal government of damaged farmland for the purpose of rehabilitation as well as a modest credit program to assist tenant farmers to purchase land.

23. Facts about Arthurdale, May 1938, and "Brief Information concerning Arthurdale," J. O. Walker to Eleanor Roosevelt, 24 May 1938, box 317, AERP. These materials contain good descriptions of the community in 1938 and also give brief histories of Arthurdale.

24. Eleanor Roosevelt, "My Day," 28 June 1938, http://www.gwu.edu/~erpapers/myday/displaydoc.cfm?_y=1938&_f=md054991.

25. Eleanor Roosevelt to E. Grant Nine, 12 October 1936, and Malvina Schneider to E. Grant Nine, 8 December 1936, A&M 3310, WVRC.

26. Eleanor Roosevelt to E. Grant Nine, 15 April 1938, A&M 3310, WVRC.

27. Eleanor Roosevelt to E. Grant Nine, 20 May 1938, A&M 3310, WVRC. Although Baruch was asked to attend the ceremony, he cabled FDR that he could not. Bernard Baruch to Franklin Delano Roosevelt, 26 May 1938, box 88, Presidential Papers, FDRL. George Bye was Mrs. Roosevelt's literary agent; it was he who encouraged her to begin writing the "My Day" column. Other clients of Bye's included John Erskine, Charles Lindbergh, Laura Ingalls Wilder, and John J. Pershing.

28. Franklin D. Roosevelt, "Address at Arthurdale, West Virginia, 27 May 1938, The American Presidency Project, http://www.presidency.ucsb.edu/ws/?pid=15647. See also "FDR Uses Speech to Attack Tax Structures," *New York Times*, 28 May 1938, 7; and Bob Sturgiss, "FDR Impressed with Project," newspaper clipping, 28 May 1938, A&M 3310, WVRC. For personal recollections of the visit, see John Maxwell, "Learning by Doing," 65; and Elsie Clapp to Eleanor Roosevelt, 6 June 1938, box 665, AERP.

29. "Report of the High School Faculty: An Analysis of the Arthurdale Community and the Student Body of the High School (1938–1939)," A&M 3310, E. Grant Nine Collection, WVRC.

30. Pickett, *For More Than Bread*, 60.

31. "Report of the High School Faculty: An Analysis of the Arthurdale Community and the Student Body of the High School (1938–1939)," 3–4, A&M 3310, E. Grant Nine Collection, WVRC.

32. Ibid., 5. The students were most likely given a version of the Stanford-Binet intelligence test. The original scale was developed in 1905, but by the late 1930s the work of Lewis Terman had led to revisions that he believed better predicted ability at the upper and lower ends of the scale. The new scale measured what at the time was called *general intelligence*. See Lewis Terman, *The Measurement of Intelligence: An Explanation of and a Complete Guide for the Use of the Stanford Revision and Extension of the Binet-Simon Scale* (Boston: Houghton Mifflin, 1916). Still controversial, intelligence tests have shown bias against poor and rural students, who may have lacked the verbal skills required the perform well on the test.

33. "Report of the High School Faculty: An Analysis of the Arthurdale Community and the Student Body of the High School (1938–1939)," 5, 7, A&M 3310, E. Grant Nine Collection, WVRC.

34. "Proposed Budget for Arthurdale School, 1938–39," 24 June 1938, and "Summary Report and Proposals for Arthurdale Schools Financing and Program," 20 July 1938, box 317, AERP. The Farm Security Administration followed the Resettlement Administration as overseer of the subsistence homesteads.

35. "Proposals of the Advisory Committee for Operating the Arthurdale School Program after 1938/39," n.d., box 317, AERP. This plan listed three "assumptions" to finance the school. Assumption 1 called for a greater contribution by the Preston County

School Board to underwrite the cost of additional teachers. Assumption 2 called for the county school board to pay the principal's salary, enabling the addition of another high school teacher. Assumption 3 asked for the WPA to cover the salaries of two teachers for the nursery school, freeing a portion of the private funds for other uses.

36. Elsie Clapp to Eleanor Roosevelt, n.d., box 665, AERP.

37. "Philosophy of the Arthurdale Schools, Arthurdale, WV," 1938, box 317, AERP. This document also contains sections on curriculum principles, a brief history of the school, and a description of the proposed activities for the 1939/1940 school year.

38. Ibid.

39. Ibid.

40. *Report of the Survey of Arthurdale School* lists the survey staff from the College of Education in the table of contents.

41. Ibid., 8e.

42. Ibid., 58.

43. Cook, *Distinctive Leaders in Teacher Education*, 63. Wheat was a native of Berkeley Springs, West Virginia, and educated in rural West Virginia schools. He held a history degree from West Virginia University and in 1929 obtained a Ph.D. from Teachers College, Columbia University. He is most noted for his introduction and support of elementary school teacher training at West Virginia University in 1951. Ibid., 67.

44. *Report of the Survey of Arthurdale School*, 130–31. Born in New York City, Baldwin received his bachelor's degree from Princeton in 1913. He also held a master's from Teachers College, Columbia University, and a Ph.D. from Cornell. He is best known for his work in leadership and school administration. He began his work at the West Virginia University College of Education in 1931. He taught for a year at the Haskell Indian Institute, a Native American boarding school. He was considered an expert on administrative and financial issues surrounding the public school and was recognized in 1964 by the American Association of School Administrators for distinguished service. See also Cook, *Distinctive Leaders in Teacher Education*, 70.

45. *Report of the Survey of Arthurdale School*, 129, 130, 8e.

46. Maloney, *Back to the Land*, 164–65.

47. *Report of the Survey of Arthurdale School*, 116. At the time of the report, the nursery school had seventy-five children enrolled and an average daily attendance of fifty. There were five groups of children broken down by age (ages two, two and a half, three, four, and five) with five teachers, a nurse, and a supervisor paid for through WPA funds. There were also eight girls helping who were funded by the National Youth Administration. Children arrived at the nursery school around 8:00 A.M. and left around 2:00 P.M.

48. Ibid., 127.

49. Ibid., 19–20.

50. Ibid., 1.

51. Ibid., 45.

52. Ibid., 6.

53. Ibid., 8.
54. Ibid., 118–19.
55. Milburn Rice, "Footnote on Arthurdale," *Harper's Magazine* 180 (March 1940): 411–19, 419.
56. Memo to General Watson, 18 May 1940, box 2700, FDRP.
57. C. B. Baldwin to James Rowe, August 1940, box 3, FDRP. This box also contains notes from James Rowe on the employment plan. Rowe was an adviser to FDR. See also Earl Beckner to Major John O. Walker, 6 August 1940, box 3, James Rowe Papers, FDRP. Blue Bell Globe had a reputation for fighting union activity and resisted attempts by the Amalgamated Clothing Workers to organize in its Kentucky and Greensboro, North Carolina, plants.
58. Arthurdale [National] Advisory Committee Report, July 1940, 3, box 336, AERP. Members of the committee included Major J. O. Walker, Elinor Morgenthau, Bernard Baruch, Mrs. Allie Freed, Clarence Pickett, Mary Switzer, Raymond Kenny, and Glen Work, the project manager. There were also representatives from the FSA present for the 31 July 1940 meeting.
59. From 1933 to 1947, the subsistence homesteads were administered by five different federal agencies: the Division of Subsistence Homesteads of the Department of the Interior, July 1933–May 1935; the Resettlement Administration (an independent agency), May 1935–December 1936; the Resettlement Administration of the Department of Agriculture, January–August 1937; the Farm Security Administration of the Department of Agriculture, September 1937–September 1942; and the Federal Housing Authority of the National Housing Agency, October 1942–liquidation in 1947. See Haid, "Arthurdale," 340.
60. Elsie Clapp to Eleanor Roosevelt, 23 January 1942, 1940, in possession of the author.
61. Elsie Clapp to Eleanor Roosevelt, 24 May 1940, in possession of the author.
62. Eleanor Roosevelt to Edgar Kaiser, 18 June 1943, Elsie Clapp to Eleanor Roosevelt, 27 June 1943, and Elsie Clapp to Eleanor Roosevelt, 5 July 1943, box 648, AERP. Kaiser was an American industrialist who later chaired Kaiser Aluminum, Kaiser Steel, and Kaiser Chemical.

7. The End of a Dream?

1. Richard Drake, *A History of Appalachia* (Lexington: University Press of Kentucky, 2001), 152, 170.
2. Thomas, *An Appalachian New Deal*, 173.
3. Roosevelt, *Public Papers and Addresses*, 3:199.
4. Clapp, "Schools Socially Functioning," 90.
5. Tugwell, "The Place of Government in a National Land Program."
6. Pickett, *For More Than Bread*, 64.
7. Thomas Hutcheson, "The Process and Content of Community Education for

Participatory Community Planning in Two Towns in Massachusetts" (Ph.D. diss., University of Massachusetts, 1993), 19.

8. Clapp, *Community Schools in Action*, v.

9. J. Wayne Wrightstone, "Vital Education: A Review of *Community Schools in Action*," *Elementary School Journal* 60, no. 10 (June 1940): 789–91.

10. Harry Carlson to Clarence Pickett, 19 January 1939, folder 3, box 2, A&M 3649, WVRC. See also Clarence Pickett to Harry Carlson, 16 February 1939, Ralph Wagner to Harry Carlson, 16 November 1938, and Malvina Thompson to Harry Carlson, 28 November 1938, folder 3, box 2, A&M 3649, WVRC. The latter refers to Eleanor Roosevelt seeking the opinion of Bernard Baruch and Pickett regarding the proposed study.

11. Wrightstone, "Vital Education," 791.

12. Howard Cummings, "Review of *Community Schools in Action*," *Social Education* 4–5 (May 1940): 369–70. Cummings glowingly compared Clapp's work to that of Lillian Wald and Jane Addams. He taught at Clayton High School, Clayton, Missouri.

13. Eduard Lindeman, "Book Review of *Community Schools in Action*," *Progressive Education* 16, no. 7 (November 1939): 521–22, 522.

14. Charlene Haddock Siegfried, *Feminist Interpretations of John Dewey: Re-reading the Canon* (University Park: Pennsylvania State University Press, 2002), 92.

15. Dewey, *Democracy and Education*, 5.

16. John Dewey, *The Public and Its Problems* (New York: Henry Holt, 1927), 148–49.

17. Dewey, *Experience and Education*, 38. Dewey understood by 1938 that there had been many misconceptions of his work and felt the need for clarification. In *Experience and Education* he critiques both traditional education and progressive education, particularly the child-centered camp addressed earlier.

18. *EW*, 2:283–84, 286.

19. Cowan, "Arthurdale," 40.

20. Maloney, *Back to the Land*, 159–60.

21. Cowan, "Arthurdale," 40.

22. Kathryn Carlson to Charles Ash, 3 December 1935, folder 4, box 2, A&M 3649, WVRC. However, Carlson also seems to have felt that the men did not demonstrate the necessary responsibility to be given more authority in the community decision-making process. Referring specifically to the proposed beer and oyster party, she wrote: "Because some of them cannot properly handle themselves socially permission to hold the supper was denied. The result was an unofficial affair that night in De Prospero's poolroom at Bretz where the social behavior was undoubtedly worse than it would have been on the property."

23. *Report of the Survey of Arthurdale School*, 1940, app. K.

24. John Martin Taylor, "A Study of the Graduates of Arthurdale High School to Determine the Influence of High School Training on Occupational Adjustment" (master's thesis, West Virginia University, 1941), 73, 78, 82.

25. Pickett, *For More Than Bread*, 46.

26. Maloney, *Back to the Land*, 95. This criticism is driven by a strong libertarian ideology that appears to dislike any form of government and certainly the New Deal, which Maloney claims is the modern progenitor of contemporary federal interference in the lives of people. He writes: "Judging by their words, actions, and writings, it is proper to say that FDR, Wilson, Tugwell, and all the rest were, at minimum extreme, reactionaries with a deep admiration for Benito Mussolini's fascism and, in the case of Tugwell, Stalin's communism." He further mentions that Mussolini and Hitler experimented with subsistence homesteads and seems to wish to link the Arthurdale planners to them. Ibid., 136. If so, this seems more than a stretch. Mrs. Roosevelt was far from politically naive, as clearly indicated in Cook's *Eleanor Roosevelt: The Defining Years*. She was involved in women's rights, civil rights, and labor issues long before FDR embarked on his national political career.

27. Eleanor Roosevelt, "Reedsville and Faith," 9 October 1934, box 1401, AERP.

28. Conkin, *Tomorrow a New World*, 242.

29. Haid, "Arthurdale," 278.

30. Lord and Johnstone, *A Place on Earth*, 178.

31. Pickett, *For More Than Bread*, 56. See also Haid, "Arthurdale," 318; and Thomas Coode and Dennis Fabbri, "The New Deal's Arthurdale Project in West Virginia," *West Virginia History* 36, no. 4 (October–June 1975): 291–308.

32. Shlaes, *The Forgotten Man*, 256; Rexford Tugwell, *The Battle for Democracy* (New York: Columbia University Press, 1935), 143. See also Maloney, *Back to the Land*, 9–10; and Lord and Johnstone, *A Place on Earth*, 12.

33. Maloney, *Back to the Land*, 194. While the term *great blunder* is Maloney's, it does describe the perception held by many in the 1940s, even many Democrats.

34. Lord and Johnstone, *A Place on Earth*, 192.

35. Haid, "Arthurdale," 311–12.

36. Maloney, *Back to the Land*, 181; Conkin, *Tomorrow a New World*, 1959. Maloney calculates that the government took an 87 percent loss on the project. (Keep in mind that the initial Homestead Act allowed FDR and eventually Secretary Ickes $25 million for the nationwide relief efforts.) See also W. T. Frazier, Records Relating to the History of the Farm Security Administration, vol. 1, 1942, NARG 96.

37. Haid, "Arthurdale," 313; Shlaes, *The Forgotten Man*, 380.

38. Lord and Johnstone, *A Place on Earth*, 183.

39. Haid, "Arthurdale," 321–22.

40. John Dewey to J. A. Rice, Black Mountain College, 16 April 1936, in Hickman, ed., *Correspondence of John Dewey*, vol. 2.

41. *LW*, 6:97–98.

42. John Dewey, foreword to Clapp, *Community Schools in Action*, x.

43. James Kloppenberg, *The Virtues of Liberalism* (New York: Oxford University Press, 1998), 105.

44. Franklin Delano Roosevelt, State of the Union Message to Congress, 11 January 1944, American Presidency Project, http://www.presidency.ucsb.edu/ws/?pid=16518.

45. Johanek and Puckett, *Leonard Covello*, 77.

46. See Paul Pierce, "The School and the Community It Serves," in *The Community School*, ed. Samuel Everett (New York: Appleton-Century, 1938), 83–124, 89; and Leonard Covello, "The School as the Center of Community Life in an Immigrant Area," in ibid., 125–63, 127 (quote). William Wattenberg ("Annotated Bibliography," in ibid., 468–69) notes Clapp's work in Kentucky. See also Samuel Everett, "An Analysis of the Programs," in ibid., 435–62; and H. A. Tape, "A Consolidated Laboratory School," in ibid., 340–76.

47. Paul Hanna, *Youth Serves the Community* (New York: Appleton-Century, 1936), 272. Hanna mentions Clapp's "A Rural Community School in Kentucky."

48. Paul Misner, "A Community Educational Center," in Everett, ed., *The Community School*, 51–82, 70.

49. Myles Horton, "The Community Folk School," in ibid., 265–97, 295–96.

50. Johanek and Puckett, *Leonard Covello*, 210.

51. Ibid., 210.

52. William Wraga, "Condescension and Critical Sympathy: Historians of Education on Progressive Education in the United States and England," *Paedagogica Historica* 50, nos. 1–2 (2014): 59–75, 65. Wraga criticizes the historical approach taken by many education historians and critics of progressive education who have divorced history from contemporary practice.

53. Lloyd Cook, "School and Community," in *Encyclopedia of Educational Research*, ed. Walter Monroe (New York: Macmillan, 1941), 1000–1005, 1002. See also Edward Olsen, *The Modern Community School* (New York: Appleton-Century-Crofts, 1953), 193. Olsen's book was essentially a sequel to Samuel Everett's *The Community School*, originally published in 1938. It contains various examples of community schools in the late 1940s and early 1950s. See also John Lund, "Education Can Change Community Life," *School Life* 31 (November 1948): 11–12; and William K. McCharon, *Selected Community School Programs in the South* (Nashville: George Peabody, 1948), chap. 2.

54. Milosh Muntyan, "Community School Concepts in Relation to Societal Determinants," *Journal of Educational Research* 41, no. 8 (April 1948): 597–609, 602.

55. Olsen, *The Modern Community School*, 200–201.

56. Maurice Seay, "The Community School: New Meaning for an Old Term," in *The Fifty-Second Yearbook of the National Society of the Study of Education, Part II: The Community School*, ed. Nelson Henry (Chicago: University of Chicago Press, 1953), 265–87, 287. Henry's yearbook gives a sense of the community school movement in the postwar years. For an extensive bibliography on community school literature prior to 1954, see Edward G. Olsen, *School and Community* (New York: Prentice-Hall, 1954).

57. Edward Krug, "The Program of the Community School," in Henry, ed., *The Fifty-Second Yearbook*, 83–99, 83. See also Harold Drummond, "The Staff of the Community School," in ibid., 100–126; James A. Lewis and Russell Wilson, "School-Building Facilities for Community Schools," in ibid., 145–55; Paul Hanna, "The Community School and Larger Geographic Areas," in ibid., 228–37; Maurice Seay and John A. Wilkinson,

"Overcoming Barriers to the Development of Community Schools," in ibid., 265–87; and L. D. Haskew and Geneva Hanna, "The Organization and Administration of the Community School," in ibid., 127–44.

58. Paul Hanna and Robert Naslund, "The Community School Defined," in Henry, ed., *The Fifty-Second Yearbook*, 49–63, 52, 62. Edward Olsen describes Hanna as a "specialist in elementary education and consultant on community education to foreign countries" and Hanna's *Youth Serves the Community* as a "casebook describing numerous service projects and programs carried on by American high school students during the early 1930s." See Edward Olsen, "Standing on the Shoulder of Pioneers," *Community Education Journal* 5, no. 6 (November–December 1975): 8–12, 10. In the article Olsen lists thinkers he believed contributed to the community education movement.

59. C. W. Hunnicutt, "The Community School as a Social Instrument," in Henry, ed., *The Fifty-Second Yearbook*, 179–94, 185.

60. Johanek and Puckett, *Leonard Covello*, 12, 234.

61. See Arthur Bestor, *Educational Wastelands: The Retreat from Learning in Our Public Schools* (Urbana: University of Illinois Press, 1953); Robert Hutchins, *Some Observations on American Education* (Cambridge: Cambridge University Press, 1956), and *Education for Freedom* (Baton Rouge: Louisiana State University Press, 1943); and Hyman Rickover, *Education and Freedom* (New York: Dutton, 1959).

62. *LW*, 5:10.

63. Martin J. Blank, "Reaching Out to Develop a Movement," in *Community Schools in Action: Lessons from a Decade of Practice*, ed. Joy G. Dryfoos, Jane Quinn, and Carol Barkin (New York: Oxford University Press, 2005), 243–58, 253.

64. William H. Kilpatrick, "The Underlying Philosophy of Cooperative Activities for Community Involvement," introduction to Hanna, *Youth Serves the Community*, 3–20, 6.

65. Johanek and Puckett, *Leonard Covello*, 227.

66. Conkin, *Tomorrow a New World*, 239.

67. Joseph Hart, *The Discovery of Intelligence* (New York: Century, 1924), 47.

Bibliography

Alberty, Harold. "The Progressive Education Movement." *Educational Research Bulletin* 8, no. 8 (April 1929): 163–69.

Antler, Joyce. *Lucy Sprague Mitchell: The Making of a Modern Woman.* New Haven, CT: Yale University Press, 1987.

Badger, Anthony. *The New Deal: The Depression Years, 1933–1940.* New York: Farrar Straus Giroux, 1989.

Bailey, Liberty Hyde. *The Country Life Movement in the United States.* New York: Macmillan, 1913.

Barney, Sandra. "You Get What You Pay For." In *A New Deal for America: Proceedings from a National Conference on New Deal Communities,* ed. Bryan Ward, 25–44. Arthurdale, WV: Arthurdale Heritage, 1995.

Baskin, Alex. "Education and the Great Depression: An Inquiry into the Social Ideas and Activities of Radical American Educators during the Economic Crisis of the 1930's." Ph.D. diss., Wayne State University, 1966.

Beard, Charles. *America Faces the Future.* Boston: Houghton Mifflin, 1932.

Beatty, Willard W. "Let Us Act to Save Our Schools." *Progressive Education* 11, nos. 1–2 (January–February 1934): 3.

Beecher, George. *Science Studies in Alamance County Schools: A Cooperative Program in Studying the Science Curriculum for Rural Secondary Schools by Elon College and Alamance County: 1938–1939.* Graham, NC: Superintendent of Public Instruction, Alamance County, 1939.

Beezer, Bruce. "Arthurdale: An Experiment in Community Planning." *West Virginia History* 36, no. 1 (1974): 17–36.

Beineke, John. *And There Were Giants in the Land.* New York: Peter Lang, 1998.

Beloc, Hilaire. *The Servile State.* New York: Henry Holt, 1946.

Bernard, L. L. "The Values of Farm Life." In *Farm Income and Farm Life: A Symposium on the Relation of the Social and Economic Factors in Rural Progress,* ed. Dwight Sanderson, John Kolb, and M. L. Wilson, 27–33. Chicago: University of Chicago, 1927.

Best, Gary Dean. *Pride, Prejudice, and Politics: Roosevelt versus Recovery, 1933–1938.* New York: Praeger, 1991.

Bestor, Arthur. *Educational Wastelands: The Retreat from Learning in Our Public Schools.* Urbana: University of Illinois Press, 1953.

Bode, Boyd H. "Education at the Crossroads: What Principles Should Determine the Curriculum?" *Progressive Education* 8, no. 7 (November 1931): 543–49.
Borsodi, Ralph. *This Ugly Civilization*. New York: Simon & Schuster, 1929.
———. *Flight from the City: The Story of a New Way to Family Security*. New York: Harper & Bros., 1933.
———. "Subsistence Homesteads, President Roosevelt's New Land and Population Policy." *Survey Graphic* 23 (January 1934): 11–14.
Bowers, C. A. *The Progressive Educator and the Depression*. New York: Random House, 1969.
Brooks, James. "Arthurdale: An Experiment in Homesteading." *Atlantic Monthly* 155 (February 1935): 196–204.
Campbell, James. *Understanding John Dewey*. Chicago: Open Court, 1995.
———, ed. *Dewey's Conception of Community*. Bloomington: Indiana University Press, 1998.
Church, Robert. *Education in the United States: An Interpretative History*. New York: Free Press, 1976.
Clapp, Elsie Ripley. "Subject Matters in Experimental Education." *Progressive Education* 3, no. 5 (October–December 1926): 370–75.
———. "Children's Mathematics." *Progressive Education* 5, no. 5 (April–June 1928): 131–35.
———. "In How Far Shall the Curriculum Be Based on Children's Interest and in How Far on Teachers' Judgment." *Progressive Education* 7, no. 4 (May 1930): 181–82.
———. "Plays in a Country School." *Progressive Education* 8, no. 1 (January 1931): 35–39.
———. "Learning and Indoctrinating." *Progressive Education* 9, no. 4 (April 1932): 269–72.
———. "Social Education in a Public Rural School." *Childhood Education* 9, no. 1 (October 1932): 24–26.
———. "A Rural Community School in Kentucky." *Progressive Education* 10, no. 3 (March 1933): 123–28.
———. "The Teacher in Social Education." *Progressive Education* 10, no. 5 (May 1933): 283–87.
———. "Schools Socially Functioning." *Progressive Education* 15, no. 2 (February 1938): 89–90.
———. *Community Schools in Action*. New York: Viking, 1939.
———. *The Use of Resources in Education*. New York: Harper & Row, 1952.
Cobb, Stanwood. "Progressive Education Today." *Progressive Education* 9, no. 4 (April 1932): 224–26.
Cohen, Ronald, and Raymond A. Mohl. *The Paradox of Progressive Education: The Gary Plan and Urban Schooling*. Port Washington, NY: Kennikat, 1979.
Collins, Bette. *Margaret and Fletch*. Staunton, VA, 1983.

Conkin, Paul. *Tomorrow a New World: A New Deal Community Program*. Ithaca, NY: Cornell University Press, 1959.

———. "Arthurdale Revisited: When Subsistence Farming Made Sense." In *A New Deal for America: Proceedings from a National Conference on New Deal Communities*, ed. Bryan Ward, 45–69. Arthurdale, WV: Arthurdale Heritage, 1995.

———. *A Requiem for the American Village*. New York: Rowman & Littlefield, 2000.

Coode, Thomas, and Dennis Fabbri. "The New Deal's Arthurdale Project in West Virginia." *West Virginia History* 36, no. 4 (October–June 1975): 291–308.

Cook, Blanche Wiesen. *Eleanor Roosevelt: The Defining Years (1935–1938)*. New York: Penguin, 1999.

Cook, Kermit. *Distinctive Leaders in Teacher Education in West Virginia University (1892–1963)*. Morgantown: West Virginia University, 1968.

Cook, Lloyd. "School and Community." In *Encyclopedia of Educational Research*, ed. Walter Monroe, 1000–1005. New York: Macmillan, 1941.

Counts, George S. "Dare Progressive Education Be Progressive?" *Progressive Education* 9, no. 4 (April 1932): 257–63.

———. *Dare the School Build a New Social Order?* 1932. Carbondale: Southern Illinois University Press, 1978.

Covello, Leonard. "The School as the Center of Community Life in an Immigrant Area." In *The Community School*, ed. Samuel Everett, 125–63. New York: Appleton-Century, 1938.

Cowan, Holly. "Arthurdale." Ph.D. diss., Columbia University, 1968.

Cremin, Lawrence. *The Transformation of the School: Progressivism in American Education, 1876–1957*. New York: Vintage, 1964.

———. *Popular Education and Its Discontents*. New York: Harper & Row, 1989.

Crunden, Robert. *Ministers of Reform: The Progressives' Achievement in American Civilization, 1889–1920*. New York: Basic, 1982.

Cruz, Feodor. *John Dewey's Theory of Community*. New York: Peter Lang, 1987.

Cummings, Howard. "Review of *Community Schools in Action*." *Social Education* 4–5 (May 1940): 369–70.

Cunningham, Nobel. *In Pursuit of Reason: The Life of Thomas Jefferson*. Baton Rouge: Louisiana State University Press, 1987.

Curti, Merle. "The Social Ideas of American Educators." *Progressive Education* 11, nos. 1–2 (January–February 1934): 26–31.

Dewey, John. "My Pedagogic Creed." *School Journal* 54, no. 3 (16 January 1897): 77–80.

———. *School and Society*. Chicago: University of Chicago Press, 1899.

———. *Democracy and Education*. New York: Macmillan, 1916.

———. *The Public and Its Problems*. New York: Henry Holt, 1927.

———. *Individualism Old and New*. 1930. Carbondale: Southern Illinois University Press, 1999.

———. "Excerpt from Philosophy and Civilization." *Progressive Education* 9, no. 4 (April 1932): 256.
———. *Art as Experience*. New York: Perigee, 1934.
———. *Experience and Education*. New York: Macmillan, 1938.
———. *The Early Works, 1882–1898*. Edited by Jo Ann Boydston. 5 vols. Carbondale: Southern Illinois University Press, 1969–1991.
———. *The Later Works, 1925–1953*. Edited by Jo Ann Boydston. 17 vols. Carbondale: Southern Illinois University Press, 1969–1991.
———. *The Middle Works, 1899–1924*. Edited by Jo Ann Boydston. 15 vols. Carbondale: Southern Illinois University Press, 1969–1991.
Dewey, John, and Evelyn Dewey. *Schools of Tomorrow*. New York: Dutton, 1915.
Drake, Richard. *A History of Appalachia*. Lexington: University Press of Kentucky, 2001.
Drummond, Harold. "The Staff of the Community School." In *The Fifty-Second Yearbook of the National Society of the Study of Education, Part II: The Community School*, ed. Nelson Henry, 100–126. Chicago: University of Chicago Press, 1953.
DuBois, W. E. B. "The Board of Directors on Segregation." *Crisis*, May 1934, 149.
———. "Does the Negro Need Separate Schools?" *Journal of Negro Education* 4 (1935): 328–35.
Durkheim, Emile. *The Division of Labor in Society*. New York: Free Press, 1997.
Dykhuizen, George. *The Life and Mind of John Dewey*. Carbondale: Southern Illinois University Press, 1973.
Eller, Ronald D. *Miners, Millhands and Mountaineers: Industrialization of the Appalachian South (1880–1930)*. Knoxville: University of Tennessee Press, 1989.
Everett, Samuel. "An Analysis of the Programs." In *The Community School*, ed. Samuel Everett, 435–62. New York: Appleton-Century, 1938.
———, ed. *The Community School*. New York: Appleton-Century, 1938.
Faber, Doris. *The Life of Lorena Hickok*. New York: William Morrow, 1980.
Fine, Sidney. "Richard Ely, Forerunner of Progressivism, 1880–1901." *Mississippi Valley Historical Review* 37 (March 1951): 599–624.
Flamm, Matthew C. "The Demanding Community: Politicization of the Individual after Dewey." *Education and Culture* 22, no. 1 (2006): 35–54.
Ford, Henry, and Samuel Crowther. *Today and Tomorrow*. 1926. New York: Productivity, 1988.
Fowler, Burton. "President's Message." *Progressive Education* 7, no. 4 (May 1930): 159.
Fraser, James. *The School in the United States*. New York: Routledge, 2010.
Froebel, Friedrich. *The Education of Man*. 1826. Translated by W. N. Hailmann. New York: Appleton, 1887.
Golin, Steve. "Defeat Becomes Disaster: The Paterson Silk Workers Strike of 1913 and the Decline of the IWW." *Labor History* 24 (Spring 1983): 223–39.
———. *The Fragile Bridge*. Philadelphia: Temple University Press, 1988.

Graham, Patricia. *Progressive Education: From Arcady to Academe (1919–1955)*. New York: Teachers College Press, 1967.
Haid, Stephen. "Arthurdale: An Experiment in Community Planning." Ph.D. diss., West Virginia University, 1975.
Hanna, Paul. *Youth Serves the Community*. New York: Appleton-Century, 1936.
———. "The Community School and Larger Geographic Areas." In *The Fifty-Second Yearbook of the National Society of the Study of Education, Part II: The Community School*, ed. Nelson Henry, 228–37. Chicago: University of Chicago Press, 1953.
Hanna, Paul, and Robert Naslund. "The Community School Defined." In *The Fifty-Second Yearbook of the National Society of the Study of Education, Part II: The Community School*, ed. Nelson Henry, 49–63. Chicago: University of Chicago Press, 1953.
Hart, Joseph. *The Discovery of Intelligence*. New York: Century, 1924.
Haskew, L. D., and Geneva Hanna. "The Organization and Administration of the Community School." In *The Fifty-Second Yearbook of the National Society of the Study of Education, Part II: The Community School*, ed. Nelson Henry, 127–44. Chicago: University of Chicago Press, 1953.
Hauser, Mary. "Caroline Pratt and the City and Country School." In *Founding Mothers and Others: Women Educational Leaders during the Progressive Era*, ed. Alan R. Sadovnik and Susan F. Semel, 61–76. New York: Palgrave, 2002.
Hefferan, Helen. "The Chicago Situation." *Progressive Education* 10, no. 1 (October 1933): 318–20.
Henry, Nelson, ed. *The Fifty-Second Yearbook of the National Society of the Study of Education, Part II: The Community School*. Chicago: University of Chicago Press, 1953.
Herring, John W., and Ethel C. Phillips. "A Reference List on Economic Problems." *Progressive Education* 11, nos. 1–2 (January–February 1934): 145.
Hickok, Lorena. *Reluctant First Lady*. New York: Dodd, Mead, 1962.
Hinitz, Blythe. "Margaret Naumburg and the Walden School." In *Founding Mothers and Others: Women Educational Leaders during the Progressive Era*, ed. Alan R. Sadovnik and Susan F. Semel, 37–60. New York: Palgrave, 2002.
Hlebowitsh, P. S., and William Wraga. "Social Class Analysis in the Early Progressive Tradition." *Curriculum Inquiry* 25, no. 7 (Spring 1995): 7–21.
Horton, Myles. "The Community Folk School." In *The Community School*, ed. Samuel Everett, 265–97. New York: Appleton-Century, 1938.
Hunnicutt, C. W. "The Community School as a Social Instrument." In *The Fifty-Second Yearbook of the National Society of the Study of Education, Part II: The Community School*, ed. Nelson Henry, 179–94. Chicago: University of Chicago Press, 1953.
Hutcheson, Thomas. "The Process and Content of Community Education for Par-

ticipatory Community Planning in Two Towns in Massachusetts." Ph.D. diss., University of Massachusetts, 1993.
Hutchins, Robert. *Education for Freedom*. Baton Rouge: Louisiana State University Press, 1943.
———. *Some Observations on American Education*. Cambridge: Cambridge University Press, 1956.
Ickes, Harold L. *The Secret Diary of Harold L. Ickes: The First Thousand Days (1933–1936)*. New York: Simon & Schuster, 1953.
Jefferson, Thomas. *Notes on the State of Virginia*. Edited by William Peden. Chapel Hill: University of North Carolina Press, 1955.
Johanek, Michael, and John L. Puckett. *Leonard Covello and the Making of Benjamin Franklin High School: Education as if Citizenship Mattered*. Philadelphia: Temple University Press, 2007.
Kilpatrick, William Heard. "The Project Method: The Use of the Purposeful Act in the Educative Process." *Teachers College Record* 19 (September 1918): 319–35.
———. *Education for a Changing Civilization*. New York: Macmillan, 1926.
———. *A Reconstructed Theory of the Educative Process*. New York: Teachers College Press, 1931.
———. "A Theory of Progressive Education to Fit the Times." *Progressive Education* 8, no. 4 (April 1931): 287–93.
———. "The Underlying Philosophy of Cooperative Activities for Community Involvement." Introduction to Paul Hanna, *Youth Serves the Community*, 3–20. New York: Appleton-Century, 1936.
———. "Bode's Philosophic Position." *Teachers College Record* 49, no. 4 (January 1948): 268–76.
Kliebard, Herbert. *The Struggle for the American Curriculum, 1893–1958*. Boston: Routledge & Kegan Paul, 1986.
Kloppenburg, James. *The Virtues of Liberalism*. New York: Oxford University Press, 1998.
Kridel, Craig. *Stories of the Eight-Year Study*. Albany: State University of New York Press, 2007.
Krug, Edward. "The Program of the Community School." In *The Fifty-Second Yearbook of the National Society of the Study of Education, Part II: The Community School*, ed. Nelson Henry, 83–99. Chicago: University of Chicago Press, 1953.
LaFeber, Walter. "Jefferson and an American Foreign Policy." In *Jeffersonian Legacies*, ed. Peter S. Onuf, 370–94. Charlottesville: University Press of Virginia, 1993.
Larabee, David. "Progressivism, Schools and Schools of Education: An American Romance." *Paedagogica Historica* 41, nos. 1–2 (February 2005): 275–88.
Lasch, Christopher. *The New Radicalism in America, 1889–1963: The Intellectual as a Social Type*. New York: Knopf, 1965.

Lash, Joseph P. *Eleanor and Franklin*. New York: Norton, 1971.
Lewis, James A., and Russell Wilson. "School-Building Facilities for Community Schools." In *The Fifty-Second Yearbook of the National Society of the Study of Education, Part II: The Community School*, ed. Nelson Henry, 145–55. Chicago: University of Chicago Press, 1953.
Lewis, Ron. "Scotts Run: An Introduction." *West Virginia History* 53 (1994): 1–6.
Lindeman, Eduard. "Book Review of *Community Schools in Action*." *Progressive Education* 16, no. 7 (November 1939): 521–22.
Lord, Russell. *The Wallaces of Iowa*. Boston: Houghton Mifflin, 1947.
Lord, Russell, and P. H. Johnstone. *A Place on Earth: A Critical Appraisal of Subsistence Homesteads*. Washington, DC: US Department of Agriculture, 1942.
Lund, John. "Education Can Change Community Life." *School Life* 31 (November 1948): 11–12.
Lynd, Robert, and Helen Lynd. *Middletown in Transition: A Study in Cultural Conflicts*. New York: Harcourt, Brace, 1937.
Maloney, C. J. *Back to the Land: Arthurdale, FDR's New Deal, and the Costs of Economic Planning*. New York: Wiley, 2011.
Marsh, Jan. *Back to the Land: The Pastoral Impulse in England from 1880 to 1914*. London: Quartet, 1982.
Maxwell, John. "Learning by Doing: Teachers Remember Arthurdale School." *Goldenseal* 8 (Spring 1962): 65–71.
McCharon, William K. *Selected Community School Programs in the South*. Nashville: George Peabody, 1948.
Mead, Elwood. *Helping Men Own Farms*. New York: Macmillan, 1920.
Mead, George Herbert. *Mind, Self and Society*. Chicago: University of Chicago Press, 1934.
Mirel, Jeffrey. *The Rise and Fall of an Urban School System (1907–1981)*. Ann Arbor: University of Michigan Press, 1993.
Misner, Paul. "A Community Educational Center." In *The Community School*, ed. Samuel Everett, 51–82. New York: Appleton-Century, 1938.
Muntyan, Milosh. "Community School Concepts in Relation to Societal Determinants." *Journal of Educational Research* 41, no. 8 (April 1948): 597–609.
National Education Association. "Current Conditions in the Nation's Schools." *Research Bulletin of the National Education Association*, November 1933, 100.
Naumburg, Margaret. "The Crux of Progressive Education." *New Republic* 63, no. 812 (June 1930): 145–46.
Olgin, Philip. "Let's Re-examine Progressive Education." *Phi Delta Kappan* 38, no. 8 (May 1957): 309–13.
Olsen, Edward, ed. *The Modern Community School*. New York: Appleton-Century-Crofts, 1953.
———. *School and Community*. New York: Prentice-Hall, 1954.

———. "Standing on the Shoulders of Pioneers." *Community Education Journal* 5, no. 6 (November–December 1975): 8–12.
Olson, Lynn. "Dewey: The Progressive Era's Misunderstood Giant." *Education Week* 18 (1999): 29.
———. "Tugging at Tradition." *Education Week* 18 (1999): 25.
Onuf, Peter S., ed. *Jeffersonian Legacies*. Charlottesville: University of Virginia Press, 1993.
Palm, Reuben. "The Origins of Progressive Education." *Elementary School Journal* 40, no. 6 (February 1940): 442–49.
Parker, Samuel. *A Textbook in the History of Modern Elementary Education*. Boston: Ginn, 1912.
Patterson, Stuart. "A New Pattern of Life: The Public Past and Present of Two New Deal Communities." Ph.D. diss., Emory University, 2006.
Perlstein, Daniel. "Community and Democracy in American Schools: Arthurdale and the Fate of Progressive Education." *Teachers College Record* 97, no. 4 (1996): 625–50.
———. "Minds Stayed on Freedom: Politics and Pedagogy in the African American Freedom Struggle." *American Educational Research Journal* 39, no. 2 (2002): 249–77.
Perlstein, Dan, and Sam Stack. "Building a New Deal Community: Progressive Education at Arthurdale." In *"Schools of Tomorrow," Schools of Today: What Happened to Progressive Education*, ed. Susan F. Semel and Alan R. Sadovnik, 213–36. New York: Peter Lang, 1999.
Pickett, Clarence. *For More Than Bread*. Boston: Little, Brown, 1953.
Pierce, Paul. "The School and the Community It Serves." In *The Community School*, ed. Samuel Everett, 83–124. New York: Appleton-Century, 1938.
Pratt, Caroline. *I Learn from Children*. New York: Simon & Schuster, 1948.
"Progressive Education." *Nature* 59 (5 January 1899): 235–38.
"Progressive Education." *School World* 4 (April 1902): 140–41.
Rader, Benjamin. *The Academic Mind and Reform*. Lexington: University of Kentucky Press, 1966.
Rainey, Homer. *How Fare American Youth?* New York: Appleton-Century, 1937.
Reese, William. "The Origins of Progressive Education." *History of Education Quarterly* 41, no. 1 (Spring 2001): 1–24.
Report of the Survey of Arthurdale School. Morgantown: West Virginia University, 1940.
Rice, Milburn. "Footnote on Arthurdale." *Harper's Magazine* 180 (March 1940): 411–19.
Rickover, Hyman. *Education and Freedom*. New York: Dutton, 1959.
Roosevelt, Eleanor. *This I Remember*. New York: Harper & Bros., 1949.
———. *The Autobiography of Eleanor Roosevelt*. 1961. New York: Da Capo, 1992.

Roosevelt, Franklin D. "Actualities of Agricultural Planning." In *America Faces the Future*, ed. Charles A. Beard, 325–50. Boston: Houghton-Mifflin, 1932.
———. *The Public Papers and Addresses of Franklin D. Roosevelt*, ed. Samuel Rosenman. 13 vols. New York: Random House, 1938–1950.
Ross, Phil. "The Scotts Run Coalfield from the Great War to the Great Depression: A Study in Overdevelopment." *West Virginia History* 53 (1994): 21–42.
Rucker, Darnell. *The Chicago Pragmatists*. Minneapolis: University of Minnesota Press, 1969.
Rugg, Harold. "Social Reconstruction through Education." *Progressive Education* 10, no. 1 (December 1932): 11–18.
———. "The Educator and the Scientific Study of Society." *Progressive Education* 11, nos. 1–2 (January–February 1934): 3–5.
Ryan, Alan. *John Dewey and the High Tide of American Liberalism*. New York: Norton, 1995.
Sadovnik, Alan R., and Susan F. Semel. *Founding Mothers and Others: Women Educational Leaders during the Progressive Era*. New York: Palgrave, 2002.
Sanderson, Dwight, John Kolb, and M. L. Wilson, eds. *Farm Income and Farm Life: A Symposium on the Relation of the Social and Economic Factors in Rural Progress*. Chicago: University of Chicago, 1927.
Schlesinger, Arthur, Jr. *The Crisis of the Old Order: The Age of Roosevelt, 1919–1933*. Boston: Houghton Mifflin, 2002.
Seay, Maurice. "The Community School: New Meaning for an Old Term." In *The Fifty-Second Yearbook of the National Society of the Study of Education, Part II: The Community School*, ed. Nelson Henry, 265–87. Chicago: University of Chicago Press, 1953.
Seay, Maurice, and John A. Wilkinson. "Overcoming Barriers to the Development of Community Schools." In *The Fifty-Second Yearbook of the National Society of the Study of Education, Part II: The Community School*, ed. Nelson Henry, 265–87. Chicago: University of Chicago Press, 1953.
Semel, Susan F. "The City and Country School: A Progressive Paradigm." In *"Schools of Tomorrow," Schools of Today: What Happened to Progressive Education*, ed. Susan F. Semel and Alan R. Sadovnik, 121–40. New York: Peter Lang, 1999.
Semel, Susan F., and Alan R. Sadovnik, eds. *"Schools of Tomorrow," Schools of Today: What Happened to Progressive Education*. New York: Peter Lang, 1999.
———. "The Contemporary Small-School Movement: Lessons from the History of Progressive Education." *Teachers College Record* 110, no. 9 (September 2008): 1744–71.
Shlaes, Amity. *The Forgotten Man: A New History of the Great Depression*. New York: Harper Perennial, 2007.
Siegfried, Charlene Haddock. *Feminist Interpretations of John Dewey: Re-reading the Canon*. University Park: Pennsylvania State University Press, 2002.
Simpson, Douglas J., and Sam F. Stack Jr., eds. *Teachers, Leaders, and Schools: Essays by John Dewey*. Carbondale: Southern Illinois University Press, 2010.

Stack, Sam F., Jr. *Elsie Ripley Clapp (1879–1965): Her Life and the Community School.* New York: Peter Lang, 2004.

———. "Guess Who Is Coming to Dinner? William Wirt and the New Deal." *Journal of the Philosophy and History of Education* 60, no. 1 (Fall 2010): 244–50.

Surdovel, Catherine Patricia. "Community Education: 1890's to the Present." Ed.D. thesis, Rutgers University, 1985.

Tanner, David, and Laurel Tanner. *History of the School Curriculum.* New York: Macmillan, 1990.

Tape, H. A. "A Consolidated Laboratory School." In *The Community School,* ed. Samuel Everett, 340–76. New York: Appleton-Century, 1938.

Taylor, John Martin. "A Study of the Graduates of Arthurdale High School to Determine the Influence of High School Training on Occupational Adjustment." Master's thesis, West Virginia University, 1941.

Terkel, Studs. *Hard Times: An Oral History of the Great Depression.* New York: Pocket, 1978.

Terman, Lewis. *The Measurement of Intelligence: An Explanation of and a Complete Guide for the Use of the Stanford Revision and Extension of the Binet-Simon Scale.* Boston: Houghton Mifflin, 1916.

Thomas, Jerry Bruce. *An Appalachian New Deal: West Virginia in the Great Depression.* Morgantown: West Virginia University Press, 2010.

Tönnies, Ferdinand. *Community and Society.* New York: Harper & Row, 1957.

Tugwell, Rexford. "The Place of Government in a National Land Program." *Journal of Farm Economics* 16, no. 1 (January 1934): 55–69.

———. *The Battle for Democracy.* New York: Columbia University Press, 1935.

———. "The Sources of New Deal Reformism." *Ethics* 64, no. 4 (1954): 249–76.

Twelve Southerners. *I'll Take My Stand: The South and the Agrarian Tradition.* 1930. Baton Rouge: Louisiana State University Press, 1977.

Tyack, David B. *The One Best System: A History of American Urban Education.* Cambridge, MA: Harvard University Press, 1974.

Tyack, David, Robert Lowe, and Elisabeth Hansot. *Public Schools in Hard Times: The Great Depression and Recent Years.* Cambridge, MA: Harvard University Press, 1984.

Urban, Wayne, and Jennings Wagoner. *American Education: A History.* New York: Routledge, 2009.

US Bureau of the Census. *Historical Statistics of the United States: Colonial Times to 1970.* Washington, DC: US Government Printing Office, 1975.

Wagner, Steward. "School Buildings: Arthurdale, West Virginia." *Progressive Education* 15, no. 4 (1938): 304–19.

Ward, Bryan, ed. *A New Deal for America.* Arthurdale, WV: Arthurdale Heritage, 1994.

Wattenberg, William. "Annotated Bibliography." In *The Community School,* ed. Samuel Everett, 463–71. New York: Appleton-Century, 1938.

Wecter, Dixon. *The Age of the Great Depression.* New York: Macmillan, 1948.

Weiler, Kathleen. "What Can We Learn from Progressive Education?" *Radical Teacher* 69 (January 2004): 4–9.
Westbrook, Robert. *John Dewey and American Democracy.* New York: Cornell University Press, 1991.
Westfall, Barry. "Elsie Ripley Clapp and the Arthurdale School: 1934–1936." *Vitae Scholasticae* 12, no. 1 (Spring 1993): 53–64.
Williams, Aubrey. "Youth and Government." *Progressive Education* 12, no. 8 (December 1935): 501–6.
———. "Rural Youth and Government." *Rural Sociology* 3, no. 1 (March 1938): 3–10.
Wilson, M. L. "The Place of Subsistence Homestead in Our National Economy." *Journal of Farm Economics* 16, no. 1 (January 1934): 73–84.
———. "How New Deal Agencies Are Affecting Family Life." *Journal of Home Economics* 27, no. 5 (May 1935): 274–80.
———. "Beyond Economics." In *Farmers in a Changing World: The Yearbook of Agriculture*, 925–27. Washington, DC, 1940.
———. *Reminiscences of Milburn Lincoln Wilson.* Oral History Collection. 1956. New York: Columbia University, 1973.
Wilson, Milburn L., and Oscar B. Jesness. *Farm Relief and the Domestic Allotment Plan.* Day and Hour Series of the University of Minnesota, no. 2. Minneapolis: University of Minnesota Press, 1933.
Woelfel, Norman. "The Educator, the New Deal, and Revolution." *Progressive Education* 11, nos. 1–2 (January–February 1934): 7–12.
Wraga, William. "Condescension and Critical Sympathy: Historians of Education on Progressive Education in the United States and England." *Paedagogica Historica* 50, nos. 1–2 (2014): 59–75.
Wrightstone, J. Wayne. "Vital Education: A Review of *Community Schools in Action.*" *Elementary School Journal* 60, no. 10 (June 1940): 789–91.
Yeager, Matthew. "Scotts Run: A Community in Transition." *West Virginia History* 53 (1994): 7–20.
Zilversmit, Arthur. *Changing Schools: Progressive Education Theory and Practice, 1930–1960.* Chicago: University of Chicago Press, 1993.
Zimmerman, Carl. "The Place of Homesteads in Our National Economy: A Discussion." *Journal of Farm Economics* 16, no. 1 (1934): 84–87.
Zirbes, Laura. "The Status of Progressive Schools." *Progressive Education* 3, no. 3 (May 1931): 359–66.
Zorach, William. *Art Is My Life: The Autobiography of William Zorach.* Cleveland: World, 1967.

Index

Addams, Jane, 5
Alberty, Harold, 10
Allen, Howard "H. B.," 39, 61, 100, 119, 123–24
American Friends Service Committee (AFSC), 26, 56, 61, 99, 109
Arthurdale: application process, 37–39; building community, 128–29, 137; closing of, 126, 134–35; community planning of, 19, 143; homesteader characteristics, 39–40; homesteader unemployment, 79–80, 88, 89, 99, 106, 113, 125; lack of racial diversity, 40; New Deal, 1; origin of, 34, 143–44; political nature of, 42, 65, 124, 138; as Reedsville Experimental Project, 36; as subsistence homestead, 36, 122
Arthurdale School: accreditation of, 103–4; budget, 57, 71, 112, 122, 124; building community of, 37, 62–64, 96, 118, 121, 128, 131, 138, 144; as county school, 104–5, 109, 113, 116, 125; curriculum, 2, 89–90, 91–93, democratic nature of, 42, 134, 138, 143; drama program, 92, 94, 101–2; early childhood emphasis of, 67–68, 82, 96; FDR visit to, 114; health care in, 97; music festival of, 102; newspaper of, 94; origins of, 7, 9, 67; philosophy of, 3–4, 8, 12, 41, 62–64, 115, 118, 137; planning of, 49, 61. *See also* National Advisory Committee

back-to-the-land movement: early supporters of, 28, 31; origins of, 7, 27–28; response to unemployment, 29–30, 136; and subsistence farming, 29
Bailey, Liberty Hyde, 27–28
Ballard Memorial School, 18; composition and enrollment of, 523–53; curriculum, 55; health-care program of, 54; as rural Kentucky public school, 51; teaching staff, 70
Baruch, Bernard: financial support of Arthurdale, 57, 66, 81, 89, 104; relation to Eleanor Roosevelt, 80, 113; support of Elsie Clapp, 85, 97–98, 106; teacher salaries, 71; and unemployment of Arthurdale, 101, 103–4, 122
Baskin, Alex, 18, 23
Beatty, Willard, 19
Beecher, George: as Arthurdale teacher, 54, 91, 78; and Fletcher Collins, 77; and John Dewey, 100; and Elon College, 105, 108; and Goddard College, 108; and science education, 91, 93
Bernard, L. L., 28
Bode, Boyd, 13, 17

Borsodi, Ralph, 28, 32
Bourne, Randolph, 65
Bowers, C. A., 16

Campbell, James, 6
Carlisle, Ethel, 74; and domestic science, 71; Lincoln School, 105; as teacher at Arthurdale, 70
Carlson, Harry, 77; and instrument construction, 77; and shop instruction, 76; as teacher at Arthurdale, 5–6, 70, 79
Chicago, University of, 4, 28, 90, 120
Clapp, Elsie Ripley: and Arthurdale School, 42–43, 51, 57, 69, 71–72, 103, 117–18; and Ballard School, 18, 51–56; City and Country School, 49; as community school progressive, 2, 14, 18, 43, 63, 68, 76, 82; *Community Schools in Action*, 105, 107, 129, 142; and John Dewey, 47, 137; early childhood education, 83; early life and education, 44–46; and experience as teacher, 48–50; experience in unemployment at Arthurdale, 85; and loss of community, 43, 88; and Milton Academy, 48–49; *My Pedagogic Creed*, 46, 52, 148; and Paterson silk workers strike, 48; and Rosemary Junior School, 49; *The Use of Resources in Education*, 58
coal industry: and coal camp schools, 37; decline of, 25, 34–35; health care in, 72; loss of community in, 58, 63, 84; racism in, 40; and social welfare, 26, 35–36, 58–59, 128
Cobb, Stanwood, 17
Collins, Fletcher: as Arthurdale teacher, 77; and drama production, 94; and Elon College, 108; folklore interest of, 77; on leaving Arthurdale, 111; and music festival, 84
community: concept of, 1–3, 143; democratic function of, 6, 33, 53, 77, 82, 118, 131, 144; loss of, 4–5, 40, 43, 56, 128; New Deal planning of, 7, 29, 31, 85; as progressive education principle, 11; schools, advocates of, 12–13, 14, 18, 47, 108; and subsistence homesteads, 26, 34, 37, 81
Community Schools in Action (Clapp). *See under* Clapp, Elsie Ripley
Conkin, Paul, 28, 30, 135, 143
Cook, Lloyd, 140–41
Counts, George, 13–14, 17–18
Cremin, Lawrence, 10–11, 65
Curti, Merle, 18, 20

Democracy and Education (Dewey). *See under* Dewey, John
de Saussure, Mme Necker, 9
Dewey, Alice Chipman, 4
Dewey, John: community and democracy, 1, 6, 10, 131; concept of community, 3–6, 138; *Democracy and Education*, 142, 147; Dewey lab school, 9, 90; early life and education, 4; influence on Clapp, 14, 43–58, 62, 76, 130; *My Pedagogic Creed*, 46, 52, 128; and National Advisory Committee, 59, 61, 99; *Philosophy and Civilization*, 17; praising Arthurdale School, 137–38; *School and Society*, 65, 90, 143; *Schools of Tomorrow*, 65; and visit to Arthurdale, 99
Dewey, Sabino, 99–100
Dickens, Charles, 27

Drake, Richard, 127
DuBois, W. E. B., 40
Durkheim, Emile, 5

Eller, Ronald, 34–35, 67

Farm Security Administration (FSA), 117, 136
Federal Emergency Relief Administration (FERA), 27, 66
Flamm, Matthew, 1
Ford, Henry, 28
Fowler, Burton, 15
Funk, Inez, 76

Gemeinschaft, 14, 150n18
Gesellschaft, 14, 151n18
Graham, Patricia, 15
Great Depression, 1, 23, 35, 127–28
Grimes, Bushrod, 39, 71, 78
Gugler, Eric, 67–68, 73

Hanna, Paul, 142
Hansot, Elisabeth, 2
Hart, Joseph, 144
Hefferan, Helen, 20–21
Hickok, Lorena, 34, 110
Hitchcock, Claude, 58
Homestead Act of 1862, 27

Ickes, Harold: on Arthurdale School budget, 57, 68; on selection of Arthurdale, 36; and subsistence homesteads, 30, 33, 35
intercultural education, 7
Ipcar, Adolph, 70, 79, 82, 109

Jefferson, Thomas, 27, 33
Johanek, Michael, 3–4, 139, 140, 142
Johnson, Harriett, 68, 82
Jones, Eunice, 70, 75, 89

Kilpatrick, William Heard: on *Democracy and Education*, 47; the project method, 13; and social reconstructionism, 14, 16, 143; and traditional education, 11
Kloppenberg, James, 138

Lindeman, Eduard, 130
Lewis, John L., 25
Liston, Sara, 76, 90
Lowe, Robert, 2
Lynd, Robert and Helen, 24

Maloney, C. J., 132, 134
McFadden, Benarr, 29
Mead, Elwood, 29, 31
Mead, George Herbert, 5
Mitchell, Lucy Sprague, 49, 59, 82, 83
Mountaineer Craftsmen's Cooperative, 68–69
My Pedagogic Creed (Dewey). See under Dewey, John; Clapp, Elsie

Naslund, Robert, 142
National Advisory Committee, 61
National Education Association, 20–21
National Industrial Recovery Act (NIRA), 26
National Miners Union, 25
Naumburg, Margaret, 13
New Deal: and back-to-the-land movement, 31; commitment to education, 41; National Industrial Recovery Act, 19, 27; political controversy of, 126, 138; and subsistence homesteads, 1, 127, 136–37
Nicholson, Bert, 77
Nine, E. Grant, 109–10, 114, 117–18

Olsen, Edward, 141

Parker, Francis, 9-10
Philosophy and Civilization (Dewey). See under Dewey, John
Pickett, Clarence: and application process for Arthurdale homesteaders, 38-39; and Elsie Clapp, 56; and government interference in Arthurdale, 134; National Advisory Committee, 59, 61; and planning of Arthurdale School, 73; relief efforts, 26, 34-35; on Arthurdale School closure, 109
Plummer, Kay, 72, 83, 96
Pratt, Caroline, 14
progressive education: and administrative progressives, 12-14; and child-centered progressives, 7, 12-15; and community school progressives, 12, 14; concept of, 2-4, 6-8, 9-11; critique of, 17-18, 56, 62, 142; and democracy, 131; diversity of, 11, 15, 16, 129; in 1930s, 62; and social reconstructionism, 12-14, 18-19, 20, 62; and subsistence homesteads, 57-58
Progressive Education Association (PEA), 11, 43, 62, 111, 142
Preston County (WV), 36
Puckett, John, 3, 139-40, 142
Pynchon, C. E., 8, 71-72

Redefer, Frederick C., 16
Roosevelt, Eleanor: and Arthurdale School, 37, 41, 42, 56-57, 68-69, 80, 95, 104, 117-18; and Bernard Baruch, 66, 71, 81, 89, 98, 101, 103, 104; and class conflict, 36; coal camp visit, 34-35; and homesteader employment, 40, 102, 113, 124; homesteader selection, 39; and music festival, 84; and National Advisory Committee, 59, 61, 99, 137; and progressive education, 58, 111-12; support of Clapp and Arthurdale School, 7, 10, 126; support of subsistence homesteads, 34, 37, 40-41
Roosevelt, Franklin Delano: and Arthurdale selection, 36; on Arthurdale visit, 114; early community planning, 31-32; election of (1932), 26; and political attacks on, 134; and subsistence homesteads, 127; State of the Union Address (1944), 138
Ross, Phil, 34-35
Rousseau, Jean Jacques, 9, 12
Rugg, Harold, 13, 19-20

Sadovnik, Alan, 7
Saunders, Carlton, 70, 76, 79, 84
School and Society (Dewey). See under Dewey, John
Schools of Tomorrow (Dewey). See under Dewey, John
Scotts Run (WV), 34-36, 37, 42, 58, 63, 68, 77, 100, 128, 144
Seay, Maurice, 141
Sedman, Mary Elizabeth, 80, 83, 96
Semel, Susan, 7
Sheffield, Elisabeth, 51, 70, 75, 78-79, 80, 90-91, 105
Social Frontier (journal), 20
social reconstructionism, 12-14, 18-19, 20, 62
Spencer, Herbert, 5
Smart, O. B., 57, 68
Stanton, Jessie, 49, 67-68, 82, 104
subsistence homestead: Arthurdale School and, 58, 63, 67, 123, 140; Arthurdale selection as, 36, 41; conception of, 1, 3, 30-31, 33-34,

35, 65, 127; Division of, 30–31; and National Industrial Recovery Act, 26; and political controversy of, 126, 134; segregation and, 40

Thomas, Jerry Bruce, 25, 59
Timbres, Harry, 72, 83–84
Tönnies, Ferdinand, 5
Tugwell, Rexford, 18, 31–33, 36, 61, 85, 99, 102, 128, 135–36
Tyack, David, 2, 13, 24, 41

United Mine Workers, 25, 36
Use of Resources in Education, The (Clapp). *See under* Clapp, Elsie

Vermont, University of, 4

Weber, Max, 5
Weiler, Kathleen, 8
West Virginia, 1; Arthurdale teachers from, 76, 89, 90; and Constitution of 1872, 40; depression economics of, 1, 25; and relief efforts in, 26, 34, 36, 59
West Virginia School Advisory Committee, 61–62, 63, 64, 67, 74, 100, 104, 117
West Virginia University, 37, 39, 56, 61, 100, 119
Whitman, John Pratt, 33, 63
Williams, Aubrey: and Arthurdale, 95; and National Youth Administration (NYA), 87–88
Wilson, Milburn: and Arthurdale School budget, 68; and building community, 56; and democracy, 32, 42; and subsistence homesteads, 31–34, 67
Wirt, William A., 65–66
Woelfel, Norman, 20

Zilversmit, Arthur, 3, 12
Zirbes, Laura, 13, 16–17, 151n28

Place Matters: New Directions in Appalachian Studies

Series Editor: Dwight B. Billings

This series explores the history, social life, and cultures of Appalachia from multidisciplinary, comparative, and global perspectives. Topics include geography, the environment, public policy, political economy, critical regional studies, diversity, social inequality, social movements and activism, migration and immigration, efforts to confront regional stereotypes, literature and the arts, and the ongoing social construction and reimagination of Appalachia. Key goals of the series are to place Appalachian dynamics in the context of global change and to demonstrate that place-based and regional studies still matter.

Appalachia in Regional Context: Place Matters
Edited by Dwight B. Billings and Ann E. Kingsolver

Literacy in the Mountains: Community, Newspapers, and Writing in Appalachia
Samantha NeCamp

Appalachia Revisited: New Perspectives on Place, Tradition, and Progress
Edited by William Schumann and Rebecca Adkins Fletcher

The Arthurdale Community School: Education and Reform in Depression Era Appalachia
Sam F. Stack Jr.

Sacred Mountains: A Christian Ethical Approach to Mountaintop Removal
Andrew R. H. Thompson

Rereading Appalachia: Literacy, Place, and Cultural Resistance
Edited by Sara Webb-Sunderhaus and Kim Donehower

Religion and Resistance in Appalachia: Faith and the Fight against Mountaintop Removal Coal Mining
Joseph D. Witt

www.ingramcontent.com/pod-product-compliance
Lightning Source LLC
Chambersburg PA
CBHW022019220426
43663CB00007B/1135